Life Beyond Liebfraumilch

Life Beyond Liebfraumilch

Understanding German Fine Wine

STUART PIGOTT

SIDGWICK & JACKSON
LONDON

First published in Great Britain in 1988
by Sidgwick & Jackson Limited

Copyright © 1988 Stuart Pigott

All maps drawn by Katharina Kelly

ISBN 0-283-99580-7

Phototypeset by Rowland Phototypesetting Limited
Bury St Edmunds, Suffolk
Printed in Great Britain by Richard Clay Limited
Bungay, Suffolk
for Sidgwick & Jackson Limited
1 Tavistock Chambers, Bloomsbury Way
London WC1A 2SG

*In memory of my father
who introduced me to wine,
and who encouraged me in my work on this book
to the very end*

The following symbols are used throughout the text:

 'Verband Deutscher Prädikats- und Qualitäts-weingüter' (the national quality wine estates association)

 'Rheingau Charta Estates Association', producers of high quality dry Riesling wines in the Rheingau

Contents

List of Maps

Acknowledgements

This book is the product of many years' travelling to the wine-producing regions of Germany. During this time an enormous number of people have helped in countless ways. There have been many matchmakers to my love affair with German wines, and it is sadly impossible to list all of them here. However, there are a number of people whose help has gone far beyond the bounds of self-promotion, and it would not be right if this selflessness was not acknowledged. Many of the wine growers listed below have either recommended to me, or introduced me to, other interesting wine producers. In some cases these introductions have been to direct competitors, something which I have never experienced elsewhere in Europe. Others have given their time *very freely* to help me increase my knowledge of viticulture, winemaking, or the problems and history of their regions. Finally, there are those who have been exceptional hosts, willing to help out when problems have unexpectedly arisen during my travels. To all these people I owe a very great debt of gratitude.

From the Moselle, Saar and Ruwer valleys: Hennes Fischer; Dr Carl and Renate von Schubert; Christoph and Graciela Tyrell; Wilhelm and Ilse Haag; Ernst Loosen and Bernhard Schug; Manfred Koll.

From the Nahe: Armin Diel; Hans and Dr Peter Crusius; Michael Prinz Salm-Salm.

From the Rhine regions: Bernhard Breuer, Carlo Runck, and Fred Prinz; Stefan and Andrea Gerhard; Maria Becker; Adam and Doreen Hulbert; Peter and Isa von Weymarn; Hajo Guntrum; Wilhelm Steifensand; the Lingenfelder family; Michael Hiller.

From Baden: Hermann Dörflinger; Hans-Joachim and Ilka von Gleichenstein.

From Württemberg: Michael Graf Adelmann.

From other parts of Germany: Mario Scheuermann (wine writer); Joachim Krieger (wine writer); Hans-Joachim Kraut-krämmer (hotelier and wine merchant *extraordinaire*); Claus Kespelher (wine broker).

From outside Germany: Chris Pies-Lintz (soon to be New Zealand wine producer).

Introduction

A century ago no type of wine was held in higher international esteem than fine German wine. Prices reflected this, with wines from the top vineyards on the Rhine regularly being sold for much more than the most renowned and expensive red wines from Bordeaux. For example, at a Christie's auction in May 1877 an 1862 Schloss Johannisberger sold for 130 shillings (about £6.50) per dozen, while 1865 (a great vintage) Château Lafite made only 90 shillings (£4.50) per dozen. On the November 1896 list of famous London wine merchants Berry Brothers & Rudd, 1862 Rüdesheimer Hinterhaus and 1862 Marcobrunn Cabinet are both priced at 200 shillings (£10) per dozen, while the most expensive red Bordeaux wine, 1870 (again a great vintage) Château Lafite, was only 144 shillings (£7.20) per dozen. In the intervening decades this position has been completely reversed, with the prices for top clarets having soared to unprecedented levels during recent years, and the prices of even the very best German wines having long declined in real terms.

Liebfraumilch, which was widely sold a century ago and is the single most popular style of wine in Britain today, is the German wine which has suffered the most dramatic reversal. On that Berry Brothers & Rudd list of 1896, Liebfraumilch is listed at 62 shillings (£3.10) per dozen, a slightly higher price than for the red wines of Châteaux Leoville, Pichon Longueville, and Margaux in Bordeaux and the red wines of Volnay, Beaune and Pommard in Burgundy. Today there is not a supermarket in the UK without a Liebfraumilch on its shelves selling for under £2 per bottle, while the very cheapest of those French wines would today cost at least 500 per cent more than a supermarket Liebfraumilch, and the most expensive more than twenty times that price! Although the quality of Liebfraumilch is now generally not up to the level of a hundred years ago, as a result of an enormous increase in the scale of its production, the best Liebfraumilch wines like Sichel's 'Blue Nun' and Valckenberg's 'Madonna' are certainly of comparable quality, and even these wines can be bought for only £3 per bottle in discount stores.

German wines reached this rock-bottom point as a result of the Liebfraumilch business being built up to a massive scale in recent years through price cutting. In this way very cheap easy-to-drink wines with little character were made available to the new generation of largely younger wine drinkers. This boom reached a peak in 1985 when 17 million cases of German wine came to the UK, and Liebfraumilch wines could be bought for a mere £1.39 in some British supermarkets. The inevitable result of these ever-sinking prices was poorer and poorer quality, and this, combined with the diethylene glycol or antifreeze scandal of 1985, put the final nail in the coffin of German wine's image. For most wine drinkers, whether casual or interested, irregular or connoisseurs, German wine is a cheap, sweet confection of low quality, often being regarded as something to be quaffed at parties when nothing else is left in the kitchen. Consumer research done in 1986 by the German Wine Shippers Committee of the Wine & Spirit Association of Great Britain and the German Wine Information service in the UK proved this to be so. No wonder few of the new generation of British wine drinkers have stayed with German wines when they started moving up the price scale; they were not, and are not, aware that Germany has anything to offer apart from rather bland sweet wines. The position in North America would appear to be little different.

Needless to say, this situation has direct commercial consequences, and the production of Liebfraumilch wines has already fallen more than 31 per cent since 1982, a massive 18.7 per cent of that fall having taken place between 1986 and the first quarter of 1987. While Liebfraumilch imports to Britain are not plummeting at quite that rate, there has been a steady and continuous decline since 1985, and it shows every sign of going further and gaining pace. Having taken over the role of world-wide bargain-basement wine from Soave and Lambrusco in the late seventies, Liebfraumilch would appear to be on the way back to where it came from: just one part of the range of white wines produced in Germany.

On the other hand, the quality side of German wine production is showing a distinct revival in export sales, with more than one million cases of German wines costing over £3 per bottle now being sold in Britain each year. Undoubtedly one of the most important causes of this revival is the many exciting new wines which the better German companies and co-operatives have recently brought out. These tend to be regional-varietal wines, Nahe Müller-Thurgau, Rheinpfalz Weissburgunder, or something similar, in bottles bearing bright, modern labels, rather than wines being sold under long, unpronounceable vineyard names in bottles with labels of kitschy rustic or pseudo-Gothic design. In fact, the tendency towards simplification and modernisation dates back to before the diethylene glycol scandal, to the spring of 1984 when Scholl & Hillebrand of Rüdesheim on the Rhine launched their 'Riesling Dry (Rheingau)'. This wine has now been followed by literally dozens of similar elegantly packaged wines, which, like it, are drier and more characterful in taste and bouquet than the Liebfraumilch and the Piesporter Michelsberg and Niersteiner Gutes Domtal generic wines that have hitherto dominated German wine exports.

The other move which has substantially contributed to the revival of finer-quality German wines is the increasingly active promotion being done by the top wine estates in Germany, who during the last decade have slowly been realising that they have to promote themselves much more actively if they are to be successful in an increasingly marketing-orientated world. Because many of them are small in terms of acreage, and individually cannot afford such lavish advertising and PR as many big Bordeaux wine estates, they have started grouping together for such activities. Initially they did this just for the German market, but since the formation of the 'Vintners Pride of Germany' group (the Schloss Vollrads, Fürst Löwenstein, Louis Guntrum, Reichsrat von Buhl, S. A. Prüm, Prinz zu Salm-Dalberg, and Fürst Castell estates) in the spring of 1987 they have also been doing so internationally. However, whether promoting their wines alone or in groups, an increasing number of the top estates have realised that it is their identity, their name, which they have to push.

This idea has already begun to alter the way German estate

wines are marketed. For example, 'Fritz Haag Riesling (Mosel-Saar-Ruwer)' is the new basic product of Weingut Fritz Haag in Brauneberg on the Moselle. It is a 100 per cent Riesling wine of very high quality, each vintage being produced with a similar balance, so that it is always dry (but not bone-dry) in taste. From now on only the top wines produced by this estate will be sold under vineyard names. Numerous other top producers are following the Haag estate along this path, though more often they are producing three wines under the estate name: one dry (Trocken), one medium-dry (Halbtrocken), and one in the sweeter style. I am sure that we will see this idea being taken a lot further in the very near future.

Much less obvious than these changes, but fundamentally far more important, is the dynamic and innovative new generation of winemakers which has been entering all sides of the German wine business since the beginning of the decade. In the few years since the diethylene glycol scandal broke they have made their influence very strongly felt, and I am sure that as a result of this a higher proportion of really fine German wines are now being made than was the case even a few years ago. This book is primarily about this new generation, the wines they are making, and the ideas about winemaking that lie behind them. However, I should immediately point out that while some members of this new generation like Ernst Loosen of Weingut St Johannishof in the Moselle are only just into their thirties, others who also belong to this 'movement', such as Karl Fuhrmann of Weingut Pfeffingen in the Palatinate, are well into their fifties.

What makes it possible to speak of these extremely diverse individuals as a group is their common belief in a small number of principles. Most importantly, for them wines made from the traditional German grape varieties vinified in genuinely traditional styles are the *only* correct basis for wine production in Germany. At the same time they are not averse to experimentation where no traditions exist, or the existing tradition seems to have little value for, or relevance to, the modern world. They and their ideas occupy centre stage here, but, without dropping some scenery in behind them, many of the reasons for their actions and beliefs, along with the wider significance of these, would be lost. Therefore, before looking closely at the present and future of German wines, it is necessary to cast a look back into the past, and to chart the progress of Germany's decline from the position of premier European wine producer to supplier of bulk wines of the most meagre quality.

The long decline

The obvious facts of twentieth-century history have had an enormous effect on the production of wine in Germany, and on the image which German wines have had internationally during recent times. However, the effect of the two World Wars has been much more complex than one might think, and the indirect results of the Second World War transformed the character of German wines, and of the German wine business. It is here that the germ of so many of the problems which have brought German wine down to its present position of low international esteem is to be found.

The years between 1914 and 1945 prepared the ground, so to speak, for this transformation. The decline began when people in England gave up drinking their once-beloved Hock (Rhine wine) during the First World War. Then came the depression of the thirties, another period when international demand for German wines slumped. However, the worst problem for Germany which these political and economic upheavals caused was not the immediate one of poor demand, though that was bad enough. It was the beginning of the decay of the wine and food culture in which German wines had played such an important role. In the years between Queen Victoria's marriage to Prince Albert, which had set the nineteenth-century fine German wine boom in Britain rolling, and 1914, it was the aristocratic and upper-middle classes who had bought and consumed fine Hock and Moselle alongside claret, champagne, port and sherry at their dining tables. The First World War not only directly killed and maimed a great many of these people; it also accelerated the social changes which were to sweep this leisured lifestyle aside.

In Germany itself many wine producers who had done very good business selling to the aristocracy before the First World War found themselves without these customers by the end of 1929, if not by 1919. Some of them even lost their wine estates as a result of the market's collapse. The estate of Dr Weil in the

Rheingau did excellent business with Kaiser Wilhelm II until 1918, and they still have a collection of imperial menu cards documenting the Kaiser's passion for their 1893 and 1911 Kiedrich wines. This business was obviously finished when the Kaiser fled Germany in the autumn of 1918. The Dr Wagner estate on the Saar did good business supplying wine to the court of the ruler of Saxe-Coburg Gotha before the First World War, but all this evaporated at the end of the twenties. As a result the Wagner family lost their sparkling wine business in Serrig, and had a long struggle to hold on to their wine estate in Saarburg.

It is against this background that the dramatic changes of the years after the Second World War must be seen. In 1945 Germany was in a state of economic ruin, and the feelings against the nation and its products in the Allied countries, among which were nearly all the traditional export markets for German wines, undoubtedly helped France ascend to its only recently challenged position of supremacy as *the* country associated with fine wine. It took even the German shippers who had traditionally done considerable pre-war business with Britain many years to begin rebuilding their markets. The house of Deinhard, for instance, did not ship any wine to England between 1939 and 1948. However, the less obvious effects of the immediate post-war conditions on the German wine business were to prove yet more significant in the long term.

In the zone of French occupation, which included the entirety of what is today the Mosel-Saar-Ruwer wine-producing region, all wine was confiscated on the arrival of the occupation forces. It was then collected together in the largest wine cellars to be found in the region. When the French left nearly five years later, much of this wine remained in these cellars, in spite of healthy French military consumption and a certain amount of wanton destruction. Much of this became the *de facto* property of the cellar owners, since in many instances it was impossible to trace whose property particular barrels of wine had once been. These stocks of wine were the foundation of the huge commercial cellars in the Moselle valley which in recent years have, in pure business terms, dominated German wine production. Some of these businesses, which buy wines in from innumerable small wine growers, blend, and resell them, have grown to gigantic proportions from the stocks which the French military left behind them.

Some of the biggest of them also happen to be the worst cowboys in the German wine business, bending the law as far as it will go, and, if rumours are to be believed, sometimes well beyond that point.

It is they who 'pioneered' German-styled EEC blended Table Wine, and turned it into the monster big-seller that it is today. These wines are usually blended from large amounts of ultra-cheap bland southern Italian wines and small amounts of acidic German wine to create a Liebfraumilch-like liquid sold under names like 'Winzermeister' or 'Winzerschoppen' at rock-bottom prices. To the average consumer this appears to be a German wine, since it looks almost identical to the cheap German wines it sits next to on supermarket shelves. This is the deepest depth to which 'German' wine production has sunk. These wines represent the bottom of the bastardisation barrel, and are totally destructive to the identity and image of Germany's own wines.

A quite different problem emerged at the same time as the big commercial cellars were starting to grow in the Moselle. This was the increasing complexity of labelling for German wines. Before the forties the naming of German wines had been the very model of simplicity, most wines being sold under village names, such as Bernkasteler, Niersteiner or Johannisberger. If the wine was exceptionally good and came from one of the best vineyard sites, the vineyard name would be used in addition to, or instead of, the village name, as in Bernkasteler Doctor, Niersteiner Brudersberg, and Johannisberger Klaus, or Marcobrunn and Steinberger. The very few, richer, late-harvested wines would have the word 'Spätlese' or 'Auslese' added after the village or vineyard name.

After the war the number of vineyard names appearing on labels multiplied rapidly, as did the words used to designate the level of richness of the wine. Such systems are not without their merits. The German system of grading wines according to richness was a product of the fact that different vineyards and vintages yield grapes of widely differing degrees of ripeness. These result in wines ranging from the very light to the almost overwhelmingly rich, and the drinker really needs to be given some guidance as to what he or she is buying. However, the pre-1971 German system potentially allowed for the grading of wines as Natur/Cabinet, Spätlese, Feine Spätlese, Feinste Spätlese, Hochfeine Spätlese, Hochfeinste Spätlese, Auslese, Feine Auslese, Feinste Auslese, Hochfeine Auslese, Hochfeinste Auslese, Beerenauslese, Goldbeerenauslese, Edelbeerenauslese, Trockenbeerenauslese, and finally Eiswein in conjunction with any of these. Only a connoisseur could possibly understand what all these terms meant.

By the mid sixties it was unusual for any non-Liebfraumilch wines not to give a village and vineyard name, together with one of this encyclopedic collection of designations indicating richness, even if it was a wine of modest quality. In the majority of cases all this extra information which had been added to the names of the producer and village of origin told the wine drinker virtually nothing of any value. Indeed, it was only a source of confusion, making ordinary wines appear to be something they were not.

This obsession with complex designations speaks volumes for the mentality of winemakers during this period. The great majority of German wines before the Second World War had been dry wines made from grape juice which had fermented through until little or no fermentable sugar was left; the only naturally sweet wines were the selected quality late-harvested Auslese, Beerenauslese and Trockenbeerenauslese wines. These amounted to no more than a few per cent of total German wine production. From the early fifties more and more German wines of the normal lighter kind were made in a sweet or semi-sweet style.

The simplest method of making sweet a wine which would otherwise ferment out to dryness is by stopping the fermentation while some unfermented sugar remains. This can be done simply by adding a large dose of sulphur dioxide, as was widespread practice in the Moselle for many decades in order to retain a little extra sweetness in the region's light Riesling wines. Instead of fermenting the wines out so that only a few grams of unfermented sugar remained (exactly how much depends on the cellar temperature during fermentation), the fermentation would be arrested just before it would do so naturally. The technology for a more precise control of the unfermented sweetness in wine, centrifuges and sterile filters, only started to become common pieces of cellar equipment during the 1950s. The careful and restrained use of such equipment to retain a modest level of sweetness would have caused no problems for Germany, but unfortunately these machines were more often used to make great quantities of cloyingly sweet wines. In these cases the sweetness did not work to accentuate the lively fruitiness of the wine, but smothered it with a blanket of sugar.

Sweet wines: the GI effect

The reasons why, when the technical possibility of making sweeter wines without a lot of sulphur dioxide became available, the potential to make such wines was turned into large-scale production are complex. Wolfgang Siben of Weingut Georg Siben in Deidesheim in the Palatinate has some very interesting theories about this development, which strike me as containing more than a germ of truth. What makes his ideas particularly interesting is that the Palatinate borders onto Alsace, and while the Palatinate went along the sweet wine path from the mid sixties, the Alsatians stuck doggedly to dry wines. Herr Siben believes that the reasons why the Germans grasped the new technology of sweet winemaking with both hands are direct or indirect products of the Second World War. He is sure that the influence of the taste for sweet drinks of the tens of thousands of American GIs stationed in Germany after the war exerted a decisive influence. The great majority of these American soldiers and airmen had been brought up on Coca-Cola and American beer, both of which are sweet. It therefore should not be surprising that they largely preferred the wines which had some sweetness.

Wolfgang Siben believes that this taste preference was then echoed by the Germans themselves, who, after the austerity of the last years of the war and the occupation years, craved fine things. Before the war the finest German wines had been the one or two per cent produced from grapes so ripe that after fermentation they still retained a marked sweetness: Auslese-style wines. With the new cellar technology this natural sweetness could be mimicked by stopping the fermentation of quite ordinary wines while considerable sugar remained unfermented or by adding clarified unfermented grape juice (Süssreserve) to dry wines. Perhaps there was also a physiological craving for sweetness at this time, because of the poor diet of the period.

The taste for such wines was undoubtedly stimulated by a number of vintages which produced substantial quantities of naturally sweet Auslese-style wines. The great post-war vintages of 1947, 1949, and 1953 were sold for low prices, owing to the economic conditions of the period, so that it was possible for those living in countries with comparatively strong currencies to drink these wines regularly. The Americans, in particular, became accustomed to such wines as something which could be easily afforded, and strong consumer expectations were thus established. The great 1959 vintage which produced very large quantities of naturally sweet Auslese wines gave this tendency a considerable further push, and extended its influence to Germany itself, since by then many Germans were prosperous enough to drink wine regularly once again. After the Germans had tasted a good number of these rich 1959 wines many of them expected such sweetness again. In Germany one often hears that the centrifuges or sterile filters came into the cellars in the early sixties; particularly in the northern Rhine regions and on the Moselle. The new style spread more slowly to the Rheinpfalz and Baden, and last of all to Württemberg and Franconia where a tradition of dry wine has always survived.

At exactly this time great efforts and investment were being made in vine breeding in Germany. The principal aims of this breeding programme, which was conducted at the state research stations dotted about the country, was to breed vine varieties which would give higher yields, higher degrees of ripeness, and greater resistance to disease. The first such new varieties introduced into the German vineyards, Müller-Thurgau (bred over a century ago), Scheurebe and Kerner, can produce very interesting wines when not over-cropped and when grown on the right soil. However, the later products of this research work, vine crossings such as Siegerrebe, Bacchus, Optima, Ortega, Huxelrebe, etc. are not far short of an unmitigated disaster in terms of the wines they yield in Germany. (Many of them are much more successful in England!)

Optima, for example, ripens so early in comparison to the traditional German vine varieties that when the last yield a grape juice which needs to have sugar added to it (chaptelisation, or *verbesserung*) to give the resulting wine enough body, Optima produces *at least* an Auslese. But, and this is a crucial but, if this

Verbesserung: "improvement" (p. 24)

Optima Auslese is compared with an Auslese from one of the traditional varieties it will taste only sweet. Auslese wines from the traditional varieties normally have an elegance, fullness, and complexity of flavour which the new crossings do not begin to match. New varieties such as Optima have done nothing but bring down the reputation of Germany's late-harvested Spätlese and Auslese wines, by making them common wines and by associating these designations with a crude sweet taste. As a result of the ease with which wines of these levels can be produced from such modern vine-crossings, some American and Japanese wine buyers still try to order the very richest of the late-harvested wines – Auslese, Beerenauslese, and Trocken-beerenauslese – by the container load! Such wines can only be produced from the traditional vine varieties in quantities of a few hundred litres, or occasionally a few thousand.

The wine law: wine by numbers

The 1971 German wine law, which could have sought to propel German wine production out of this ever-deepening mire, sadly did the opposite. It only succeeded in institutionalising the grading system of German wines in a form which encouraged the further extension of all these unfortunate developments; this is called the Prädikat system. The only criterion on which a German wine earns itself a place within this system is the amount of sugar in the grapes at harvest as measured by the specific gravity (density) of the grape juice. But wine contains more than water, sugar, and the product of sugar's fermentation by yeast: alcohol. Anyone who has tasted more than a few wines will realise that these other constituents in wine, the various kinds of acidity, mineral extracts, and complex organic substances, play a crucial role in determining both the character and quality of the wine. They also determine such fundamental things as whether it is white or red. The German wine law takes no notice of the levels of these substances in determining the quality grade of a wine.

Worst still, although this law sets higher minimum must weights for non-traditional grape varieties to reach each Prädikat level than for the late-ripening traditional grape varieties, these differences are not nearly great enough. As far as the 1971 wine law is concerned, an Optima Auslese from a flat vineyard on ground which used to produce sugar beet is every bit as good as a Riesling Auslese from one of the top steep vineyard sites of the Rhine or Moselle valleys which has been planted with vines for more than a millennium! This has encouraged a flood of cheap 'Spätlese' and 'Auslese' Prädikat wines of a quality that is meagre compared to Spätlese and Auslese wines from the traditional grape varieties. It is these wines as much as the bargain-basement Liebfraumilch wines which created the image of German wine as bland and sweet. The only difference between the effect of the two different types of wine is that cheap Liebfraumilch, Piesporter Michelsberg and Niersteiner Gutes Domtal gave ordinary wine drinkers this impression, and the cheap Prädikat wines gave more sophisticated wine drinkers this impression. Thus, the 1971 wine law actively penalises those who have been producing real Spätlese and Auslese wines for decades or even centuries by directly attacking their markets, and indirectly by eroding the image of their finest products.

At the same time as this infernal machine was set in motion, the AP number was introduced. Every German wine producer who intends to sell a wine as a Qualitätswein (QbA, the German equivalent of Appellation Contrôlée), or Qualitätswein in conjunction with a Prädikat level (QmP), has to submit a sample of this wine for testing. The most important part of this testing is a tasting by members of the wine trade, at which wines have to pass with a certain minimum mark (1.5 out of 5 for Qualitätswein). These tastings are conducted very quickly indeed, and I know from personal experience that many of the tasters feel a sense of obligation to pass a large proportion of the wines which come before them. In fact only about 3.5 per cent of wines submitted fail to get an AP number, and every now and again one comes across some really poor wines that have somehow got through. Those who administer this system work very hard to make it operate effectively, but the task presented to them is beyond human capacity, such are the number and diversity of wines needing to be tested.

The AP number tells the consumer almost nothing about the wine he or she is about to buy, save that it has been judged 'acceptable' and 'typical'. Even these terms are applied in the testing in such a loose and undefined manner as to have little meaning. Some less reputable members of the wine trade also use the AP number as an all-purpose alibi, saying 'it's got an AP number, it must be OK', often with reference to old stock which has lost any fruitiness it may once have had. At the same time the AP number's requirement of 'typicality' means that while some inferior, but typical, wines get numbers, some excellent wines fail just because the winemaker has been inventive.

By the mid eighties the consequences of the imperfections and loopholes in the 1971 wine law, and of the wider tendencies which it put into legal form, had been realised by the majority of German wine producers. Moves to overcome or circumvent these difficulties had already started by the time the 1985 diethylene glycol scandal broke. Although nobody was killed or even made ill by DEG, in contrast to the methanol scandal in Italy in 1986 which killed about thirty people, the effects have been grievous. German wine is now perceived by many not only to be thin, crude and sweet, but full of additives, whereas the first is clearly the real problem. However, in spite of the crisis into which this has plunged the German wine industry, the end result may yet be good, for the crisis is already stimulating drastic changes.

For example, whereas its critics once despaired of ever changing the 1971 German wine law, a series of changes are in the process of going through at the time of writing. These are designed to impose limits on the yield of all German vineyards, and to make the AP number testing a more effective guarantee of quality. However, while it is encouraging to see the authorities finally moving in a positive direction, the real impetus for this has come from developments which have already taken place in German wine production. These have already done much to overcome the confusions which complex labelling, sweetened-up wine styles, inferior grape varieties, and pretentious Prädikat levels have caused for Germany on a national level. The importance of regional identity and regional style has been rediscovered in a big way. This is the foundation of the brighter, clearer future for German wines.

Liebfraumilch: the good, the bad, and the ugly

For several years Liebfraumilch has had to be sold as a regional wine, and must declare itself to be either from the Rheinpfalz (the Palatinate), Rheinhessen, Nahe, or Rheingau, though in practice the last region's name never appears on Liebfraumilch labels. While I am sure the EEC law which states that every quality wine must be sold under a regional designation is right and proper, this goes against the idea behind Liebfraumilch as we know it: a trans-regional designation for wines from the Rhine regions made from the Riesling, Silvaner, and Müller-Thurgau grapes. In fact, by luck rather than design, the change to regional Liebfraumilch fits in very well with the current general trend towards regional wines in Germany. However, since Liebfraumilch has been accommodated within this tendency only by an accident of history, and its name rather than the regions it comes from remains *the* name most associated with German wine, it is worth taking a look at what makes a good Liebfraumilch. Then the kaleidoscopic diversity of new regional and varietal German wines currently joining it on supermarket and wine store shelves around the world will make much more sense.

For many wine drinkers and many more wine merchants Liebfraumilch is an object of amusement, disdain, or even derision. One British wine merchant recently went so far as to advertise himself with the slogan 'We sell no Liebfraumilch', and many of his colleagues and competitors agreed with his assessment that Liebfraumilch is not a serious wine. Some of the cheapest Liebfraumilch wines available are indeed crude, sugary, and thin. However, in assessing a wine like Liebfraumilch one should take into account the market aimed at: primarily wine drinkers who do not want to have to think too much in choosing a wine, who want something easy to drink and not too expensive. Liebfraumilch wines should be fresh and reasonably fruity, but should not possess any marked character which might offend some drinkers. They should therefore be fairly light, lowish in acidity, and have a modest sweetness which makes them round and soft. So the theory has gone these last few decades, the law having introduced only one or two new factors such as the addition of the Kerner grape variety to the traditional Liebfraumilch varieties as the required base of any Liebfraumilch blend (one or a combination of these grape varieties must make up at least 51 per cent of all Liebfraumilch wines).

This has been the line which the traditional producers and

1865 Liebfraumilch 1te Qualität
Eigenes Gewächs.

P. J. Valckenberg. in Worms a. Rh.

exporters of Liebfraumilch have followed since the war. Easily
the most important of these producers are P. J. Valckenberg of
Worms and H. Sichel Söhne of Alzey (both companies situated
in Rheinhessen). It was Valckenberg who made Liebfraumilch a
well-known name in many countries, including England, during
the last century. Sichel were, unintentionally, the creators of the
first branded Liebfraumilch when they put a picture of nuns
gathering grapes on the label of a 1921 Liebfraumilch wine
during the early twenties. This wine quickly became known to
their customers as 'the blue nun wine', though the nuns on the
label wore brown habits and only the sky was blue, well, bluish.
Blue Nun Liebfraumilch, which was already being blended to a
consistent style before the Second World War, was the trail-
blazer in establishing the kind of branded Liebfraumilch we are
so familiar with today. Valckenberg quickly followed Sichel's
marketing strategy by naming their Liebfraumilch 'Madonna',
and both proceeded to establish these names as global brands.
These have never been cheap wines, partly because of consistently good quality standards, and partly because a brand name
cannot be maintained without spending money. On this level,
Blue Nun or Madonna are quite comparable with Moët et
Chandon, Martell, Budweiser, or Coca-Cola.

To achieve consistency of style and quality is not easy, and in
the end there are certain things which cannot be economised on
if these are the aims of Liebfraumilch blending. Wilhelm Steifensand, the young co-owner and export director of Valckenberg,
insists on 25 per cent or more Riesling in Madonna, 'because

otherwise the wine would lack character, especially in poorer vintages. This is crucial in achieving the quality we want, and we just have to accept the extra cost'. Sichel employ six brokers, two of them full-time, to select the wines worth considering for inclusion in Blue Nun blends. This is expensive, but they feel that it provides them with the best choice of raw materials. Many of the small growers that both companies buy from have sold to them regularly for decades, and their picking and pressing of the grapes and fermentation of the resulting wine can be trusted to be of a good standard.

Rainer Lingenfelder, Sichel's young but highly experienced winemaker, who is also winemaker at his family's excellent estate in the Palatinate (see Weingut Lingenfelder, p. 89), believes that quality control of the wines accepted for blending, and of the finished wines which leave under Blue Nun labels, is the secret of the wine's great post-war success. He says that 'even those growers who have sold to us for a long time know that we won't automatically accept their wines, and when we are putting together a blend we always have bottles of previous blends there as quality and style benchmarks'. Both here and at Valckenberg it is necessary that the base wines which come in are filtered and fined to make sure that they are clear, since many come from small growers who do not have any sophisticated equipment.

They must also be treated to ensure that tartrates will not crystallise out of the wine after it leaves the plant. These are the small clear crystals which form in many German (and other) wines, falling to the bottom of the bottle, and alarming some people since they look as though they might be ground glass. In fact they are harmless, but in the case of wines like these which are sold around the world, it is not certain that every customer will understand that.

Sadly, this degree of care for the character of Liebfraumilch wines is exceptional in Germany. There are many companies whose Liebfraumilch wines do not have any recognisable character from the Riesling, Silvaner, or Müller-Thurgau grape varieties. These inferior Liebfraumilch wines are largely composed of wine from the new vine crossings developed in Germany from the beginning of this century onwards, and are generally much sweeter than the Liebfraumilch wines from the better producers. They come from the southern part of the Palatinate and the western part of Rheinhessen: areas with no great tradition of viticulture. The majority of these vineyards have been planted in the last two and a half decades as a result of government subsidies which inadvertently encouraged sugar-beet growers to switch to viticulture. The result is a great lake of poor-quality wines sloshing around at rock-bottom prices, and, as Wilhelm Steifensand said to me, 'most of this goes out through the Liebfraumilch hole'.

Many German wine companies were only concerned in expanding the scale of their business when they hopped on the Liebfraumilch bandwagon which Sichel's and Valckenberg's success had created. A price war between these companies ensued, during which Liebfraumilch prices on the shelf in England plummeted below £1.50 per bottle. The catastrophic effect on the image of Liebfraumilch which all this had, and the world-wide trend towards drier white wines, have caused both Sichel and Valckenberg to develop new drier-style wines.

Unlike their Madonna Liebfraumilch wines, Valckenberg's Riesling Dry is a pure varietal: it is produced entirely from grapes of the Riesling variety. Like the Riesling Dry wines also produced by Deinhard of Koblenz and Scholl & Hillebrand of Rüdesheim, it is a return to the classic style of German wines.

✻'Before the war,' points out Wilhelm Steifensand, 'nearly all German wines were dry. Only those which were late-harvested could have a natural sweetness. The taste for this classical dry style is now returning both in Germany and around the world.'✻ These new wine styles are very much concerned with bringing German wines back to the dining table. Wilhelm Steifensand is no dogmatist intent on convincing people that any and every dish can be complemented by a German wine, and he gladly talks about the wines from other countries which he frequently drinks with meals at home, but he feels that drier German wine undoubtedly deserves a place on menu cards and dining tables around the world, 'basically because they go with many dishes much better than most of the high alcohol–low acidity wines from France and the New World'.

The same intention lies behind Sichel Dry. This is a yet more revolutionary German wine, though it is made from Silvaner and Müller-Thurgau wines similar to those which go into Blue Nun Liebfraumilch blends. The base wines used to make up a Liebfraumilch blend arrive at the producer's cellars as dry wines, nearly all the sugar having been converted to alcohol during fermentation. After blending they are sweetened by adding clarified unfermented grape juice, or Süssreserve, to them. When Sichel decided to develop a completely dry wine, Rainer Lingenfelder and Riquet Hess reviewed their normal base wines and decided that however they were blended they would make a wine that would be too dry for many people's taste unless it was softened in some way. They therefore conducted a lengthy series of experiments, eventually rejecting new-oak ageing in favour of malolactic fermentation as the means of this softening.

French wines normally undergo a second, or malolactic, fermentation after the alcoholic fermentation (though many producers in Champagne, Alsace and the middle Loire valley try to avoid it), as do the wines from most of the more southerly wine-producing countries. Its effect is to turn the aggressive unripe, or malic, acidity in the wine into the softer lactic acid. This is conventionally regarded as a fault in Germany, where the tradition is for wines which have a lively fruitiness not mellowed by the effects of malolactic fermentation. (Indeed, the high acidity of many German wines makes it difficult for the malolactic fermentation to start.) As a result, many German wine producers have derided Sichel Dry as a mistake without even having tasted it.

Lactic acid, as its name suggests, has a milk-like taste. If a wine producer whose wines undergo malolactic fermentation does not understand the process, then the result can be a horrible sour cream smell and taste. However, malolactic fermentation can also contribute a most attractive buttery-oily character to white wines, making them taste richer and more complex. One can argue whether this makes a German wine too untypical, but the success of the test marketing in Holland and Denmark would seem to indicate that there will be an international demand for this wine. Like Britain and North America, Denmark and Holland were also countries where until recently only sweet German wines were sold. There must be tens of thousands of wine drinkers in these countries who want to drink dry wines, but find much of what is on the market too sharp for their taste. It is to them that Sichel Dry ought to appeal.

The origins of regional character

Because of its unconventional style, Sichel Dry can hardly be said to have 'regional character', though in fact it is made from grapes of the traditional varieties of a single region, Rheinhessen. The factors which determine the characteristic tastes of a wine-producing region are its climate, soil types, grape varieties and winemaking traditions. Changes to the latter two factors, which are under human control, can overnight make traditional-style wines a thing of the past. This has not only been the experience of Germany during recent decades, and I am sure that in the future the wine producers of many other countries will regret that they pulled up their traditional grape varieties and planted the fashionable Cabernet Sauvignon and Chardonnay varieties, then started slavishly copying Burgundian and Bordelais techniques in their cellars.

The 'natural' factors affecting the character of a region's wines are not quite as immutable as is often supposed. For example, the recent canalisation of the Saar river has markedly improved the microclimate there, on account of the greater surface of water created. In the Rheingau, the reorganisation of the Rüdesheimer Berg vineyards more than a decade ago changed

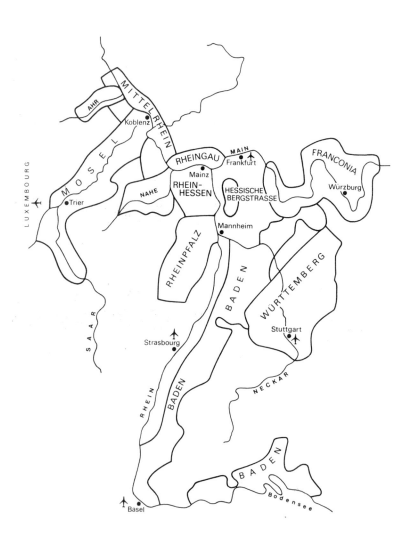

The eleven wine-growing regions of Germany

the soil structure there, and sadly for the worse in some places. It is very expensive and time-consuming to put that right. Such manipulations of the climate and soil are not uncommon, but their effects are generally limited to small areas. On the truly regional scale the natural factors are much more constant, and they have a great influence on the character of the wines produced in a particular region.

The vineyards of northern Germany are at the northern border of the area where viticulture is practical, because of simple climatic factors. Here every fraction of a degree Centigrade or sunshine hour gained makes a significant difference to the wines. There may not appear to be much difference between the Moselle's annual average temperature of 9.8°C and 1574 sunshine hours, and the 10.1°C and 1712 sunshine hours in the more southerly Palatinate, but the success with which peaches, apricots, almonds and figs can be grown in the Palatinate, and the rarity of these trees in the Moselle, shows what a substantial difference these fractions make. The product of this difference is grapes with consistently greater ripeness in the southerly regions of Germany. In terms of taste this extra ripeness means more body (alcohol), and less acidity. This might appear to be all to the good, but in practice it can mean wines which are a little heavy and lacking in freshness: problems that particularly afflict parts of Baden and Württemberg. The refreshing acidity so typical of the wines of the Moselle, Ahr, Middle Rhine, Rheingau and Nahe can certainly be unripe, can sometimes be what most wine drinkers think of as 'acid'. However, it can also be very positive, giving a marvellous vivacity and crispness to the wines of these regions.

There is an east–west variation in Germany's climate, as well as the more obvious north–south one. This affects the regions of Franconia and Württemberg, along with some parts of Baden. These areas have a much more continental climate than the Moselle and Rhine regions, experiencing far greater extremes of temperature. I learnt this the hard way in 1985 when I visited Franconia in early October, then again in mid-November. On the first of these visits it was so hot I need not have brought a jacket, while on the following visit there was over a foot of snow and temperatures down to −15°C! Early and late frost can be a real problem for the vines in Württemberg and Franconia, as well as being uncomfortable. However, this rather rugged climate can also be positive for the wines of these regions. In good vintages like 1979 the grapes in the more easterly areas of Germany achieve a very high degree of ripeness, and wines with as much as 15 degrees of alcohol can be produced.

The influence of the various rivers after which many of the wine regions are named, and about which their vineyards are planted, is also considerable. Any large body of water acts as a moderator of air temperature. In certain places the sunlight reflected from a large river can also significantly increase the total amount of light reaching a vineyard. All these effects are to be found in parts of the Moselle, Middle Rhine, Rheingau, Rheinhessen (around Nierstein and Oppenheim), Franconia (along the Main valley), and Württemberg (along the valleys of the Neckar and its tributaries). The other important aspect of river valleys which greatly influences the wines produced there is the concentration of solar radiation on the sloping banks. The steeper the slope the greater this effect. All these are positive influences which make for ripe and finer wines, that are less likely to have an aggressive acidity.

Features of a wine region's landscape can also have a negative effect on its climate. Thus it is often supposed that the reason for the lesser ripeness and steely acidity in wines from the Saar valley, compared to the fuller, riper wines from the Middle Moselle, is due to the Saar being the more northerly area. In fact it is the other way round, the Middle Moselle being more northerly than the Saar. Its climate is more advantageous in spite of this, because the steepness and winding nature of the Moselle valley protects the vineyards there from cold wind. In contrast, the Saar vineyards are very exposed to wind from the east and north-east, which means that the vines there start growing later, and the grapes start ripening later too. On the other hand, in very hot years the Saar wines' extra spur of acidity can make them the finest of all Germany, because of the extra elegance this brings.

The regional-varietal revolution

Grape varieties can hardly be separated from soil types when speaking about the traditional style of any region's wines. The flavour components a wine gains from the soil depend very largely on the grape variety. In the wines they give, some vine varieties strongly reflect the soil on which they are grown. This is particularly true of Riesling and Chardonnay. Other varieties, such as Gewürztraminer and Müller-Thurgau, tend to impose their own character over that which the soil gives the wine. The classic German example of the combination of soil, vine variety, and winemaking style working together to produce a traditional regional style of wine is Silvaner grown on the heavier clay soils of Rheinhessen, and then fermented to bone dryness. The full body, round, rather neutral, fruitiness, and pronounced chalky earthiness of these wines is *the* traditional taste of the region.

One of the most important of Germany's new regional-varietal wines for everyday drinking is 'RS', the Rheinhessen Silvaner whose production is monitored and approved by the Rheinhessen wine development organisation, Rheinhessen-wein. This is made by nearly two hundred producers to a set of analytical criteria which ensure that the result is in the traditional regional style for Silvaner wines. These producers include some fine estates, and the region's largest co-operative cellars. Their wines are quality tested by Rheinhessenwein, and the wines which make the grade receive the common labels used by all RS producers. Each producer adds his name in small print to one side of the striking black and yellow RS label, and must then market the wine at or above an agreed minimum price. (Sekt in the same style is also produced.)

Riesling produces an amazing diversity of flavours and aromas as a result of being grown on different soils. Although it always needs a good vineyard site and good exposure to the sun, it adapts well to slate, sand, loess, chalk, limestone, loam, clay, marl, porphyry, quartzite, and some other soil types. This means that Riesling is very widely planted in Germany, being at least represented in all eleven of the wine-growing regions and important in nine of them: a major reason why the character of German wines varies so much while they retain a strong family resemblance.

Another important and valuable aspect of the Riesling vine is that its grapes do not have to reach full ripeness to give good wines. However, it does need a certain minimum amount of body, of alcohol, to make a fully satisfactory wine. The wines of other grape varieties are no different; few Chardonnay wines with less than 12 degrees of alcohol are really satisfactory, for example. Under this level of body they tend to be rather thin and insubstantial. If made as a dry wine, Riesling requires less alcohol than Chardonnay, at least 9 degrees in the Moselle, 10 degrees in the Rheingau and Nahe, and 11 degrees further south. Made with some sweetness, Riesling wines can manage with less still, and a fine Moselle, Saar or Ruwer Auslese may have only 7 degrees of alcohol.

The French have been very clever about the addition of sugar to wines, which is often necessary to achieve the alcohol level that will give the finished wine the necessary body to underpin the fruit character of the grape variety, and the flavours which come from the soil. They call this process 'chaptelisation', and speak of it as though it were a tradition going back into the mists of time, rather than being the invention of Napoleon's minister of agriculture. Without this legally approved additive even the wines from the great Bordeaux châteaux would only be good two or three vintages every decade. However, this image of chaptelisation as a traditional practice has led to its being abused in some French regions (Burgundy still being the principal offender), with the result that many wines are made over-alcoholic.

The Germans, who are generally much more circumspect about adding anything to their wines, have been very stupid in their presentation of this necessary practice. They have called it 'Verbesserung', which translates as 'improvement' in English, and conjures up images of soap powder and lists of E numbers. They have also introduced a legal distinction between wines to which sugar has been added, which are called Qualitätswein or QbA, and those to which it has not been added, Qualitätswein mit Prädikat or QmP wines. This distinction does not necessarily say anything about the real quality of the wine bearing these different designations, nor would it if applied to Bordeaux or other French wines. A chaptelised wine can be excellent or poor, as can an unchaptelised one.

In the past, German wine producers concentrated much too much on QmP wines, because these had a good image as a result of having no sugar added to them. This was a mistake, because in the north of Germany about half of all the wine produced as QbA has to have sugar added to have enough body to be harmonious. However, as a result of consumer suspicion of Prädikat, or QmP, wines in the wake of the diethylene glycol scandal, which affected only such wines, an ever-expanding selection of high-quality QbA wines have come on to the market. At the same time as the anxiety about QbA status has been thrown out of the window in the cause of better winemaking and continuity of supply, unpronounceable vineyard names have also been abandoned. Almost without exception all these new wines state the grape variety and region of origin prominently on the label; everything else is then printed as small as the law will allow.

They are a marked contrast to the German QbA wines with which we are all familiar: Liebfraumilch, Piesporter Michelsberg, Bernkasteler Kurfurstlay, and Niersteiner Gutes Domtal. Apart from Liebfraumilch, these wines are all sold under 'Grosslage' names. A 'Grosslage' is a collective site, which means that wines from a wide area can be sold under this name rather than having to be sold under the individual vineyard name. This sounds good, but unfortunately these Grosslage names invariably *appear* to be a village name followed by a vineyard designation. In fact the majority of Piesporter Michelsberg wines have nothing whatsoever to do with the pretty little village of Piesport on the Moselle, or its excellent steep slate-soil vineyards. Most Piesporter Michelsberg comes from flat vineyards around the village of Leiwen that produce distinctly inferior wines. These are cheap, whereas any wine from the good Piesport vineyards would be far too expensive to sell under the Michelsberg name. The same unfortunate problem applies to all the famous Grosslage names.

The new regional-varietal QbA wines renounce this confidence trick in favour of telling us what we really need to know about wines of this quality level: where they come from, and the style of the wine. Perhaps the most important producers of these new-style wines in Germany are the large regional co-operatives. Given this, placing a regional designation no more precise than Rheinhessen, Rheinpfalz or Baden on the label makes sense, for that gives them the chance to draw the component wines for these blends from any of their members. That is good for the quality of the wine. It also makes it easy for us, since we only need to learn a very few regional names. The grape variety and whether the wine is dry, medium-dry, or sweet tells you the style. Bottle shapes and colours are also being used to indicate this, clear glass generally indicating dryness.

One of the best examples of such wines is the new 'Master Class' range from the Rietburg co-operative in the Palatinate. In

RHEINPFALZ
QUALITÄTSWEIN

1986 ER
GRAUER BURGUNDER
TROCKEN
BEREICH SÜDLICHE WEINSTRASSE
A.P.NR.   5062052-48-87   Alc. 11,0% vol.

ERZEUGERABFÜLLUNG DER
GEBIETSWINZERGENOSSENSCHAFT RIETBURG EG,
RHODT/SÜDL. WEINSTR.   0,75ℓ e

many respects these wines are the brain-child of Rietburg's
Mancunian – yes, Mancunian – export director, Philip Scammel.
It is hard to convey the sense of shock I felt the first time I visited
the Rietburg and found myself met by someone with a broad
Manchester accent, but clearly the world really is a small place
these days. Undoubtedly Philip Scammel's directness of
approach, and the fresh perspective he brought to the Rietburg,
were crucial to the creation of their Master Class range. When he
arrived in 1985 Philip Scammel carefully examined their full
range of wines, and while he found most of them to be of
acceptable or very good quality, he felt that they did not realise
the potential which the co-operative's good vineyards and wide
range of grape varieties made possible.

'Some of our members,' he told me, 'will insist on harvesting
their grapes as late as possible, whether it's good for the wine or
not. Often this means that these grapes have very little acidity
when they are harvested, and the wine is then rather flabby. I
know this late harvesting is a tradition in Germany, but there's
no use producing lots of Spätlese and Auslese if almost nobody
wants these wines.' He felt that with their thirty-plus grape
varieties there was great scope for tailoring the winemaking to
each of these and producing high-quality varietal wines. 'Take
Müller-Thurgau, for example. Most of it is made really sweet in
this part of Germany, and then it's rather boring, characterless.
However, made very cleanly and with only a touch of sweetness
it's a lovely, refreshing, fruity wine you can drink a whole bottle
of.'

He was also worried by the complexity of the labelling, and the
sheer number of different wines they had on their list. 'If you
think there's something important enough about one of your
wines that people should look for it again, then the label and the
bottle has got to virtually shout this at them.' The old Rietburg
label was, if I am completely honest, one of the ugliest and
clumsiest going, with far too many decorative scrolls and different typefaces to be easily legible. The label is surely 'first base'
for any wine trying to appeal to a large number and wide range of
people. Who is going to pick up a bottle of wine with a near-
illegible label? And, if someone does pick up such a bottle, how
are they going to know what it is they have bought? How will
they ask for it again?

The Master Class, which was released in May 1987, is the fruition of many months of consideration of Rietburg's strengths and problems, and many months of development. It is composed of four dry and two medium-dry white wines, and one red wine. All seven varieties are traditional to the Palatinate, and though Müller-Thurgau, a vine crossing, is included, it has been grown there since the beginning of the century. None of these wines is quite bone-dry, as their acidity is relatively high compared to dry white wines from other countries. The minimal touch of unfermented sugar in each of the dry varietals has been adjusted to bring out the full fruitiness of the wine and to round its acidity. The two medium-dry wines, Gewürztraminer and Müller-Thurgau, are from varieties judged to need rather more sweetness to bring out their more aromatic character. The taste of these is definitely medium-dry, though, not medium-sweet. Although in good vintages the Master Class blends will be largely composed of wines which have not had any sugar added to them, that is Prädikat or QmP wines, they will always be sold as QbA (Qualitätswein) so that the label will stay the same from one year to the next, apart from the vintage changes.

Rietburg's aim is that each of the Master Class wines will show a clear varietal character, and that they will all be harmonious dry wines with enough body for the dinner table. This means 10.5° alcohol for the medium-dry wines, 11.0° for the dry whites, and 11.5° for the red. The softer Müller-Thurgau and Gewürztraminer also drink beautifully on their own. The rich dry Weissburgunder (known as Pinot Blanc in France), which unlike the other Master Class wines has had some malolactic fermentation, is also most attractive to drink on its own. Several of the range are quite serious for wines being discussed in an everyday drinking context, particularly the dry Riesling which is quite a firm, masculine wine. It would have no difficulty being served with game (so long as the meat was not cooked in, or served with, a red wine sauce).

Having made these wines to be drunk with food, Rietburg have bottled them in clear Burgundy-shaped bottles to emphasise this. The very modern-looking artist label is a highly impressionistic vineyard landscape. The packaging is designed to fit the new style of wine; winemaking, presentation, and marketing working together, rather than simply being a matter of old wines in new bottles. Compared to the old mixture of somnolent worship of tradition for tradition's own sake and ad hoc modernisation which used to typify much of the German wine business, this represents a great leap forward in sophistication.

More and more of the co-operatives and commercial cellars in Germany are coming up with wines in similar styles. Recently a concept similar to RS was launched for Baden wines, for example (though in this case there are seven dry varietal wines). The co-operatives are also starting to work together bottling similar-style wines from different regions and grape varieties under common packaging. There is a veritable explosion of drier-style varietal wines coming on to the market. I am sure that it will not be long before we take these wines to our hearts as firmly as an earlier generation took Liebfraumilch. Then Germany will once again offer a truly balanced selection of wines which offer a range of possibilities at every price level, not just Liebfraumilch and Piesporter Michelsberg at one end and much more expensive estate-bottled wines at the other. Then we shall be able to *drink* German wine regularly with pleasure, rather than just quaff it.

Understanding German fine wine: a selection of the best in German winemaking

It is often said that German fine wines are complex and technical, difficult to understand in comparison to other wines. To a large extent this is nonsense. Just imagine how difficult it would be to try to understand the wines of France from scratch if there were not dozens of books on the subject, many knowledgeable wine merchants, and a lot of educational television and magazine advertising to offer a path through the complications of the Bordeaux classifications, the hierarchy of Burgundian vineyards, the Grand Cru system of Alsace, etc. The problem with Germany is largely due to unfamiliarity with the country and its wines. While wine writers sometimes write about the way French wines are made even in national newspaper columns, some of these writers sadly do not even understand how German wines are made. Little guidance is available to anyone wanting to learn more about German wines.

Any wine-producing country or region approached for the first time can seem daunting. Undoubtedly, the easiest way to get to grips with a new wine region is to actually go there, and to talk to the people who make the wines. The following profiles of some of Germany's top wine producers try to come as close to that experience as possible. Each one focuses on one aspect of the character or making of German wines generally, of which this producer is a particularly good example. All the producers are important figures in their regions, well-known to neighbouring growers, and a few are famous well beyond Germany's borders.

Wine producers always have strong opinions, no matter from which country they come, and these often conflict with those of their neighbours and colleagues. These points of difference between winemakers as to what is the correct way of doing things are precisely what gives each producer's wines their own particular character, or style. For this reason, no attempt has been made to harmonise the opinions of these strong personalities. Winemaking in Germany, and beyond, is half an art and half a science, and to try to reduce it to the latter is to give a false picture of it. There are therefore more than a few seeming contradictions in the following pages!

It is important to point out that these producers are not my selection of *the best* winemakers of Germany. The wines of many of the estates and co-operatives featured in the Directory section of this book are just as fine as those from the following selection of producers. Indeed, they include some of my favourite German wine producers.

The vineyard area of each estate is given in both hectares and acres. There are 2.47 acres to the hectare. In calculating acreages the figure has been expressed to the nearest half-acre.

Weingut Fritz Haag, Mosel

Wilhelm Haag (owner).
Weingut Fritz Haag,
Dusemonder Hof,
D 5551 Brauneberg/Mosel.
Tel: 06534 410.

5 hectares/12.5 acres.
100% Riesling.

Wilhelm Haag's small estate in Brauneberg epitomises the wealth of great German wines which remain virtually unknown in England. From the first time Wilhelm welcomed me to his estate in the spring of 1986, I was convinced that he was not only one of the best wine producers in the Moselle valley, but one of the greatest white wine producers of the world. Yet, at this time not one single bottle of his wine was coming to England!

For those who have only experienced the popular face of Moselle wines, the Piesporter Michelsberg or Bereich Bernkastel QbA wines which line so many supermarket shelves, the first taste of a Fritz Haag wine will be either a revelation or a profound shock. Mass-produced commercial Moselle wines are very soft, sweet, and neutral in flavour. They are made predominantly from Müller-Thurgau grapes from vines which have been so mercilessly over-cropped that the wines they yield are virtually a cocktail of water, alcohol and sugar. Wilhelm Haag's Riesling wines, which come principally from the great Brauneberger Juffer and Brauneberger Juffer-Sonnenuhr vineyards, are the very opposite of this. They are extremely intense, and always marked by a scintillating interplay of fruit flavours and racy acidity.

In the Moselle region only wines made from the Riesling grape can have this kind of vigour, concentration, and flowery complexity. However, if such wines are made in an unmanipulative, uncompromising style like that of Weingut Fritz Haag, then in their youth they can be every bit as aggressive as an immature top-class red Bordeaux wine. The power and aggression of young Château Latour or Château Mouton Rothschild come principally from the tannins and alcohol which form their structure. In Riesling wines the acidity and mineral extracts fulfil the same role, which can be quite as mouth-puckering as the 'skeletal' structure of a red wine. However, without a good quantity of these, Riesling wines can be nearly as soft and characterless as the mass-produced Moselle wines.

At a tasting in the surprisingly modern Dusemonder Hof, a quite attractive piece of 1960s architecture, it is hard not to be bowled over by the sheer enthusiasm and excitement with which Wilhelm Haag talks about his young wines. Though in his late forties, Wilhelm has the energy of a much younger man, for whom every new vintage offers many surprises and challenges. While the majority of German wine producers still measure the success of a vintage by whether they get a high enough sugar level in the grapes to be legally allowed to sell their wines as Spätlese or Auslese, for Wilhelm Haag a vintage is good if the wines are crystal clear, and if the majority have nine or even ten grams per litre of acidity.

To put this acidity content in perspective, it is about one and a half times as much as that of a fine Champagne! However, and this is the critical point, because the great majority of Wilhelm Haag's wines come from the steep south-south-west-facing slope of the Brauneberg their acidity is almost never sharp. Haag wines are not 'acid' in the negative sense of the word as it is normally applied to wine. In such good vineyard sites a good proportion of the acidity in the grapes is the ripe-tasting *tartaric* acid. In lesser Moselle vineyards, which either have poor exposure to the sun, and/or are not steep enough to concentrate the sun's warmth, the acidity in the wines will be almost exclusively the harsh, unripe-tasting *malic* acid. The Germans have graphic words for these two kinds of acidity: tartaric acid is '<u>Wein</u><u>saure</u>' or wine acidity, and malic acid is '<u>Apfelsaure</u>' or apple acidity.

Weingut Dusemonder Hof - Brauneberg / Mosel

FRITZ HAAG
1985er
Brauneberger Juffer-Sonnenuhr
Riesling - Auslese
Erzeugerabfüllung - Qualitätswein mit Prädikat
750 ml   A. P. Nr. 2 577 050 19 86   Alc. 7,1 % by Vol.

With a high but ripe enough acidity, a Riesling wine from the Moselle or the best areas on the Rhine can age like no other white wine. At wine tastings Wilhelm Haag likes nothing more than to astonish his guests by serving a wine from his cellar blind, and to confound everyone by showing how much older than their guesses the wine actually is. The most extreme example of this that I have experienced at the Dusemonder Hof was a 1935 Brauneberger, a wine of the most ordinary quality grade from a forgotten vintage. It showed no old character whatsoever. Indeed, on the contrary, it had a vigorous youthful fruitiness which suggested a wine of half a dozen years of age! In less rarefied territory, some of the Haag wines of the excellent 1975, 1979 and 1985 vintages will not reach their peak until well into the next century.

When fine Riesling wines start to mature, which is to say after they have been in the bottle for at least three or four years, then each wine starts to develop a highly individual character. The remarkable variety of fruit, spice, herbal, vegetal, and honeyed tones which the bouquet and flavour of Riesling wines gain as they age makes them unique amongst white wines. When they are young the fruitiness of fine Rieslings is reminiscent of green fruits, apples, or white peaches. With age this is transformed in the most extraordinary ways. A Haag Brauneberger Juffer-Sonnenuhr Auslese from the great 1953 vintage that I tasted last year with Wilhelm had exactly the smell which comes up from a forest floor after heavy rain. (This is no poetic exaggeration, for all those present had precisely the same impression of the wine.)

Wilhelm Haag's approach to winemaking is to preserve and cultivate these individual characteristics of each barrel of wine in his cellar. Hence the importance of the barrel or lot number, which is the number printed in bold in the AP code number on every one of the estate's labels. In the Moselle, wines are traditionally made in 1000 litre barrels called 'Füder', but many of the larger producers have exchanged these for much bigger tanks (normally of stainless steel). An entire vintage at Weingut Fritz Haag, which on average is a mere thirty-five Füder barrels, would not begin to fill just one tank at the large regional co-operative a few miles away! Needless to say, to mix all these barrels together would be to mix up and lose the individual character of each of these wines.

As a result of the Haag policy of cultivating individuality, in any particular vintage there are Weingut Fritz Haag wines which are light and flowery and develop quite quickly, and there are powerful, more earthy wines, and also steely wines which will age almost indefinitely. The Moselle wines of the 1975 vintage are, for instance, normally very elegant, 'classic' flowery Rieslings; even the late-harvested Auslese wines are refreshing rather than rich and powerful. Most of Wilhelm's wines are beautiful examples of this, but he also has an Auslese which is very full-bodied and heavy, and yet another Auslese which is still extremely firm and undeveloped. The latter has a considerable amount of unfermented sweetness (about 60 grams per litre), but tastes almost dry because of the very powerful acidity in the wine.

The winemaker's decision as to how much sweetness each

wine should retain after fermentation is critical in determining
whether it has the balance which will allow its own particular
character to be best expressed. Today many German winemakers can state quite simply how they balance the level of
unfermented sugar in their wines. Owing to the current obsession of many German wine drinkers with absolutely bone-dry
wines, there are wine producers who on principle only produce
wines which have fermented out to analytical bone dryness. At
the other extreme there are producers who give all their
Kabinett wines 35 grams per litre of sweetness, all their Spätlese
45 grams per litre of sweetness, etc. In the Moselle neither of
these is a recipe for harmony.

Wilhelm Haag's answer to a direct question as to how he
decides the level of sweetness that a particular Füder of wine
needs sums up his entire winemaking philosophy. 'There is no
easy answer at all, it depends on the degree of ripeness of the
grapes, which part of the Brauneberg they have come from, the
weather conditions we had during the summer and the weeks
before the harvest . . . These decisions are all based on years of
experience. As each bin of grapes comes into the press house
during the harvest I look it over, smell it, and taste from it, then I
drink a glass of must from each pressing. All my impressions,
together with the details of which parcel of vineyard the grapes
came from then get recorded in a book which I have kept since I
started making the estate's wines. By tasting the finished wines,
and comparing them with what is recorded in the book I have
slowly refined the way in which I make my wines.'

In principle, the making of the Weingut Fritz Haag wines is at
the same time extremely pedantic, yet as straightforward as
possible. The sweetness which the Brauneberger Juffer-
Sonnenuhr wines retain is entirely their own natural sweetness
from the grape must, the fermentation being stopped before the
yeast has consumed all the sugar in the fermenting must. The
Brauneberger Juffer wines are all made dry or medium-dry now,
and the dry ones are fermented through until the yeast is no
longer active. Even so, between four and nine grams of sweetness per litre remain in them, and this does much to harmonise
these wines without giving any taste sensation of sweetness. To
retain their vibrant freshness, all the wines are bottled early,
normally in March or April. However, because of the variation

in their character some do not reach the list until many years later.

While Wilhelm Haag's estate has had a great reputation in the United States for many years, fame has come only recently in Germany. If it comes to England too, then the name of the Brauneberg may yet return to the height of renown which it enjoyed during the last century.

Wine has always been something of a fashion industry, and the modern taste has been for the cleaner, more polished elegance of the wines of the Wehlener Sonnenuhr vineyard. Maybe taste is changing again, and the more solid, masculine Brauneberg wines with their distinctive, but not dominant, earthiness will once again be deemed to belong to the very first class of Moselle wines, and of white wines as a whole.

Maximin Grünhaus, Ruwer

Dr Carl Ferdinand von Schubert (owner),
Alfons Heinrich (cellarmaster).
C. von Schubert'sche Gutsverwaltung,
D 5501 Grünhaus bei Trier.
Tel: 0651 5111.

33 hectares/81.5 acres.
95% Riesling, 5% Müller-Thurgau and Kerner.

During the last few years the name of Maximin Grünhaus has become more and more closely identified with the finest-quality Riesling wines, not just in Germany but around the world. The consistently high quality and distinctive character of the wines from this estate, combined with its equally unmistakable art nouveau label, and the fact that all three of its vineyard sites – Bruderberg (3 ha/7.4 acres), Herrenberg (17 ha/42 acres), and Abtsberg (13 ha/32.1 acres) – are in the estate's exclusive possession, have worked to create its remarkable reputation.

In spite of this, rather little has been written about the way the wines at Maximin Grünhaus are made, which is surprising since the estate's methods highlight many of the critical factors in making fine Riesling wines generally. Although the Maximin Grünhaus estate has always had a very good name, it is since Dr

Carl von Schubert arrived as full-time owner late in 1981 that it has risen to its present heights. This is not because Carl is a brilliant publicist, though he does have a very natural gift for explaining the estate's aims and methods such that even those with no technical knowledge can understand them. The real reason is that he has done much to refine and rationalise the way the estate's grapes are processed after harvesting and the resulting wines are made.

Perhaps the most distinctive quality of the Maximin Grünhaus wines is their delicately herbal/flowery bouquet, and the great delicacy of their flavour. In these respects they are the apotheosis of fine German Riesling. Although the Grünhaus wines are remarkably long-lived, their seeming fragility was real enough when they were at the grapes and grape must stage. Dr Carl von Schubert explained this to me very succinctly when I stayed at the estate for the first time. 'At all costs we want to retain the lively fruitiness of the wines. For this reason we are very careful not to leave our wines too long in the barrel, and for the same reason I introduced our new system in the press house in 1982.'

To understand the influence of barrel maturation on German wines, one should descend into the cask cellar at Maximin Grünhaus. The nineteenth-century buildings stand a short distance away from the original estate house, which dates back to the early Middle Ages. It used to house a part of the abbey of St Maximin from which the estate takes its name. One would hardly know that the cellar buildings are of a different period, though, because the member of the von Schubert family who bought the estate in 1882 and built them made sure that all his many additions harmonised with the existing building. Below ground the cellars extend under a large part of the park-like garden, and the bottle cellar is of Roman origin.

The extensive casks cellar houses a 'palette' of casks from 228 litres in size, up to 500-litre Halbfüder and 1000-litre Füder, plus a few 7000-litre casks. The smallest barrels are in fact Limousin oak 'barriques', but they have already been used at another estate (Schlossgut Diel, p. 54) where all the oak flavour has been removed from them. The aim here, as at all other traditional German estates, is to use the wooden barrels only to 'ripen' the wines, not to give them any oak flavour as is common in France. This 'ripening' process which wine stored in an old oak barrel undergoes is a result simply of the slow passage of oxygen through the wood of the barrel, and it is something Carl von Schubert passionately believes in. For him, 'with a good Riesling wine this opens out the flavour and bouquet, and the wine becomes more complex. From the 1983 vintage, for example, we had the equivalent of 180 Füder of wine from Qualitätswein up to Trockenbeerenauslese and Eiswein, and even then almost every wine spent some time in cask. Fifty years ago our wines would have been aged in cask for two or three years. Today, our wines normally spend about six months in cask.'

The best wines at Maximin Grünhaus also ferment in cask, and this is part of the reason for the range of cask sizes: small barrels for the rare Beerenauslese, Trockenbeerenauslese and Eiswein dessert wines, big casks for the dry-style QbA wines. The reason why the latter are made in the big casks is not just that Carl von Schubert has increased the production of wines in this style, but also because if made in Füder barrels they would naturally stop fermenting before all the sugar had been turned to alcohol. In the large barrels they ferment a bit further, and the taste of many German customers for really bone-dry wines can be satisfied. On the other hand, the Spätlese and Auslese wines in the traditional sweeter style are deliberately fermented in Füder or Halbfüder casks in the coldest part of the cellar. Here the fermentation stops naturally whilst considerable sweetness remains. (The sweeter QbA and Kabinett wines of more modest qualities are made in tanks, where pressure is used to stop the fermentation.)

Down in the cellar the Grünhaus motto is 'as little handling of the wine as possible, but as much as necessary'. This is also true upstairs in the press house, where Carl von Schubert's grape handling system is operated. This requires no pumps whatsoever, all movement of the grapes and pressed grape must being done by gravity. When the grapes arrive in wooden boxes they are tipped into a mill where they are broken open. From here they drop into the pneumatic press, from which the must runs into settling tanks on the level below. Here it sits at least overnight, so that any solid matter can naturally settle out; centrifuges assist this separation process only after very difficult harvesting conditions. Finally the clear must runs down into the cask and tank cellar. This could hardly be simpler, as is all the best winemaking.

Just as important as this careful handling of grapes and must is the sheer speed with which the grapes come from the vine to the press. 1982 was a difficult vintage in Germany as a result of torrential rain at harvest time, which meant a lot of rotten grapes and many unclean wines. The worst offenders were the largest estates, who could not cope with the massive quantity of grapes that year. In their press houses bins of grapes stood around for many hours or even days waiting to be pressed. At Maximin Grünhaus the grapes come straight from the vineyard into the press house, which stands at the bottom of the single continuous slope of the Herrenberg, Abtsberg and Bruderberg vineyards. As a result of this, the 1982 Maximin Grünhaus wines are delightful: fresh, clean and typical in bouquet and flavour.

What happens when grapes sit around, and if wines stand too long in cask, is that oxidation starts to take place, which makes the wine less fruity and rather blunt in taste. The remarkable finesse of the best Grünhaus wines depends on the fruitiness of the wine being unimpaired by oxidation. In France some white wines are macerated on the skins to give them more flavour, which means that after the grapes have been broken open in the mill the resulting mash of grape pulp, juice and skins is deliberately left to stand for some hours. The resulting wine gains extra flavour from the grape skins, but a degree of oxidation accompanies this. In Germany few producers will risk this for fear of losing the flower-like freshness which they seek. German wines may rarely have the sheer power of, say, great white Burgundy, but this is not what they are about. They are not made with the same aim in view, and they should not be judged in foreign terms.

Carl von Schubert loves to taste wines from other regions and countries, and has a private cellar full of fine claret going back into the last century. What he looks for most of all when tasting any wine is a distinctive regional or varietal character. 'I don't like this modern tendency for the wines of every country to taste alike,' he insists. 'I'm very glad that there is nowhere in the world which has yet produced wines like ours. I don't want to use new oak casks to mature my wines, and try to pretend that Grünhaus

Riesling wines can be like Chablis, and I would hate to find that someone in another region was trying to imitate us. With so many things today becoming standardised, I think that the special character of our wines is something we must hold on to.'

While Carl has personally done much to cultivate the special character of the estate's wines, the cellarmaster, Herr Heinrich, is a crucial factor too. He has been in charge of both the cellar and the vineyards at Maximin Grünhaus for more than three decades. As he said to me, 'How can I make a wine if I don't know where the grapes came from? Each part of the Abtsberg, Herrenberg and Bruderberg has its own qualities, and I have to know about these when deciding how I am going to make the wine from each parcel of vineyard. For example, we indicate that some Auslese grade wines are of special quality by putting a cask number on the top label, and in 1983 the best of these was the Abtsberg Auslese 190. When I tasted through the 1983 wines in cask with Dr Carl von Schubert, I told him that because of where in the Abtsberg this wine came from it would be the best Auslese. He was not immediately convinced. This Auslese is neither the richest we made that year, nor the one with the highest acidity. However, by bottling time I was shown to have been correct in my judgement.'

At Maximin Grünhaus there is also another vital link between vineyard and cellar. This is the yeast which comes into the cellar on the skins of the grapes. Natural yeast communities in vineyards develop over decades, and the proportions of each strain in each individual vineyard can differ markedly. These natural yeast strains ferment wines differently from each other, and from cultured strains.

The wine scandals in Germany during the early 1980s have given German wines the image of being at worst artificial, and at best the result of a lot of manipulative techniques. In fact, at the top end of the quality scale, they are amongst the purest and most 'natural' wines in the world. Maximin Grünhaus is a shining example of this.

Weingut St Johannishof, Mosel

Ernst Loosen (owner),
Bernhard Schug (cellarmaster).
Weingut St Johannishof,
Postfach 1308,
D 5550 Bernkastel.
Tel: 06531 3426.

8.0 hectares/20 acres.
97% Riesling, 3% Müller-Thurgau.

To take ripe Riesling grapes from good Moselle vineyards and turn them into quite nice wines is not so difficult, but to make great wines from these same vineyards requires a level of involvement, and an attention to detail, which to an outsider would probably look like obsession. The Loosen family, which originates from Ürzig, has been making good wines in the Moselle valley for generations, but until recently wine has always taken second place to politics.

Ernst Loosen, who recently took over control of the family estate, never really wanted to be a wine producer until he found that he was one. Though he went through three years of study at

the Geisenheim viticultural and winemaking school, he was much more interested in archaeology. It was only when his father's health problems forced him back to the family estate from Mainz University, and he had to make the 1983 vintage at a moment's notice, that he discovered a real passion for wine-making. From the rather hesitant beginning with that vintage the wines of Weingut St Johannishof have come on in leaps and bounds, the best 1985, 1986, and 1987 wines from the estate being of the very highest quality.

The jump in quality already achieved required an enormous amount of work. Wine production is in many ways one of the arts, but it is also like a complex engineering problem; really great wine comes about when both these aspects are highly developed, and then nature adds the best it can give. However, from a short meeting with Ernst Loosen one would never think that he is capable of the kind of application and rigour necessary to make great wines. Even most of his neighbours amongst the wine estate owners misjudge him in this respect. Ernst Loosen could hardly be more relaxed and casual in manner. He seems, at first glance, only too happy to drop work to enjoy a few glasses of wine with friends or visitors. The often chaotic state of his office also seems to speak against his possessing the necessary organi-sational abilities . . .

What his neighbours have not seen, though, and what is also not apparent to casual visitors, is the depth of seriousness behind the joking front. In the last few years Ernst has visited numerous wine producers in Chablis, the Côte de Beaune, Alsace, Gaillac, California, Switzerland, and England to expand his experience of winemaking techniques and philosophies around the world. There have also been innumerable critical private tasting ses-sions of his own and other Moselle wines, at which nobody is harder on the St Johannishof wines than Ernst and his young cellarmaster, Bernie. The smallest weaknesses are picked out and analysed, and each is felt as a reproach for not having been more careful with this detail of the handling of the must, or with the selection of the grapes, or with the cellar work.

For Ernst all this is essential to raising his estate up to being one of the very best in the region. 'How can I expect to improve our wines if I don't learn about all the other methods which I could use, and if I don't look for the tiniest problems in the wines we've already made? In winemaking the smallest differences in each stage of the process all show up in the finished wine. We have vineyards in five villages along the middle part of the Moselle valley, and the wines from each of these five villages has its own character. A few mistakes in the cellar and the subtle tones which give each its individual character can be lost or covered up. This is what we want to avoid at all costs. What I am after is wines which though they are light in alcohol are rich and complex in flavour.'

For Ernst, the biggest mistake of the last generation was that too many wines were made with too much sweetness. The effect of this was to cover up the special tastes which come from the different soils in the villages of Erden, Ürzig, Wehlen, Graach, and Bernkastel where the estate has its vineyards. Until recent vintages the majority of St Johannishof wines were not just lacking in elegance, but also in character. The only wines which rarely suffered from this problem, the only ones which were really nurtured, were the Erdener Prälat wines. This vine-yard has a red sandstone soil which gives its wines a completely different character from normal 'slaty' Moselle wines. It is the light, flowery Riesling wines from the vineyards with slate soils which have made the Moselle famous, but much more serious complex wines come from the heavier soils in Ürzig, Erden, the Brauneberg, and parts of Graach. These have been ignored and forgotten during recent decades, because they do not square with our expectations of what Moselle wines should taste like.

Ernst is a great fan of these earthier, more complex Moselle wines, and has been conducting many experiments on how to get stronger flavours from the soil into the wines he makes from the Bernkasteler Badstube vineyards, and the world-famous Wehlener Sonnenuhr site. Here the wines have a comparatively clean, lightly slatey (flinty) character, though in Wehlen this can be combined with an exquisite richness and piquancy. Ernst has reduced the yield in his vineyards in these sites in order to achieve this extra concentration. This was done simply by chang-ing the pruning system to the less labour intensive 'Vertico' form.

It makes a fascinating tasting to line up a group of wines from the Erden and Ürzig vineyards, which lie next to one another at the crook of one of the Moselle's great loops. Here the vineyards rise very steeply from the bank of the Moselle, many clinging to the small patches of precipitous soil around the red sandstone cliffs which separate the Ürziger Würzgarten to the west and the Erdener Treppchen to the east. Below these cliffs in a position almost perfectly sheltered from wind is the Erdener Prälat. This great wall of red rock and vines is undoubtedly one of the most stirring vineyard views in the world.

The richest of the wines from this favoured corner of the Moselle valley are from the Erdener Prälat, owing to its exceptional microclimate. The vineyard faces south-southwest, the perfect aspect, giving it all the sun of the day and the evening, and the rocks above it retain the warmth of the sun, radiating it back at night. Directly in front of the vineyard is the Moselle itself, which also acts as a heat reservoir. The sum of all this can be tasted in the wines, which have a unique combination of the special rich earthiness which comes from red sandstone in the soil, and the extra ripeness from the remarkable microclimate. On the opposite bank of the river here is a classic example of the Moselle region's problems: a great expanse of flat vineyards planted with non-traditional grape varieties during the past fifteen years. The quality produced from this pancake of a vineyard that is completely exposed to the wind, with its heavy clayey soil, is miserable.

Weingut St Johannishof's 1977 Erdener Prälat Spätlese and 1984 Erdener Prälat Kabinett were classic examples of what this very special vineyard site can produce. Both were minor vintages in which the great majority of Moselle wines were Qualitätswein. In marked contrast to the unripeness of the majority of the region's wines in these vintages, these wines are ripe and concentrated.

The character of the Erdener Treppchen wines reflects that of the vineyard's exceedingly steep slope, where the soils are lighter and slatier than the Prälat's. The Treppchen wines share a little of the Prälat's earthiness, but are altogether nervier and more filigraine. Because they are lighter in weight they also develop a little more quickly, and from reasonably ripe vintage they can be very attractive from eighteen months of age. They can age just as long as the Prälat wines, though, and from a vintage with perfect balance such as 1971, 1985, or 1987 will live for many decades. Like fine red wines, they should be decanted if drunk in their youth, since contact with the air helps open up their bouquet. The most pungent of all the wines from this corner of the Moselle are those from the Ürziger Würzgarten, which have a luscious exotic fruitiness in ripe vintages.

We tend to assume that power in white wines comes only from alcohol and new-oak character (tannins). While white wines can certainly have power as a result of having good amounts of these components, they can also have power which comes from acidity, and from mineral extracts. This is epitomised by the wines of Weingut St Johannishof, where Ernst Loosen seeks to make wines with modest alcohol and no oak flavour, but real power. The style of the estate's wines is the most direct possible expression of Ernst Loosen's personal taste. He much prefers strongly flavoured, spicy food such as the Cajun cuisine of Louisiana to international-style Haute Cuisine. Even though Moselle wines are from their alcohol content amongst the lightest in the world, Ernst Loosen wants every one of his wines to make a strong impression on those who drink it. At all costs he tries to avoid making wines which are neutral, which will not evoke any response from those who drink them. In this his winemaking is diametrically opposed to the characterlessness which sadly typifies so much Moselle wine. He will surely become a model for the new generation of winemakers in the region, though perhaps not for the organic wine producers; Ernst organically produced Müller-Thurgau wines are too well made and he is too well organized, for them!

Weingut Dr Heinz Wagner, Saar

Heinz Wagner (owner).
Weingut Dr Heinz Wagner Nachf,
Bahnhofstrasse 3,
D 5510 Saarburg.
Tel: 06581 2457.

7.5 hectares/18 acres.
100% Riesling.

Saar is has great natural pot'l for wine, tho its wines are inherently light (p48)

It often happens that a wine-producing region becomes identified with one great producer, and that however good his or her neighbours may be they remain in the shadow of this one bright star. The vineyards which cluster around the Moselle's most westerly tributary, the Saar, produce Riesling wines of a unique kind, which during the decades since the last war have become ever more closely identified with the name of Weingut Egon Müller-Scharzhof (p. 137) *In fact, although this world-famous estate certainly deserves its stratospheric reputation, there is a remarkable concentration of fine producers on the Saar (pp. 137–43). The reason for this is that whilst the Moselle valley has problems arising from the planting of what was hitherto poor arable land with vines that produce untypical wines, the Saar hardly suffers from this at all.*

Of the many top Saar estates none is less well known than Heinz Wagner of Saarburg, yet he is one of the small handful who can produce wines which it would do Egon Müller no disservice to sell under his name. His vineyard possessions epitomise the virtues of the Saar, since they are all steeply sloping slate-soiled sites planted 100 per cent with Riesling. And at the Wagner estate 100 per cent means not a single vine of any other variety. All this land has been cultivated as vineyards for at least a century and much of it for many centuries.

Heinz Wagner is undoubtedly the most completely committed wine producer I have met anywhere in the world. In spite of clearly being into middle age he personally oversees all the vineyard work, and does all the winemaking and cellar work at his estate. For several years this enormous workload has meant that he has not been away from the estate for more than a weekend at a time, and then on business! However, for Heinz Wagner the basis for the quality of his wines is not just his work, but is at least as much the excellent quality of his vineyards. It is hard to visit the estate without getting a vineyard tour, not just to see the hillsides where the Wagner vineyards are situated, but to see all the individual plots he owns and cultivates. These are all in the very heart of the classic, steeply sloping Saar vineyard sites: sites so steep that no mechanisation of the vineyard work is possible.

However, because of the Scharzhofberg vineyard's great fame which Egon Müller's success has greatly enhanced, the names of the sites where Heinz Wagner has his vines will probably be unfamiliar. Of these the Ockfener Bockstein and Ayler Kupp have some reputation outside Germany, but the Saarburger Antoniusbrunnen, Kupp, and Rausch (see Weingut Forstmeister Geltz Zilliken, p. 141) are completely unknown in Britain. The excellent Schodener Saarfeilser Marienberg, of which Heinz Wagner has just acquired a large part, is not only unknown, but well-nigh unpronounceable. Yet these unknown sites, and particularly the Saarburger Rausch, give Heinz Wagner's finest wines.

What makes the Rausch a special vineyard is that in addition to having the typical qualities of a top Saar vineyard – precipitous steepness, southerly exposure, a grey slate soil – the soil is not quite so rocky here. This gives the Rausch wines a touch more weight and depth, and a wonderful delicate touch of spiciness. Heinz Wagner's large plot in the centre of this site (recently replanted) also gives grapes of a remarkable ripeness in difficult vintages. There could be no better example of this than his 1984 Saarburger Rausch QbA, which was easily the best wine produced on the Saar that year.

The harmony of wines like this, where the steely acidity typical of Saar wines is very pronounced, is greatly helped by Heinz Wagner's very conservative winemaking. During the last twenty or more years there has been a general tendency in Germany towards hi-tech winemaking, an obsession with cleanness of flavour which has tended to result in some of the substance being stripped out of many wines. Saar Rieslings are inherently light, and to lose even a fraction of their modest body can leave them thin and hard. This is anathema to Heinz Wagner, who recently decided not to spend many thousands of pounds on a new press precisely because it might 'clean up' his wines to the point of making them weaker in flavour.

Another side of the estate's conservatism is Heinz Wagner's exceptionally unmanipulative cellar work. Whereas most estates in the Moselle valley have to stop the fermentation of all the wines which they want to retain some sweetness, Heinz Wagner's icily cold cellar largely does this for him. The extensive cellar under the elegant mansion at Bahnhofstrasse 3 is about a hundred years old, and consists of three long galleries. There is enough space to make much more wine than the estate currently produces, so, in marked contrast to some of his neighbours, Heinz Wagner has a lot of elbow room in his cellar. A tasting of young wines from barrel during the early months of the year down here is a painfully cold experience. Though the temperature when the wines are fermenting does not drop quite so low, the cellar is cool enough for many wines to stop fermenting with between 5 and 30 grams per litre of unfermented sweetness remaining.

The final level of sweetness in the bottled wines is achieved by carefully blending barrels of dry and slightly sweeter wines. This traditional technique is once again coming into fashion in the region as a whole, and is now used at the recently revived Karthäuserhof estate in the Ruwer (p. 143), for example. Using this technique, it is possible to make wines with a certain amount of sweetness which taste fruity rather than just sweet. The advantage of this method of balancing Riesling wines from this part of Germany was made very clear with the 1986 vintage, from which the Wagner and Karthäuserhof estates produced some of the finest wines of the region. Even their sweeter wines were beautifully fresh and vigorous, and showed well from the moment they first came on to the market.

Sweetness and acidity are the two components which are most important in determining the harmony of a Saar Riesling wine. The way in which Heinz Wagner works to ensure that the pronounced acidity of his wines is racy rather than sharp and aggressive, is by maturing his wines for up to ten months in wooden Füder casks. This has to be done with great care, as Riesling wines held in cask for this long can easily acquire a slight oxidised tone. However, if this is avoided, then the character of the wines' acidity is greatly mellowed, and both the bouquet and flavour expanded.

The slow-developing Saarburger Rausch wines benefit from this extended cask maturation most of all. At the other extreme, the lighter, flowery, more quickly developing Saarburger Kupp wines need early bottling. These distinctions mean that the development of each cask has to be continuously followed. During this period when the barrels of wine lie in the cool, dark, dank atmosphere of the cellar their contents can change very rapidly. In May and June 1987 I was able to follow the development of Heinz Wagner's 1986 wines in barrel at roughly fortnightly intervals. During this time the Saarburger Rausch Riesling Kabinett wines gained considerable fruit, becoming more and more complete and satisfying, slowly losing their initial aggression.

Nothing delights Heinz Wagner more than tastings like this where he can directly show off his work. Then his normal reserve instantly vanishes, and an almost child-like enthusiasm effervesces from his slender frame. Without winemakers with the animation of Heinz Wagner, and wines with the animation of his fine Saar Rieslings, the world would be a dreary place indeed. Though many people may find the powerful acidity in his wines too much for them, Heinz Wagner is determined to stick with the classical style of his region. 'This is what our wines are really like. When they lack a bit of acidity then they usually lack fruit and flavour too, so I don't think we should compromise on this. We must stand by what has made us famous. Wouldn't it be sad if I took the excellent wines which the Rausch, the Bockstein, and the Saarfeilser Marienberg give me and then remodelled them to make them more immediately attractive? I know the answer to this question, because once I went a little way along that path to satisfy the wishes of some American customers. The results weren't at all good.'

Though Heinz Wagner is by no means a member of the young generation of German wine producers, in this respect he is completely at one with the new ethos which has been permeating the German wine scene during the past few years. Indeed, some of the most extreme 'classicists' amongst this new generation could learn a great deal about what is classical from Heinz Wagner.

Weingut Hermann Dönnhof, Nahe

Helmut Dönnhof (owner).
Weingut Hermann Dönnhof,
Bahnhofstrasse 11,
D 6551 Oberhausen an der Nahe.
Tel: 06755 263.

6.5 hectares/17 acres.
66% Riesling, 34% Müller-Thurgau, Kerner and Scheurebe.

More than any other German wine-producing region the Nahe is appallingly underrated. Though two of its producers are famous, the great Niederhausen-Schlossböckelheim State Domaine (p. 155) and the Crusius estate at Traisen (p. 153), few people directly associate them with the Nahe. Even as recently as 1971 it was quite legal to sell Nahe wines as Rhine wines without naming the region! Such a dire lack of regional identity will take a long time to overcome, but the extraordinarily high-quality wines from young wine producers such as Helmut Dönnhof are already doing much to make people in Germany sit up and take notice of the region once again.

The Dönnhof estate is only a short stroll across the Luitpold bridge over the Nahe from the State Domaine buildings on the upper part of the river's course. The Dönnhof cellar buildings look just like a beautifully maintained stone-built barn, which is precisely what they once were. However, as the door is slid open one is in for a shock, for inside, neatly parked in a corner, is a gleaming, stainless steel, computer-controlled press.

This contrast typifies the approach of Helmut Dönnhof. A quiet, very sure man in his mid thirties, he believes that most German wine producers are like children before the companies manufacturing chemicals and machinery for winemaking. 'As a conscientious winemaker trying to produce individual wines with elegance and finesse you just don't need all this hi-tech stuff, which I'm sorry to say many colleagues buy and use with little or no thought. Of course I do need some machines for key parts of the winemaking process, and then I must have the very best available, but I don't want to collect machines like toys!' While most German wine producers who still have them speak of their wooden casks as though they performed some mysterious and miraculous transformation on the wines stored in them, Helmut spoke of his as 'part of the essential technology for the style of wines I am trying to produce. I also need stainless steel tanks for keeping wines which are ready for bottling. Neither new technology nor old technology gives you a guarantee that you will end up with good wines. I use each as it is appropriate, so although I'm pleased with the new press, I also need my little nineteenth-century basket press for making icewines.'

One of the first wines which Helmut made after returning from the Geisenheim viticultural school to run the family estate was

Stück is 1200l

an icewine (Eiswein) from the 1977 vintage. Icewines are great rarities which have been made by chance for two centuries, but have only been actively sought since the early 1960s. They are made from frozen grapes, which normally have to be harvested in the early hours of the morning and rushed to the press before they melt. The effect of the freezing is to remove part of the water from the juice (as ice), so concentrating the sugar, acidity and flavouring substances. Because one usually has to wait many weeks after the normal harvest to get cold enough weather for icewine – weeks during which the grapes could easily get so rotten as to be unusable – this is a highly risky business.

Dönnhof's 1977 Eiswein was not a great success, being far too acidic for his taste. To give an idea as to what he means by this, his top 1983 Eiswein had 16.4 grams per litre acidity (roughly two and a half times as much as champagne!) and is beautifully balanced. It was this wine which attracted the first German press attention to his estate, since its incredible concentration and great elegance matched that of the top icewine from the State Domaine across the river. In fact the two wines had been harvested on the same night from virtually neighbouring plots of vines; Dönnhof's is from his monopole vineyard, Oberhäuser Brücke, and the State Domaine's from their monopole vineyard, Niederhäuser Hermannsberg.

However, for Dönnhof these wonderful rarities which can only be produced in miniscule quantities are very much the top of the icing on the cake. It is making the best possible Riesling Qualitätswein each year that is the focus of his attentions. Because they have sugar added to them to build up their alcohol content, and because the majority of QbA wines sold outside Germany are cheap and boring, Qualitätswein does not have a very good international image. Certainly this was the correct judgement of even most estate-bottled QbA wines in the past, when many estates put all their efforts into their higher-grade wines (Kabinett, Spätlese, etc.).

A Dönnhof Riesling Qualitätswein, however, is every bit as elegant and refined as the Kabinett and Spätlese wines of many other Nahe producers. This is principally because the wines have modest alcohol levels, and are made individually in Stück and Halbstück wooden casks. There is absolutely no mixing of wines from different grape varieties, or from different vineyards.

Tasting Dönnhof wines one can immediately recognize the different character of each of the vineyards. The 'problem' with this approach is that there are thirty-seven different wines on the list of this small estate!

On a recent visit to Weingut Hermann Dönnhof a German wine writer, Armin Diel (see p. 55), pointed out the commercial madness of this, and suggested that at least Helmut should blend together all his dry 1986 Riesling QbA wines. This is something many estates across Germany are doing now, both to simplify their sales and to give themselves more room for manoeuvre in winemaking. A trial blend was even put together to prove what a fine wine this would be. Helmut sat attentively listening through the exposition of this proposal, though with a slightly strained look on his face. On tasting the sample of '1986 Dönnhof Riesling QbA Trocken' he agreed that it was better than each of the components which made it up, adding, 'the only thing I should point out, though, is that I'm simply not going to do it. It's against my principles.' Six months later, when the wines had settled down after bottling, it was possible to see Helmut's point very clearly. Each of the wines which might have been mixed together had an absolutely distinct character unlike any other in the group; the Oberhäuser Leistenberg racy with a pronounced slaty/flintiness, the Oberhäuser Felsenberg richly appley with a strong earthiness underneath, the Oberhäuser Brücke really ripe with a very refined peach-like fruitiness.

Of all the vineyard sites in the picturesque rocky upper stretch of the Nahe, the Oberhauser Brücke is the smallest at a meagre one hectare, or 2.5 acres. It and the neighbouring Niederhauser Hermannsberg, Schlossbockelheimer Kupfergrübe and Schlossböckelheimer Felsenberg vineyards are amongst the best vineyard sites in the whole of Germany. Almost all the important Nahe estates – the State Domaine, Crusius, Paul Anheuser (p. 151) – are substantial vineyard owners here. Although there are some very good sites around Bad Kreuznach and Dorsheim, outside this corner of the Upper Nahe there is only one great Nahe vineyard: the Traiser Bastei at the foot of the gigantic Rotenfels cliffs. The soil of the Bastei is of red porphyry, and it gives the wines a uniquely rich perfume which defies description. This is also an important element of the soils in Schlossböckelheim, particularly in the Felsenberg. The other sites have various mixtures of porphyry, lotite, rhyolite, sandstone, loess, slate, clay and loam. This exotic-sounding catalogue of minerals is reflected in the complexity of the wines, which can age for quite as long as any from the Rhine or the Moselle.

The most extreme examples of this ageing capacity are the State Domaine wines from the precipitous Schlossböckelheimer Kupfergrübe, which hardly seem to begin developing until they have been in the bottle for five years or more! Helmut Dönnhof's 1983s and 1985s are equally serious wines which deserve to be cellared for at least four or five more years. In the case of the Auslese and Eiswein a minimum of ten more years will be necessary for these wines to reach their peak. Modern-style top red Bordeaux wines of the same vintages will be crumbling badly by the time these top Nahe Rieslings start to show their best.

Sadly, today we tend to regard all white wines as being for early consumption. The most expensive white Burgundies occasionally escape this headlong rush to pull corks, but those white wines which have the best potential of all for long ageing, clasically made Riesling wines, are almost never given the chance to show their wonderful mature character. The world used to be very different. Four decades ago, when Helmut Dönnhof's grandfather had an excellent reputation for his Rieslings, the majority of his customers aged the wines they bought from him. We should learn from their example.

Schlossgut Diel, Nahe

Armin Diel (owner),
Heribert Kastell (cellarmaster).
Schlossgut Diel,
D 6531 auf Burg Layen.
Tel: 06721 45045.

9.7 hectares/27 acres.
80% Riesling, 10% Grauburgunder (Pinot Gris),
5% Weissburgunder (Pinot Blanc), 5% Traminer.

There is hardly another wine producer in all Germany who is the cause of such controversy, whose name draws either such high praise or derision from wine writers and other producers as Schlossgut Diel. The obvious cause of this fiery controversy is the fact that since the 1984 vintage a proportion of the Schlossgut Diel wines have been aged in new oak barrels in the French manner. What people think of these wines depends very much on their prejudices about the merits or demerits of making wines in a traditional way. For some wine drinkers in Germany these wines are something very special, remarkable innovations, while for others they are the ultimate in blasphemy. Putting these wines, about 30 per cent of the estate's production, aside for the moment, though, I have no doubt that the conventionally made dry Riesling wines of Schlossgut Diel are amongst the most refined and elegant dry wines being made in Germany today.

Things were not always like that at Schlossgut Diel. Armin's father, Dr Ingo Diel, from whom he has recently taken over full control of the estate, had a radically different winemaking philosophy. Until Armin started to have an influence on the Schlossgut Diel wines in the late 1970s, the estate produced primarily sweet wines, of which a large proportion were dessert wines made from experimental new grape varieties. Dr Ingo Diel took a special pride in being the first to plant the most exotic of these new vine crossings, and in making a huge range of Beerenauslese and Trockenbeerenauslese dessert wines from them. In this the estate was not unique, the planting of new vine crossings being very much in vogue at the time. However, they led this trend with genuine fervour. Dr Ingo Diel once told a student working at Schlossgut Diel that 'in ten years only un-sophisticated growers will have the old varieties, Riesling and so forth, in their vineyards.'

For Armin, the majority of wines made by the estate during this period are beyond the pale, bad jokes best forgotten. For him the traditional grape varieties are 'the only correct basis for winemaking here on the Nahe, and in Germany generally. Here that means most of all the Riesling, then Grauburgunder, Weiss-burgunder and Traminer. Since the very hard frosts a couple of winters ago, that is effectively what we have at Schlossgut Diel. The remainder of our vineyards planted with non-traditional grape varieties have been replanted, or leased away. I don't even want Müller-Thurgau any more, though many people say it's become a classic variety because it's been around for a hundred years.'

The next critical element of the new philosophy which Armin

has introduced to Schlossgut Diel is the fermentation of all the estate's wines to dryness, without any manipulative influence to try and make them drier or a little sweeter. All the Schlossgut Diel wines have been dry since the 1984 vintage, and in future only Beerenauslese and Eiswein will be lightly sweet. Armin believes that while sweetness is a necessary part of the character of these wines, it definitely should not be part of the make-up of the more normal-quality ones. However, Schlossgut Diel has not simply 'turned the controls' to dry instead of sweet, as many German wine producers have done during the last few years. For Armin a dry Nahe wine with the racy acidity he is looking for must have 11 degrees of alcohol in order to make a harmonious wine. Therefore if the grapes do not reach the necessary degree of ripeness for this, sugar will always be added to the wine so that this alcohol level is reached. Therefore there are no Kabinett wines produced at Schlossgut Diel, and they offer nothing between QbA and Spätlese on their list.

Schlossgut Diel have equally clear objectives when it comes to the acidity content of their wines. I visited them at the beginning of the 1986 harvest, and when I arrived Armin immediately led me down into the capacious cellars under the elegant estate house to their small laboratory. Here the young cellarmaster Heribert Kastell was measuring the sugar and acidity content of samples of grape must from their different vineyards. The acidity content is now the most important factor in determining the picking date for each plot of vines on the estate, but as luck would have it this was no problem with the 1986 vintage.

A few yards away from the laboratory is the cask cellar which lies under the burg, the medieval castle, of Burg Layen. Here sit the mixture of conventional German wooden Stück casks and new oak barriques in which the Schlossgut Diel wines are matured. In fact not all these barriques are French, for the Grauburgunder 'Barriquewein' is matured in new 300-litre barrels made of German (Hunsrück) oak. The strong, broad flavour of this oak suits the fullness of this grape variety's wines very well. Only the Riesling 'Barriquewein' is matured in actual 228-litre French casks of Limousin oak (from Tonnellerie François Frère in Saint Romain, Burgundy), which gives the wine a distinct vanilla tone. Armin is always anxious at this point to stress that he is not trying to copy French wines. 'I certainly don't just want to produce clones of wines from other countries, though I do think that there's a lot we can learn about winemaking from the French. Also, these wines with new oak character will always be just one side of what we do, for people who particularly like this style. The traditionally made Riesling wines will always remain in the majority.'

Though the new-oak-aged wines are casually referred to as 'barrique' wines at Schlossgut Diel, no legally defined term of this kind exists. Indeed, there is no way in which these wines could even acquire an official AP number that would entitle them to be sold as QbA wines. Therefore they are sold as Table Wines (Tafelwein) with just Schlossgut Diel, the vintage and the grape variety printed boldly on the label. There is more than an echo of 'Sassicaia' and 'Tignanello' in all this. (These two high-class Italian red wines, which, because they are made wholly or partly from French grape varieties, are also sold as Table Wine (Vino da Tavola), are now cult wines which sell for very high prices.)

All these barrels, and the care of their contents, takes a great deal of work. This is most ably undertaken by Heribert Kastell, who has a remarkable knowledge of winemaking for his age, and a lively wit which makes him an immediately appealing person. Both he and Armin have strong personalities, but seem to work together remarkably well, Heribert's more down-to-earth character perhaps balancing Armin's expansiveness and unabashed ambition. They often go to important wine tastings together, and one gets the feeling that a very important exchange of ideas takes place as a result of this camaraderie.

Unusually for Germany, as much care is taken with the packaging and marketing of the estate's wines as with their making. The idea of having to sell wines from more than thirty different grape varieties, as his father did, gives Armin apoplexy. He has worked systematically to reduce the range of wines the estate offers, the 1986 vintage comprising just seven wines (compare Weingut Hermann Dönnhof's thirty-seven, page 53), and he thinks that even this is too many. 'I'd really like to have just one, but in Germany we have this tradition of not blending together the different grape varieties, and I want to stick with that.'

While many other German wine producers have replaced their kitschy old labels with kitschy modern labels during the last

few years, Schlossgut Diel's packaging is the very model of classicism and clarity. Care has even been taken to ensure that the paper on which the labels are printed, and the glue which sticks them to the bottle, do not fail when bottles are placed in an ice bucket for several hours. I watched these experiments, and the critical examination of the results under both natural and artificial light were of an almost scientific exactitude.

As well as being a wine producer, Armin Diel also works as a wine writer (never commenting on his own wines), and as a restaurant critic. As a result he has a lot of friends in the hotel and restaurant business. Indeed, it was almost only as a result of pressure from one top German restaurateur, Andreas Schmitt of Restaurant Schweizer Stuben in Wertheim-Bettingen, that the Schlossgut Diel barrique-aged Riesling came into being. Very few people outside Germany realise that Germany's restaurants have the second highest number of Michelin stars of all the European countries, after those of France, and that Munich, Baden, and the Rheingau are among the gastronomic centres of Europe.

As a result of their very high quality, and the excellent PR the placement of these wines on so many top restaurant lists brings, demand for Schlossgut Diel wines already far outstrips production. Since the 1985 vintage the wines have been sold by subscription, 'en primeur', shortly after the harvest. The 1985 vintage was sold out by Christmas of that year. The Schlossgut production could only be increased by the purchase of further vineyards, since Armin has fixed the yield at between 5000 and 6000 litres per hectare. He has therefore introduced a second label, Schlosskellerei Diel, under which wines made from bought-in grapes or grape musts are sold.

Armin always prefers to buy in grapes from growers with whom contracts have been made well before the harvest, 'because that way we can control what we are getting as much as possible. We work together with the grower, instructing him or her how we want the vineyard managed, and when we want the grapes picked. In this way we can achieve quality which sometimes matches that of the Schlossgut wines. We also use the Schlosskellerei name as a second label for the wines from our own vineyards which we consider fractionally below the minimum standard for the Schlossgut label. This system works very well.'

Those outside Germany who deride dry German wines as 'not serious', or 'lacking in elegance', should take note of this commitment to quality and harmony, and try some of Schlossgut and Schlosskellerei Diel's scintillating wines. If anyone needs proof that there are adventurous and innovative winemakers in Germany as well as in the New World, it is to be found here at Schlossgut Diel.

Vereinigung der Charta Weingüter, Rheingau

The Charta Association of Rheingau producers currently has thirty members, a full list of which is given at the end of this section. The following estates are featured below as examples which illustrate the Charta's aims and ideals:

Bernhard Breuer (owner,
and Charta director).
Weingut Georg Breuer,
Grabenstrasse 8,
D 6220 Rüdesheim.
Tel: 06722 1027.

10.5 hectares/25.5 acres.
82.5% Riesling, 4% Reichensteiner, 13.5% Müller-Thurgau
and Silvaner.

*Erwein Graf Matuschka-Greiffenclau (owner,
and Charta director).
Schloss Vollrads,
and Weingut Fürst Löwenstein
D 6227 Oestrich–Winkel.
Tel: 06723 5056.*

*Schloss Vollrads: 50 hectares/123 acres.
98% Riesling, 2% Ehrenfelser. (The vineyards of Schloss
Vollrads all bear the estate's own name, and are in the
exclusive ownership of Graf Matuschka.)
Fürst Löwenstein: 17.7 hectares/44 acres.
96% Riesling, 4% Müller-Thurgau.*

*Hans Hermann Eser (owner).
Weingut Johannishof,
Im Grund 63,
D 6222 Geisenheim–Johannisberg.
Tel: 06722 8216.*

*18 hectares/44.5 acres.
100% Riesling.*

*Gerko Freiherr von und zu Innhausen und
Knyphausen (owner).
Weingut Freiherr von Knyphausen,
Klosterhof Drais,
D 6228 Eltville–Erbach.
Tel: 06123 62177.*

*16.5 hectares/41 acres.
84% Riesling, 6% Spätburgunder (Pinot Noir), 10%
Müller-Thurgau, Ehrenfelser and Kerner.*

The wines that I used on the first page of the Introduction as
examples of how highly fine German wines were regarded in
Britain a century ago were all classical Rheingau Rieslings. The
renown of Rheingau wines can be used as a kind of barometer for
the reputation and respect accorded to German wines as a whole
since that time. If this is done then the Rheingau and Germany
reached rock bottom at the end of the 1970s and the beginning of
the 1980s when the great Schloss Eltz estate was broken up and

two of the other great aristocratic estates of the region were sold off to large industrial concerns.

However, this was not to be the end of the line for the region, but rather a crossroads. On 12 July 1984 Erwein Graf Matus-chka-Greiffenclau of Schloss Vollrads and Weingut Fürst Löwenstein, Dr Hans Ambrosi, director of the Rheingau Staats-weingüter, Professor Dr Helmut Becker of the Forschungsan-stalt (viticultural and winemaking school) in Geisenheim, and Bernhard and Heinrich Breuer of Weingut Georg Breuer and Scholl & Hillebrand signed the document which founded the Rheingau Charta estates' association. The most concrete part of the association's aims is the production and promotion of classi-cal Rheingau Riesling wines of a guaranteed quality, and the more general aim is to bring the reputation of Rheingau Riesling wines back to its late nineteenth-century zenith.

RHEINGAU RIESLING

A Tradition of Quality.
Only Rheingau Riesling wines
of the highest quality with healthy
acidity and produced under
the stringent CHARTA-regulations
may bear this symbol.
The balanced dryness of these wines
makes them especially suitable
for fine dining.

The testing used to guarantee the quality of Charta wines is rigorous. Each of the thirty member estates can submit cask or tank samples of any 100 per cent Riesling wines produced from their vineyards which have at least the minimum acidity level, and the degree of ripeness required for them to gain Charta status.* These are tasted blind by a professional panel which has to decide whether the wines are well above average quality for the Rheingau. Over a quarter of the wines submitted fail at this point, and only those which pass are then bottled in the distinctive long brown flute-shaped Charta bottle with the association's Romanesque window emblem embossed on it. However, before a single bottle is sold the wine must pass the taste assessment for a second time, to make sure that the wine which passed the first time is the one which has actually been placed in the Charta bottles. Even then, the wine cannot leave the producer's cellar until the beginning of the October following the vintage.

The promotion of these selected wines is paid for by a contribution which each member pays into a central fund. Normally these presentations take the form of dinners, since the Charta sees the dining tables of the world as the proper place for their wines. This was, after all, where a great proportion of fine Rheingau wines was consumed during the region's heyday.

This part of the Charta association's philosophy comes directly from Erwein Graf Matuschka-Greiffenclau, who has put so much energy into the promotion of wine and food in connection with his own wines that even those wine writers who normally ignore German wines know of him. When Graf Matuschka left his job as marketing director for Olivetti in Germany in 1977 to run Schloss Vollrads the estate was in a run-down condition. Even the winemaking had slipped during the seventies, and the fourteenth- and seventeenth-century buildings were crumbling in many places. Rheingau wine and food was the concept he developed to promote his wines, so that he could support the massive investment needed to revive the estate.

Books about entertaining or cookery from the last century recommend what appear to our white-wines-with-fish-and-

---

*Charta wines must have an acidity of at least 7.5 grams per litre, and very little of unfermented or residual sugar. Minimum grape must weights (sugar content levels) are 65° Oechsle for QbA, 78° Oechsle for Kabinett, and 88° Oechsle for Spätlese, all significantly higher than the legally stipulated minimums for wines of these quality grades.

white-meat and red-wines-with-red-meat perspective to be ludicrous combinations. Rüdesheimer Berg Riesling with saddle of roebuck (venison), Schloss Vollrads Riesling with lobster, and Steinberger Riesling with roast lamb were then perfectly accepted marriages of food and wine; so was mature Château Lafite with sweet pastries, and the lusciously sweet Sauternes Château d'Yquem with oysters! Fine Rheingau wines were then an important part of gastronomic culture.

However, rather than relying too directly on what worked a hundred years ago, Graf Matuschka has attempted to put the partnering of food and wine on a slightly more logical and 'scientific' basis. He has also stressed how logical is the combination of light, medium-dry Rheingau wines and today's lighter style of cooking. Since 1977 he has been taking his wines around the world demonstrating that they can be drunk with almost any kind of meat or fish so long as it is correctly prepared, and that many cheeses actually go much better with white wines that have a refreshing acidity than they do with a heavy red wine.

In dealing with restaurateurs, who can have amazingly closed minds when it comes to the question of wine and food, he sometimes has to adopt a positively combative approach. For example, in southern California recently he strode into a restaurant and challenged the owner that his wines could harmonise with any of the restaurant's sauces better than the most expensive Californian Chardonnay on their wine list. The logic of the challenge to a sauce and wine tasting is that in almost every dish it is the sauce which has the strongest flavour: the only point quickly conceded by the restaurateur. The stakes for this challenge were that if Graf Matuschka won he should have a selection of his wines taken onto their list, and that if he lost he would bring a big party there for dinner that evening. The waiters and chef would act as judges.

Anyone who has been to one of Graf Matuschka's food and wine presentations will not be surprised to hear that the restaurateur was bitterly disappointed to find how badly his excellent and extremely expensive Grgich Hills Chardonnay went with every single one of his sauces. The reason is simple. Sauces are made by reduction of stock that involves an element of caramelisation, or they are thickened with cream or *crème fraiche* which also results in a sweetness. The lively fruity acidity of a Rheingau Riesling cuts the sweetness and fat in sauces, refreshing the palate. Graf Matuschka has christened this the 'sorbet effect', and it won three of his wines places on this restaurant's list. The way in which he won gave the waiters an excellent story to tell the restaurant's customers, which has hardly held back consumption of his wines there!

In order to give himself a slightly greater variety of wines to offer customers, and to increase the total quantity of wine which he has to sell, Graf Matuschka took a lease of the Fürst Löwenstein estate in Hallgarten in 1979. The wines from here are slightly fuller and broader than the very racy Rieslings from Schloss Vollrads. If the Vollrads wines can sometimes be very firm in their youth, the Fürst Löwenstein wines are often attractive from the word go. However, for long ageing there is almost no other wine in the Rheingau to touch Schloss Vollrads. I have tasted wines of their most ordinary quality grade from the 1959, 1964, 1966 and 1967 vintages which have all been very fresh and lively; the 1966 at twenty years old was vibrantly youthful and quite delicious! At the celebrations for the 775th anniversary of the Greiffenclau family's recorded involvement in wine production in the autumn of 1986, a bottle of 1862 Schloss Vollrads was opened and was still very much alive.

The success which Graf Matuschka had with promoting the classical drier style of Rheingau Riesling as a partner for fine cuisine, and by emphasising the great ageing capacity of these wines, did not escape the notice of other Rheingau producers for very long. In particular, Bernhard Breuer of Weingut Georg Breuer and the wine merchants house Scholl & Hillebrand had begun feeling very disaffected. By the beginning of the eighties he found that he was drinking classical dry Rheingau wines at home in the evenings and at weekends, but selling sweetened-up German wines during the week. 'I was getting to the point where my existence was virtually schizophrenic!' he says, looking back on that period.

Like the great majority of Rheingau wine producers, his estate and Scholl & Hillebrand had drifted into sweetening wines up during the 1960s. Making wines to meet the growing demand had seemed to simplify the selling side of things. However, by 1980 when Bernhard had established himself at the head of the family firm after taking over from his father in 1975, he decided that at least with the wines from the Georg Breuer estate there was to be no more of this. Since that time he has refined the making of these wines to the point where Weingut Georg Breuer now virtually has just a selection of Charta wines from the great vineyard sites of Rüdesheim (the Rüdesheimer Berg Schlossberg wine bearing a specially created artist label each year), and a Rüdesheimer Riesling QbA Dry.

From being a relatively typical Rüdesheim producer, Bernhard's estate has rapidly risen to being arguably the top producer of Rüdesheim wines. The superb 1986 vintage will undoubtedly hasten international recognition of this. It has not come without an enormous investment of effort, money, and thought, though. The system for deciding the time of harvest had, for example, to be changed to take account of how quickly the grapes on the steep slopes of the Rüdesheimer Berg can lose acidity in hot weather. The cellar work has also had to become much more pedantic, and the wines are allowed to take their time instead of being made more immediately accessible with sweetness. In particular, it can take the wines from the great Berg Schlossberg vineyard a full year from the time of harvest till they even begin to show their real qualities in the barest outline; to reach their peak they need a further decade or two.

Though Bernhard is convinced that the reason for the Charta's success is the guarantee it offers the purchaser of the style and quality of the wine he or she is buying, he passionately believes that this does not mean that all Charta wines taste the same. 'Quite the opposite,' he maintains; 'one of the central ideas of the Charta is to encourage the Rheingau producers to care for the reputations of the great vineyards again. At the beginning of this century and earlier we sold the more straightforward wines as Rheingau Riesling, as Scholl & Hillebrand have been doing once again since the spring of 1984, and then only the top-quality wines were sold under a vineyard name. Those names – Rüdesheimer Berg, Johannisberger Klaus, Steinberg, Marcobrunn – were then as famous as any of the top Bordeaux Châteaux or Grand Cru vineyards of Burgundy, and this is something I am sure we can bring back.'

From Bernhard's austerely modernistic house high up behind Rüdesheim he has a fine view over a good many of those top vineyards. Pointing out of the window he says, 'where we are at the top of the "Oberfeld" the slope of the vineyards isn't very great and the soil is deep, limey loess and loam. Over in that direction is the Rüdesheimer Berg where the vineyards are steep to precipitous and the loamy soil contains a great deal of slate and quartzite. These differences result in very different tastes, even if the wines which come from these two areas are identical as far as chemical analysis goes. The wines from the Berg will always be racier, more elegant and delicate, the wines from up here rather simpler. Such differences in taste are not just what gives each wine its identity, but are also very useful when it comes to making combinations of food and wine, because they give us a palette of flavours to work with.'

Another of the Charta's central concerns is to bring back the ecological balance in the region's vineyards. In recent decades traditional viticultural practices have been replaced by a tendency to plough the ground and spray with herbicides until the vineyards look like French formal gardens. It may look satisfying to the grower, who can then tell himself that he has removed all the plants which could compete with the vines for nutrients and water, but the long-term result can be a serious deterioration of the soil structure. Quite quickly this rebounds on the vines which start to grow poorly. There is also, needless to say, both the literal and environmental cost of all the ploughing and spraying.

Among the Charta members there is some divergence of opinion as to how vineyards should be returned to green cultivation, but this is hardly surprising, given the region's diverse soils and the difference in rainfall between the villages near the river and those high up by the Taunus forest. In some areas it is possible to let the weeds grow without interference; in other areas it is better only to let them grow between every other row. This is what the excellent Dr Weil estate in Kiedrich (p. 170) has done since 1966, yet in spite of the success of the estate during this time not a single producer in Kiedrich has followed their example! Thankfully the Rheingau as a whole is not so narrow-minded, and already 30 per cent of the vineyards are green all year round, and fully 75 per cent are green at least over the winter months.

Of the Charta estates Hans Hermann Eser in Johannisberg has perhaps the most highly developed and individual system of vineyard cultivation. While the majority of his colleagues plant their vines close together, each year training the new growth about one metre up from the main stem, Herr Eser's vines are giants. In his vineyards the rows are just over two and a half metres apart, the vines within each row being separated by the same distance, and the growth rising up to about the same height above the soil. He believes that this form of training 'builds a big leaf area which can feed the ripening grapes. The growth mustn't be too vigorous, or all the vine's energy will go into that, but without a healthy plant with enough leaves to support the grapes you end up with a poor level of ripeness, and consequently thin wines.'

The Eser family is one of those great rarities, a wine family which works together with a common intensity of commitment. They are in complete agreement on the goals towards which they are working, and the general route they should take to reach them. The one point on which there was once disagreement was at the beginning of the sixties, shortly after Hans Hermann Eser took over from his father and introduced the new vineyard system. When his father heard that instead of the scrupulous vineyard cleanliness which had hitherto been their ideal, corn would be planted between the rows of vines during the winter, he threw up his arms in horror.

However, the corn was planted in August and by vintage time there was what looked like a lawn between the rows of vines. As a result it was easy to pick even in the wettest weather, and the ploughing into the soil of the corn in late spring gave the stony loam soils of Johannisberg the humus they need for a good structure. The system took several years to prove its full worth, since soil structure cannot be changed overnight. Now, almost all the vineyards have been turned over to this form of cultivation, which not only improves the health of vines, soil and environment, but has reduced costs quite dramatically. This is principally because now ploughing only needs to be done once annually. This is also good for the soil since the wheels of tractors tend to compact it too much. Like lawns, vines need well-aerated soils to grow well.

All this would be a little academic if the wines of Weingut Johannishof were not amongst the most refined and elegant in the entire Rheingau. All the estate's wines are fermented in the eighteenth-century cask cellar nine metres below the Johannisberg vineyards. A small spring runs through this narrow gallery filled with Halbstück casks, ensuring 100 per cent humidity year-round. The temperature is an equally constant 8°C, and to make wines which comply with the Charta's criteria for only a slight sweetness Hans Hermann Eser simply has to leave the barrels of wine to ferment through by themselves. The vineyards of Johannisberg rarely give wines which lack in acidity, so the Charta's minimum acidity level is not a problem. Weingut Johannishof is a classic example of how the Charta style can be a perfectly natural balance for Rheingau Riesling wines.

Herr Eser's use of wooden casks for the fermentation and maturation of the great majority of his wines is today unusual in the Rheingau. The more normal position is a mixture of wooden casks and tanks, as at Weingut Freiherr von Knyphausen in Erbach. Gerko Freiherr von und zu Innhausen und Knyphausen is a model representative of the most positive kind of 'modernism' in the Rheingau. He has a small cellar of old wooden casks and a much larger more modern one of tanks, 'because what we need to care for with the majority of wines is to retain the lively fruitiness, but there are also wines which are too aggressive or a bit awkward in their youth, and these can greatly benefit from a short period in cask. That's why I always want to have the option of using wooden casks available to me.'

Even before the Charta's formation Gerko was a champion of Rheingau wines of the medium-dry style rich in fruity acidity, which is approximately the balance of Charta wines. For him, a Rheingau Riesling which retains its full natural acidity content will often be a little hard if it is absolutely bone-dry. On the other hand, he believes that the kind of sweetness which would satisfy the sweet tooth of some uncultivated wine drinkers smothers the fruitiness of Riesling wine.

Though all the members of the association also produce wines which are bone-dry and/or sweeter than the Charta allows to bear its emblem, and many are involved in the VDP and engage in other activities, the ideal of making the Charta wines as internationally renowned as the finest red wines of Bordeaux or Burgundy is common to all. The Charta's organisation makes it possible for the smallest grower, who can do little to promote his wines alone, to add his or her weight to this common striving. It also encourages him to work yet harder for the best possible qualities. Already the commission of professionals who undertake the taste-testing of potential Charta wines has noticed a distinct rise in the general standard of wines submitted for their approval.

The apogee of the Charta's activities to date was the magnificent Riesling-Gala banquet held in the Laiendormitorium of the medieval abbey of Kloster Eberbach on Sunday, 15 November 1986. This was the final event of the first 'Three Glorious Days for Rheingau Riesling' festival which was jointly organised by the VDP Staatsweingüter and Charta. Four hundred people sat down to what was the finest banquet I have ever attended. The quality of the food was up to Michelin starred restaurant standard, in spite of having been prepared using makeshift equipment in a tent in the monastery grounds! This was a miracle performed by Egbert Engelhardt, chef of the 'Graues Haus' restaurant in Winkel (owned by Graf Matuschka). A series of ten Charta wines beautifully accompanied the six courses, and somehow every wine was there at just the right moment. If any proof were still needed that the Charta association's wines deserve a place on every sophisticated dining table and in every sophisticated wine cellar, it was provided that day.

The following estates are also members of the Charta association. Those marked with an asterisk are discussed above, or in the Directory section.

Rheingauer Weinkellerei
  Lorch,
Binger Weg 2a,
6223 Lorch.
Tel. 06726/375.

Weingut Friedrich Altenkirch,
Binger Weg 2,
6223 Lorch.

*Weingut Georg Breuer,
Rüdesheim.

Weingut Fritz Perabo,
Inh. Christof Perabo,
Schauerweg 57,
6223 Lorch.
Tel. 06726/302.

*Weingut Balthasar Ress,
Eltville–Hattenheim.

Weingut August Eser,
Friedensplatz 19,
6227 Oestrich–Winkel.
Tel. 06723/5032.

*Weingut Johannishof,
Geisenheim–Johannisberg.

Weingut Jakob Jung,
Eberbacher Strasse 22,
6228 Eltville–Erbach.
Tel. 06123/62359.

Weingut Josef Kessler,
Heimatstrasse 18,
6228 Eltville–Martinsthal.
Tel. 06123/71235.

Weingut F. Fendel Erben,
Marienthaler Strasse 46,
6220 Rüdesheim am Rhein.
Tel. 06722/2555.

*Verwaltung der
  Staatsweingüter Eltville,
Eltville.

Scholl & Hillebrand GmbH,
Geisenheimer Strasse 9,
6220 Rüdesheim am Rhein.
Tel. 06722/1028.

*Weingut Dr R. Weil, Kiedrich.

*Weingut Freihern von
  Knyphausen,
Eltville–Erbach.

Weingut Hans Lang,
Rheinallee 6,
6228 Eltville–Hattenheim.
Tel. 06723/2475.

Weingut Schumann–Nägler,
Nothgottesstrasse 29,
6222 Geisenheim.
Tel. 06722/5214 + 6564.

Weingut Schönleber–Blümlein,
Kirchstrasse 39,
6227 Oestrich–Winkel.
Tel. 06723/3110.

Freiherr von Zwierlein,
Schloss Kosakenberg,
6222 Geisenheim.
Tel. 06722/8307.

Weingut Hupfeld Erben,
Rheingaustrasse 113,
6227 Oestrich–Winkel.
Tel. 06723/3307.

Weingut Wilfried Querbach,
Dr Rody Strasse 2,
6227 Oestrich–Winkel.
Tel. 06723/3887.

*Schloss Vollrads,
Oestrich–Winkel.

*Weingut Fürst Löwenstein,
Oestrich–Winkel.

Weingut der Forschungsanstalt,
Blankechstrasse 19,
6222 Geisenheim.

Graf von Francken–Sierstorpff,
Rheinstrasse 7,
6222 Geisenheim.
Tel. 06722/8042.

*Wegeler–Deinherd
(Gutsverwaltung Wegeler
  Erben),
Oestrich–Winkel.

Weingut Fritz Allendorf,
Kirchstrasse 69,
6227 Oestrich–Winkel.
Tel. 06723/5021.

Weingut Bernhard Mehrlein,
Urbanstrasse 29,
6227 Oestrich–Winkel.
Tel. 06723/2934.

Weingut Hans Barth,
Bergweg 20,
6228 Eltville–Hattenheim.
Tel. 06723/2514.

*Weingut Eberhard Ritter und
  Edler von Oetinger,
Eltville–Erbach.

Weingut Josef Freimuth,
Schmittstrasse 3,
6222 Geisenheim.
Tel. 06722/8568.

Freiherrlich Langwerth von Simmern'sches Rentamt, Rheingau

Helmut Kranich (director),
Josef Schell (cellarmaster).
Freiherrlich Langwerth von Simmern'sches
*   Rentamt,*
Langwerther Hof,
D 6228 Eltville.
Tel: 06123 3007.

50 hectares/99 acres.
95% Riesling, 1.5% Spätburgunder (Pinot Noir), 3.5%
Müller-Thurgau, Weissburgunder (Pinot Blanc).

Josef Schell, the cellarmaster of Langwerth von Simmern, once told me, 'You could come here for a year, and I could carefully teach you how I work in the cellar. However, even then you would only have learnt 98 per cent of what I actually do. The last 2 per cent is in my fingers. I've only acquired that 2 per cent by actually making wine for many years.' Tacit knowledge of this kind is the mark of a real cellarmaster. Josef Schell's three decades of totally dedicated work at Langwerth von Simmern have made him *the* cellarmaster of the Rheingau region.

Langwerth von Simmern has a long tradition for making wines with a restrained touch of sweetness, wines in a highly refined version of the style of German wine familiar to us all. It was this style of wine which Josef Schell learned to make when he came to the estate in 1958. Langwerth did not jump on the dry wine bandwagon which started rolling in Germany during the mid seventies. As a result, for many years people said that Langwerth were the greatest in the Rheingau for the wines with sweetness, but that one really had to go elsewhere for good dry wines. However, in the last few years Josef Schell has also mastered this style, the 1986 vintage dry wines of Langwerth von Simmern being among the finest in the Rheingau; no small achievement for a man who from his age might be expected to have begun getting set in his ways.

What makes all this yet more remarkable is that Josef Schell undertook little formal study or training in winemaking. He is a classic example of the self-taught winemaker. The first principles of his work are very simple: scrupulous cleanliness, minimal handling of the wines, and at all costs the preservation of the distinctive character of each individual wine. The first of these costs a lot of work in cleaning fermentation tanks and maturation casks, the second great restraint, and the latter an enormous amount of work preparing numerous different lots of Süssreserve.

Süssreserve, or clarified unfermented grape juice, is the traditional method of sweetening wines in the Rhine regions. Sadly, this is normally done in a crude manner, every wine being dosed with a great big dollop of a single Süssreserve, rather than the wines of each vineyard and Prädikat level being dosed with their own Süssreserve. That this easy way out is normally taken should be no surprise if one considers the extra trouble preparing a dozen or more small lots of Süssreserve is, compared with preparing just one. If one single Süssreserve is furthermore made from another grape variety (worst of all from inferior modern vine crossings), then the resulting wine will not even have typical Riesling character. Only if Süssreserve is of the same grape variety, quality grade, and place of origin as the wine to which it is added are good results obtained, as at Langwerth.

However, wines are not only made in the cellar. Without the right vineyard management and organisation of the harvest, without the right raw material in the form of ripe clean grapes, it is not possible for great wines to be made. If Josef Schell is the master of cellar work, then Langwerth's director Helmut Kranich is the master of harvest organisation. In spite of the romance associated with grape picking, it is never easy work. In 1987 it was a really close shave for Langwerth; they gathered in the last of their grapes literally as the first drops of really heavy rain started coming down!

The products of this rigorous organisation of the harvest at Langwerth von Simmern have been numerous. Since Helmut Kranich's arrival they have made the only Riesling Auslese in the Rheingau in 1982 (Erbacher Marcobrunn), the only Riesling Trockenbeerenauslese in the Rheingau in 1983 (Hattenheimer Nussbrunnen), and several beautiful Riesling Kabinett wines in 1984, when the great majority of growers produced only QbA

grade wines. These were all hard-won prizes, since in 1982 there were a lot of grapes with rot which had to be removed from the vineyards before there was the remotest chance of top qualities being harvested. In 1983 there was hardly any of the noble rot necessary to produce Beerenauslese and Trockenbeerenauslese dessert wines, and in 1984 only the very best grapes were ripe and clean enough for the resulting wine not to require some added sugar to have adequate body.

A difficult vintage like 1984, which the press dismissed as being unripe and thin before tasting a single wine, is the greatest test of a wine producer's mettle, and the superb quality of the wines of this vintage at Langwerth is the best possible proof of the estate's capabilities. They hardly have a hint of the greenness which was typical of the vintage and marked even a good number of the better examples in their infancy. From the first tasting after bottling they overflowed with fresh fruitiness, and rippled with racy acidity.

Because vintages like this are always overlooked by the trade, these wines offer remarkable value for money. However, they should not be drunk too young. Helmut Kranich is not alone in thinking that Rheingau wines from such vintages need long ageing. 'The wines from really good vintages are ripe in taste

Flaschenreife : bottle age

from the beginning, though they are certainly finer if matured for some years before drinking. However, the wines of the unripe vintages *need* many years of slow maturation in the bottle to gain ripe flavours, what we call "Flaschenreife", or bottle ripeness. Then they can be quite delicious.'

Such remarkably high-quality wines from problematic vintages are only possible from the very best vineyards. Langwerth are lucky to own 13.2 hectares/32.5 acres of vineyards on the short slope which rises from the bank of the Rhine between Erbach and Hattenheim. This is one of the best hillsides along the entire length of the Rhine. One can walk along the road at the bottom of this hillside in little more than five minutes, yet in that short distance there are six individual vineyard sites which each give a distinct type of fine Riesling wine.

It is instructive to taste a single wine of the same vintage from each of the sites of which Langwerth owns a slice: the Hattenheimer Mannberg (90 per cent in von Simmern's ownership), Hattenheimer Nussbrunnen, and Erbacher Marcobrunn vineyards. The differences are often strikingly clear. The Marcobrunn will always be the heaviest wine with a rich earthiness not shared by the others. Nussbrunnen will have the fullest fruit and probably a pronounced peachiness, whilst the Mannberg will be the lighest and raciest. Traditionally Marcobrunn is rated top amongst the Erbach–Hattenheim sites, but it is really a matter of taste, and some of the greatest German wine connoisseurs do not share Thomas Jefferson's enthusiasm for Marcobrunn wines.

The nicest way to taste wines like these is without too much ceremony at the Langwerther Hof, the estate buildings in Eltville. These are a fine collection of architectural styles, ranging from fourteenth-century Gothic to seventeenth-century Renaissance revival, which form a large enclosed square. In the middle of this is a park-like garden where von Simmern have a wine stand during the various wine festivals which occur during the summer months in the Rheingau. One of the unsung virtues of German winemakers is that even those at the very top are not above mixing with customers and drinking a few glasses of wine with them in the garden. I do not believe that the Domaine de la Romanée Conti or Château Margaux are particularly renowned for this.

This kind of relaxed enjoyment or the dinner table are the perfect situations for the regular-quality wines, the QbA and Kabinett wines, produced by top estates such as Langwerth von Simmern. Such wines will age very well, but should also be enjoyed for their youthful freshness. However, with the very top wines, which always have a marked sweetness in spite of their high acidity levels, a grander situation is called for. Wines like the Langwerth von Simmern 1983 Auslese, Beerenauslese and Trockenbeerenauslese are produced in such minuscule quantities, a few hundred litres, that every half-bottle is precious, and the idea of a single one being drunk without due respect is nothing short of horrendous.

If Riesling QbA and Kabinett wines made with the kind of care that von Simmern lavish on the tanks and casks of wine in their cellars will last ten, fifteen or more years, then the top wines really need a minimum of that many years' ageing before being drunk. Those who produce such remarkable products surely deserve the title of artists.

Weingut J. B. Becker, Rheingau

Hans-Josef Becker (owner and winemaker),
Maria Becker (owner and director).
Weingut J. B. Becker,
Rheinstrasse 6,
D 6620 Walluf.
Tel: 06123 72523.

11 hectares/27 acres.
80% Riesling, 15% Spätburgunder (Pinot Noir), 5%
Müller-Thurgau.

Not all the most creative people amongst the top German wine producers are happy to work together with others in organisations like the VDP or Charta. Indeed, some of the most gifted winemakers in Germany are determined individualists who feel compelled to take their own path. Hans-Josef Becker, more than any other wine producer in the Rheingau, is his own man. He is without any doubt the producer of the finest dry Riesling wines in the entire region, and many of his medium-dry wines are excellent examples of this style, always elegant and harmonious.

There again, in spite of his excellent reputation in Germany for dry wines, when a great vintage comes along he produces some of the very finest rich Auslese wines in the Rheingau. Yet even these wines are not Hans-Josef's first love: that is his red wines.

Hans-Josef's individualism is apparent from the moment one meets him, or perhaps I should say from the moment one meets him and his majestic moustache. (Never did a winemaker have a more magnificent personal trade mark.) To a certain extent, how things go from there depends on his mood, and what he thinks of his visitor. If a visitor is judged to be sufficiently serious, he may get a tour of the cellars during which the details of Hans-Josef's winemaking will be explained. This is as individual as Hans-Josef himself. To winemakers from other estates and regions the cellar work at Weingut Becker can look decidedly eccentric. I shall never forget the surprise on the face of Hermann Dörflinger of Müllheim in Baden (p. 221) when he saw the large old-fashioned pump which Hans-Josef uses when filtrating his wines. It may not be high technology, but it does what he wants, and that is all that matters to Hans-Josef.

The filtration this pump is used for is equally unusual. For some years Hans-Josef Becker has used only membrane filtration, unlike most estates which use large sheet filters. He uses precious little of even this gentle form of filtration, though. The Becker Rieslings are made extremely simply (failing any problems which difficult weather conditions during the harvest might create). Whereas most estates rush to bottle all their wines to be able to serve even the most distant export markets for the Christmas following the vintage, Hans-Josef only begins thinking about bottling wines in the August or September following the vintage, not having tried to push them to an artificially early stability by reducing their acidity artificially, or over-filtering them. He knows that they need time to reach the necessary maturity in cask before bottling.

The red wines take even longer, and are rarely bottled until nearly two years after the vintage. While the village of Assmannshausen in the Rheingau has a historical reputation for red wines, Walluf had no name for them until Hans-Josef's grandfather produced some quite serious red wines at the beginning of the century. The red wines his father made had a little touch of sweetness, which was typical of German red wines during the post-war decades. Hans-Josef's red wines are bone-dry, have a classical red wine fermentation on the skins (for fourteen or more days), are fined with egg whites like the very best French red wines, and never have much below 12° of alcohol. In recent years their reputation has spread tremendously, and the 1985 Becker red wine was sold for 22 DM (about £8/$15) direct from the estate. In spite of this it is already sold out (at the time of writing, November 1987)!

One of the reasons for the high price is the remarkably low yield: in 1985 less than 3000 litres per hectare/1200 litres per acre, which makes the Burgundians' famous low yields look distinctly greedy. This is partly due to the great age of half the Spätburgunder vines planted in the great Wallufer Walkenberg vineyard, which date back to Hans-Josef's grandfather.

Hans-Josef himself does much of the work in this steeply sloping strip of vineyard which runs from the edge of Walluf by the Rhine up towards the Taunus forest. It is not at all unusual to call and find that he is out in the Walkenberg just finishing off some work on the estate's caterpillar tractor. In fact, he lives out in the vineyards somewhat further from town. There he has a converted barn which he shares only with his horses. Few visitors are taken there, as Hans-Josef greatly values his time alone. There is a big party there every Christmas Eve, though.

The best place to meet Hans-Josef is without doubt the Beckers' Wine Garden on the bank of the Rhine just across the road from the fine estate buildings. This is run by his sister Maria, who also manages the wine estate, organises the sales, and runs a wine-broking business with her brother. (Both the Beckers work incredibly hard.) 'The Wine Garden' is open every day between May and October from five o'clock in the afternoon (two pm on Saturdays and Sundays), until late, which means really late if it is a warm night. It is also open at weekends during the winter, given good weather.

Nearly everyone who comes to The Wine Garden drinks the red wine, or one of the dry Rieslings. The latter is fully accepted amongst Hans-Josef's and Maria's customers as the normal style, to the extent that the great majority of the estate's production is made dry or medium-dry. Whereas the completely dry Riesling wines from many growers in the Rheingau are a bit blunt and

Spiel: "play" of fruit & acidity on the tongue

lacking in fruitiness, Hans-Josef's dry Rieslings are always full of animated fruitiness, or what the Germans call 'Spiel'. This wonderful word, which like so many foreign taste descriptions cannot be directly translated into English, means play; the play of fruit and acidity on the tongue.

The secret of the elegance and harmony of these dry wines is a very careful selection of the grapes, and then of the casks of wine for this style. Over-ripe grapes, or grapes with too much unripe acidity, will not make an attractive dry wine. They need a little touch – and for Hans-Josef it really is no more than a little touch – of sweetness, to accentuate the fruit. However, when the right balance is achieved Hans-Josef believes that it is the dry wines which will age best of all. 'If you want to drink my Riesling wines young, then I strongly recommend you to take one of the Halbtrocken wines,' he says, 'because early on the dry wines are too aggressive, and the sweet wines . . . well, they taste sweet. However, after a few years of ageing the position is rather different, for the firm edge of the dry wines has been rounded and the full intensity of their flavour is developed. The sweeter wines also taste better then, because their sweetness has receded into the background making them harmonious. However, I'm sure that even then the dry wines are purer in character and more elegant.'

The relaxed way in which Hans-Josef and Maria hang over the bar in The Wine Garden and chat about wine or gossip with regulars belies the depth of experience they have. Hans-Josef believes that it takes a winemaker as long as ten years to find exactly the right methods for himself. He made his first wines with his father in 1964, and his first wines alone in 1971. However, in contradiction to his own rule he made some bad mistakes in 1982, and much of the wine was not up to his normal standards. It can happen to anyone, and it was hard to have to sell so much of that vintage away in bulk. None the less the rule stands, and by its reckoning Hans-Josef is well into his prime.

This is certainly the impression one gets when tasting his best wines from the last few vintages, or better still drinking them in The Wine Garden. Even so, some of the first wines he made by himself are excellent – most of all the 1971 Wallufer Walkenberg Auslese (No. 3) which is the most perfect Rheingau wine I have drunk from this great vintage. Here is the perfect marriage of *Botrytis* and Riesling character, neither swamping the other, the wine extremely clean and refreshing in spite of its great richness. Amazingly, it is still available in small quantities, owing to the Beckers' tradition of holding stocks of the best wines from older vintages. Equally ravishing, though in quite a different style, are the dry and medium-dry Wallufer Walkenberg Riesling Spätlese wines from 1983.

A tasting at Weingut Becker should always finish with the red wines, though, which my colleague Harry Eyres called 'the Chambertin of the Rheingau' when he tasted them for the first time in Walluf. The 1983 and 1985 Spätburgunder Kabinett Trocken wines are really first-class, deep and full, but without the heaviness or harshness (from over-chaptelisation and over-extraction) which mars so much red Burgundy. I had better not admit just how many bottles of these wines I have drunk in Walluf . . .

Weingut Heyl zu Herrnsheim, Rheinhessen

Isa von Weymarn (owner),
Peter W. von Weymarn (director).
Weingut Freiherr Heyl zu Herrnsheim,
Mathildenhof,
Langgasse 3,
D 6505 Nierstein.

28 hectares/69 acres.
60% Riesling, 20% Müller-Thurgau, 16% Silvaner, 4%
Weissburgunder (Pinot Blanc), Traminer and Kerner.

Rheinhessen has a reputation for sweet, rather soft, blowsy wines that tend to be appreciated by old women and the unsophisticated. However, as well as producing large quantities of wine in that style the region is also home to a small number of wine estates who make Riesling wines of great elegance. Weingut Heyl zu Herrnsheim in Nierstein is undoubtedly the greatest of these estates, their best Rieslings being amongst the finest Rhine wines.

That this estate is barely known in Britain is the result of an accident of business history, but is none the less a scandalous reflection on the lack of interest that the British wine trade has shown in fine German wines during recent years. Heyl is not a new star on the German wine scene; they have been great wine producers since at least 1893 when they started to use their unique blue monk label. The wines on their list, including the special supplement of rarities, which stretch back over three decades, are a living testament to a continual commitment to quality unmatched in the region.

For Peter and Isa von Weymarn, producing the finest possible wines is nothing less than a matter of honour, and this is one of the few larger German estates where the owners really want to hear any and every critical comment about their wines. Tastings here are a delight; to rush through in order to make another appointment would be to miss a great deal, and not to respect the seriousness of the von Weymarns. In warm summer weather tastings normally take place on the balcony of the spacious Mathildenhof overlooking the beautiful park-like garden. Peter von Weymarn brings only a few wines at a time, because he wants to be able to talk about them, and more generally about the problems of the German wine law, organic wine production, and a dozen other things.

Most people are taken aback when they discover that Peter von Weymarn does not come from a family with any history of winemaking, and that he never undertook any formal training in winemaking or viticulture. In fact he was a physicist working at the Max Planck Institute until he married Freifrau Isa von Meding-Heyl. In the years since 1969 when Isa and Peter took over control of the estate they have learnt and achieved an enormous amount. 'I think my training as a physicist taught me some very useful things,' Peter von Weymarn maintains. 'Firstly that you must have a systematic approach, and secondly that you must pay attention to every small detail. If you lack the first of these then everything can fall down because just one part of the winemaking process isn't receiving proper care and attention. If you lack the second then you'll never make great wines, because the difference between making a good wine and a great one is precisely due to the sum of many small details of method in every aspect of the winemaking process.'

For Peter von Weymarn winemaking begins not just with the cultivation of the vines, but with the soil. If its structure is not good, the vines will not grow well enough to produce good-quality grapes. This applies even more to the organic wines which Heyl produce than to the regular ones, and these now account for fully 10 per cent of the estate's production. If chemical fertilisation is to be completely renounced, Peter von Weymarn believes, the special red slate soils of Nierstein (excepting the Kranzberg which has a loess soil) must be prepared for this over a period of five or more years. The great majority of the Heyl vineyards are now 'green', the weeds being allowed to grow between the rows of vines and ploughed back into the soil once a year. This contributes both minerals and extra humus to the soil.

However, Peter von Weymarn is no 'green' who is against the use of any chemicals in winemaking. He regards the idea that modest levels of sulphur dioxide in wine (which are essential if the wine is to remain fresh) cause health problems as ludicrous and hysterical. 'There are, it is true, a few people who have a real allergy for sulphur dioxide, but this is very rare. What we should be much more worried about is the fact that some of the modern insecticides can get into the bottle. This is a problem which affects all wine-producing regions, and it's one of the reasons why we are so interested in organic wine production. None the less this matter must also be kept in proportion; yeast is a very good cleansing agent, reducing the concentration of many undesirable substances in fermenting wines by as much as a thousand times.'

Peter also considers the picking of the grapes critical for the quality of the wine. 'Much more than in France the grapes in our vineyards vary in quality and must be selected. For us this is quite as important as how big the yield is. This selection of grapes is a German tradition. I don't think our estate is so unusual in doing this, but perhaps the rigorousness here isn't something you'll find everywhere.' How strict a selection has to be made depends very much on the conditions during late summer and the vintage time. Heyl's best vineyard is their monopole, Niersteiner Brudersberg, the only steep south-facing vineyard next to the Rhine during its long sweep southwards from Nackenheim, past Nierstein and Oppenheim towards Worms. In 1984 Peter and Isa von Weymarn had to make the strictest possible selection to get a (brilliant!) Kabinett quality wine from the Brudersberg. Though 1986 was not a great vintage, in the first days of the harvest they picked grapes of Auslese quality in the Brudersberg without any selection at all!

Those Auslese-quality grapes did not automatically become an Auslese wine, though. Peter and Isa have very strict minimum quality criteria for each Prädikat or quality grade, and the final stage in determining if a particular wine is good enough to bear a particular designation is the taste of the wine. This is how the better wine producers had always decided which wines could bear the quality designations like Spätlese and Auslese, before the 1971 wine law came along and handed everybody a lot of analytical criteria. Even some good wine producers now work strictly by the legally prescribed quality criteria, saying, 'I've achieved the minimum level of sugar in the grapes for a Spätlese, so why shouldn't I sell it as a Spätlese since I'm legally entitled to do so?'

For Peter von Weymarn this is only one of the 1971 wine law's many absurdities. Another which he finds very frustrating is the way in which any wine with less than 9 grams per litre sugar is legally speaking Trocken or dry, and any with more than this (but less than 18 grams per litre) is Halbtrocken or medium-dry. As he points out, it is easy to find Trocken wines with very low acidity which taste sweet, whilst his Halbtrocken wines from 1984 with high acidity taste really dry. Peter von Weymarn's solution is to give each wine a pair of numbers indicating the ratio of sweetness to acidity in taste, and these are printed in the estate's price list. In this system 1:0 means bone-dry and 1:5 really sweet. Unfortunately it would be impractical, and illegal, to put such taste-coding numbers on the label.

With the aid of this system Peter and Isa von Weymarn are able to persuade their customers that even some wines which analytically have considerable sweetness can go very well with food, because they *taste* dry. This kind of balance in some 'sweet' wines is possible because at Weingut Heyl zu Herrnsheim there is almost no 'deacidification'. The lowering of acidity in German wines through the addition of large quantities of calcium carbonate has a catastrophic effect on them. It instantly knocks the stuffing out of the wines, and they can only deteriorate from that point on. (Handled very carefully, the double salt method of deacidification can be useful in making the wines from very difficult vintages in northern Germany more harmonious, since it only removes the unripe malic acidity.)

This virtual renunciation of deacidification would not be possible if the von Weymarns did not make their wines almost exclusively in wooden casks. This enables the wine to find its own equilibrium, excess acidity crystallising around the inside, and dropping to the bottom, of the casks. However, they work very carefully with the casks, wary of the danger of losing freshness if wines remain here too long. As soon as each wine has gained the right degree of rounding and mellowing from the cask, it is immediately transferred to a stainless steel tank to await bottling. Here the wine will hardly change at all, even over a period of many months.

However, even after bottling their work has not finished, for the right moment to present the wine to their customers for the first time must be carefully selected. The better Riesling wines are almost never made available until at least two years after the vintage. Substantial stocks of the wines with the greatest potential for long maturation in bottle are also put aside. Hence that list of wines going back to 1953! This is not to say that all the best wines from Heyl have to be drunk after long ageing. Their bone-dry Silvaner Trocken wines can be enjoyed during their first few years after bottling.

The Silvaner wines at Heyl zu Herrnsheim have been fermented to dryness since 1976, and have got better and better with almost every vintage. The 1985 Niersteiner Öelberg Silvaner Spätlese Trocken could not have been better, having the typical rather neutral Silvaner character, but also astonishing elegance. It was a revelation to many people in the German wine business, as well as to me, and in May 1987 it tasted wonderful with the asparagus au gratin at the Mathildenhof.

Weingut Rappenhof, Rheinhessen

Dr Reinhard Muth (owner and director),
Klaus Muth (owner and director).
Weingut Rappenhof,
Bachstrasse 47–49,
D 6526 Alsheim.
Tel: 06249 4015.

30 hectares/74 acres.
38% Riesling, 15% Spätburgunder (Pinot Noir),
Weissburgunder (Pinot Blanc), Ruländer (Pinot Gris) and
Chardonnay, 10% Silvaner, 10% Müller-Thurgau,
10% Kerner, 7% Gewürztraminer, 10% Portugieser and
others.

Though Weingut Rappenhof produces a good quantity of Riesling wines in both the dry and sweeter styles, and these can be very fine in vintages like 1985, 1979, or 1975 where they have a nice refreshing acidity, the estate's real forte is the Burgundian grape varieties. Nobody else in Germany has the complete range of these in cultivation and production, and even Weingut Rappenhof only has Chardonnay in its vineyards by special permission of the state as an experiment! Globally, no other grape variety is being more widely planted than the Chardonnay; Germany is almost the only wine-producing country where it is not being widely planted.

Although other EEC countries also have rules which prescribe the varieties which may be used to make quality wines, and forbid the planting of vine varieties which have special disease or pest problems, normally any grapes can be used to make Table Wine. In Germany, the rules about which grape varieties can be planted are very strict, with the consequence that there are some totally illegal experiments with classic French and Italian varieties going on.

Another aspect of the wine-control authorities' narrow attitude that frustrates Dr Reinhard and Klaus Muth is their often highly restrictive idea of what is typical, and hence capable of receiving Qualitätswein or Qualitätswein mit Prädikat status. The Muths and Graf Adelmann in Württemberg (p. 109) are almost the only German wine estates to produce red wines with a distinct oaky character which none the less pass the AP number testing, and can be sold as QbA or QmP.

Weingut Rappenhof is one of the German estates where there are no particularly fine buildings or wonderful views of the Rhine or Moselle, but a lot of very exciting and often unusual wines in the cellars. Dr Reinhard is very open and extremely even-handed when speaking of his neighbours and competitors. His son Klaus is rather more excitable and jovial, but both are very charming. They speak perfect English, and at least some of a handful of other European languages between them. The reason for Dr Muth's great linguistic abilities, and for their experimentation with 'foreign' grape varieties and winemaking techniques, is that for some years he has been the president of the German wine growers' association. It was on one of the trips he made in this capacity, to Piedmont in Italy, that he decided to

Ruländer = Pinot Gris

start work with new oak casks. 'We visited someone there who was experimenting with many different types of wood ageing for his wines, and I was so fascinated by the results that I knew we had to try this too.'

At Weingut Rappenhof the cellar currently contains tanks for white wines and for the 'nouveau'-style red wine made from grapes from the Portugieser variety, old wooden Halbstück, Stück and Doppelstück casks for Riesling and lighter red wines, and new oak 228-litre 'barriques' for the best wines from both the red and white Burgundy varieties. (The barriques come from Tonnellerie François Frère in Saint Romain, Burgundy.) Two types of oak are used: Limousin from south-west France for the red wine casks, and Vosges from Alsace for the white wines. Both types of wood must be well seasoned before being turned into the small casks. 'The chemical changes which take place during this seasoning are very important. Without this the wood tannins which the wine absorbs from the cask would be too aggressive, and they'd quickly overwhelm the wine. It's this long seasoning as much as the scarcity of the wood and the skilled work which goes into making the casks, which makes them expensive.'

Though the high price of barriques adds significantly to the cost of the wines aged in them, it is these wines which Weingut Rappenhof sell out of first. The superb 1985 vintage new-oak-aged Weissburgunder Tafelwein (a declassified bone-dry Auslese) was all sold to a single customer before ever reaching the list! Even with the barrique-aged red wines, of which the production is considerably greater, Weingut Rappenhof is fast approaching the point where only wines from the last vintage will be available.

The Rappenhof style is, as Klaus Muth explained, 'light and fresh for the normal white wines, without enough acidity to enable them to develop in bottle for many years. With the varieties that can sometimes easily lack acidity we deliberately harvest early. If we didn't do this with the Ruländer, for example, it would be a flat heavy wine, but with early harvesting we can really produce something special with this variety here.' Klaus Muth trained as a lawyer, which is quite a normal course of study for the sons of top estate owners. Surprisingly, it seems to prepare many of them very well for being wine producers (see also Weingut Mönchhof, p. 123). Certainly Klaus has a very firm grasp of every aspect of Rappenhof's winemaking.

I was lucky to be able to visit the estate in the middle of the 1986 harvest, the one time when visitors are not normally welcomed with open arms, on account of the enormous work load. Klaus was able to show me the various stages of the red wine fermentation, since several pickings had already been made and were at different stages in the process. As soon as the red grapes arrive they are sorted, since even a few rotten grapes can ruin the colour of a red wine. Then the sound bunches are milled to break open the skins, and this pulp or mash is pumped into large open-topped vats to ferment on the skins for 8–10 days. During this time the 'cap' of skins which floats to the surface is pushed down into the pulp and juice twice a day to help extract the colour from the skins. Then the juice is drained off and the pulp lightly pressed. This press wine is usually added to the 'free run' wine, and after settling the wine goes down into new or old casks.

In recent decades, even if they have been made dry, German red wines have normally been more like a rosé in colour, and have not had any tannin. Tannin is the principal cause of the mouth-drying or puckering aftertaste of red wines. It is also the major ingredient in the structure of serious red wines, without which they cannot live very long or develop a more complex character through ageing in the bottle. The significantly higher tannin content of claret in comparison to Beaujolais is the principal reason why good examples of the former are laid down to mature, and the latter generally cannot be aged for very long.

By having noticeable tannin in all their red wines except the nouveau-style Portugieser, Rappenhof firmly assert that theirs are serious red wines. The colour is, in comparison to French red wines, never less than respectable and often deep. They rarely have less than 12 degrees of alcohol, and have a solid, warm, red wine fruitiness, combined with some obvious acidity: another important element of the Rappenhof hallmark (the red wines here do not undergo a second or malolactic fermentation). This balance enables them to age very well for at least five or six years, and in some cases much longer.

When barrique ageing has been used, the new-oak flavour is always pronounced. If it is never as strong as in top clarets, it is certainly comparable to the level of oakiness of many top red Burgundies. This is controversial enough for Germany, though, and Dr Reinhard Muth is very anxious to make his position on oak-ageing very clear. 'I don't want to take a dogmatic stand on the barrique question, but I feel that some of my opponents are taking up a dogmatic position. They don't want wine drinkers to even have the choice to drink wines with oak character! The most ridiculous thing is that if I suddenly changed to making all my wines very sweet and abandoned dry wines, then it would be exactly such a restriction of consumer choice they would charge me with!'

The barrique-aged white wines are a stark contrast to the vividly fruity, clean 'normal' Riesling, Silvaner, Ruländer and Gewürztraminer wines from Rappenhof. They are as clearly marked by oak character as the barrique-aged red wines. The lightest of these, the 1984 Weissburgunder Tafelwein, had 11 degrees of alcohol, but Klaus Muth believes this is really the practical minimum for a wine to be able to benefit from new-oak maturation. He and his father are much happier with their 1985 Weissburgunder Tafelwein (13 degrees of alcohol), the 1986 Ruländer Tafelwein and Chardonnay Tafelwein (both with around 12 degrees of alcohol). These wines have enough body to carry the oak, though Dr Reinhard Muth went very carefully with the Chardonnay. 'We only fermented it in the new oak, then transferred it to an old oak Halbstück cask. Already it's got more oakiness than the majority of Chablis, but is still very fruity. We felt that this style was better for us, rather than trying to make a big fat wine.'

However, it is not just these atypically German Rappenhof wines which will shock those who think of German wines as soft, sweet and bland. The Rappenhof dry Gewürztraminer wines can also be very fine, with the classic rose petals-lychees character of the grape variety. The Muths are rightly proud of these wines, which have a delicacy and elegance not often achieved with Gewürztraminer. 'Richard Spiers, a UK importer, took one of our dry Gewürztraminers with him on a trip to Alsace, and showed it to the Hugel family. They just couldn't believe it came from Germany, and immediately sent it to their lab, and wanted to know exactly how it had been made!'

Weingut K. & H. Lingenfelder, Rheinpfalz

Rainer Lingenfelder (owner and winemaker),
Karl Lingenfelder (owner and director),
Hermann Lingenfelder (owner and director).
Weingut K. & H. Lingenfelder,
Hauptstrasse 27,
D 6711 Grosskarlbach.
Tel: 06238 754.

9.7 hectares/24 acres.
22% Riesling, 15% Scheurebe, 14% Spätburgunder (Pinot
Noir), 12% Kerner, 37% Müller-Thurgau, Dornfelder,
Ruländer (Pinot Gris) and Morio-Muscat.

Weingut Lingenfelder is one of the rising stars of the Palatinate, which is itself the rising star amongst the German wine regions. There are an astonishingly large number of good estates and co-operatives here (pp. 194–209), and a great many of these have only emerged from obscurity during the last few years. Weingut Lingenfelder has a much longer reputation than this, Karl Lingenfelder having dedicatedly worked for high qualities for more than twenty-five years, but it has certainly come a rung or two further up the quality scale since Karl's son Rainer Lingenfelder has been winemaker.

Rainer is only in his early thirties and seems even younger, having a seemingly inexhaustible supply of energy. As well as supervising the winemaking at his family estate, until recently he was also chief oenologist for H. Sichel Söhne in Alzey, makers of Blue Nun liebfraumilch. Rainer's training gave him the kind of diversity and breadth of experience which very few other German winemakers acquire in their entire lives. Prior to and during his studies at the Geisenheim viticultural and winemaking school he worked in the Barossa valley of South Australia for Penfolds Wines, Basedow Wines, and Kaiser Stuhl Wines; in Gisbourne, New Zealand, for Montana wines; and in Bordeaux for Château Grand Puy Lacoste and Château Ducru-Beaucaillou. Then he spent a year and a half in Egypt as supervising consultant on a winery modernisation project. And if this was not enough, Rainer has more recently made two trips to study winemaking techniques in California!

Although Rainer's technical interests are very diverse, a thread runs through them all: the study of phenolic compounds in wine. This obscure-sounding and disturbingly named group of substances make up most colouring matter in wine, and the tannins present in all white wines as well as reds. However, it is on phenolics in red wines that Rainer's attention has been focused, since getting the right kind and quantity of these in red wines is, in Rainer's words, 'crucial to their harmony, ageing capacity, and, most importantly, their taste'.

The reason for this consuming interest is very down-to-earth, though, for until the beginning of this century the area of the Palatinate where the Lingenfelders live was a red wine region. Even today, there is a large acreage of red grapes (mostly Blauer Portugieser) in the area immediately around and to the north of Bad Dürkheim, stretching as far as Grosskarlbach. However, for Rainer what is made from the vast majority of these grapes is barely even red wine. After a big regional tasting we attended recently he said to me, 'What wonderful Riesling wines, but how can they present Pinot Noir wines like that? They were far too pale, thin, acidic, and mostly lacked any real red wine character . . .' The red wine tradition in the Palatinate has well and truly been lost, and is only just beginning to emerge again as a result of the work of people like Rainer Lingenfelder and Werner Knipser (p. 194).

All this would not be worth recounting if Weingut Lingenfelder had not already got four vintages of their new-style Palatinate Spätburgunder behind them. Of these one has to be singled out, since the 1985 is the full realisation of what Rainer Lingenfelder has been trying to achieve with Pinot Noir. The first time I visited Rainer in May 1986 this wine was lying in the cellar, where we tasted it from cask. I was absolutely stunned when Rainer turned the lights on in the small vaulted red wine cellar under the Lingenfelders' beautiful neo-classical house, and I saw rows of barriques with 'Château Grand Puy Lacoste' stamped on them.

Rainer had bought these barrels after they had been used at the Château for maturing three vintages, so that most of the oak flavour had already been leached out of them. This might seem a perverse thing to do – buy and ship barrels half across Europe when the very substance for which they are normally used had

Racking can intensify the colors + fruit of red wines

already been removed – but it was a very carefully thought out decision. 'Although we managed to get 13 degrees of alcohol in our 1985 Pinot Noir entirely naturally,' Rainer maintains, 'even then it doesn't have the weight of a red Burgundy. As a result I don't think that our red wines can take new-oak flavours. Remember, even in Burgundy most growers only replace a few of their wooden casks each year. What I want the wine to get from its time in these small casks is a steady, very gentle contact with the air through the wood. This causes the tannins in the wine to soften and the acidity to mellow, creating a much better harmony than if we aged the wine in a big barrel where it would have much less air contact.'

To prove this Rainer recently presented me with two cask samples of the 1986 Pinot Noir. One was significantly deeper and more purple in colour, with greater intensity of fruit, and a more classic red wine character. This was the wine aged in the *small* casks. What makes this so surprising is that all the wine books say that a red wine gets browner and less fruity as a result of contact with air; for instance, as it matures when laid down for many years. However, this is simplistic. When certain compounds in the phenolic group are in contact with oxygen they undergo chemical changes with results exactly opposite to what the simple 'the older the wine the browner it will be' rule would lead one to expect. This chemical transformation is vital to red wines, and is the reason that whilst winemakers are generally very nervous of their white wines having any contact with the air, they are happy to rack a red wine from one barrel to another by pouring it through several feet of air many times during cask ageing.

Rainer has not simply congratulated himself on this wine, though. Every knowledgeable visitor to the estate – a German or English wine writer, a young winemaker from New Zealand, or Peter Sichel, President of H. Sichel Söhne Inc. (New York) – is subjected to a blind international Pinot Noir tasting. Needless to say, at least one of the Weingut Lingenfelder Spätburgunder wines is always included. The comments on all the wines are carefully noted by Rainer, and the tasters are asked to guess which wine is the Lingenfelder.

However, though Rainer is very flattered by comments such as that by my colleague Andrew Barr, who said, 'I think Rainer

Scheurebe: Silvaner x Ries, 1916 by Georg Scheu

Lingenfelder probably knows more about red winemaking than all the growers of certain Burgundian villages put together!', he would not want his interest in the red wines to obscure the white wines which make up the majority of the estate's production. Indeed, it was one of these wines, the 1983 dry Riesling Spätlese (a late-harvested wine from the fine Freinsheimer Goldberg vineyard) which first attracted my attention to the estate. Early in 1986 I tasted this wine with Rainer's then importer in England, and was so impressed by its depth and elegance that I wrote saying I thought it was better than the equivalent wines produced by the world-famous Weingut Dr Bürklin-Wolf (p. 198) and Weingut Reichsrat von Buhl (p. 202) estates. The very day after my letter arrived, Rainer received a copy of the latest issue of the Swiss wine magazine *Vinum*, in which were the results of a tasting of 1983 Rheinpfalz dry Rieslings where his wine was placed above those from Bürklin-Wolf and von Buhl!

Rainer's dry Riesling and Scheurebe wines are a far cry from the present image of dry German wines in Britain and America, where they are regarded as being thin, highly acidic wines that fundamentally lack fruit and harmony. This particular dry Riesling from Lingenfelder had a very respectable 11.4 degrees of alcohol, which, combined with its excellent ripe fruitiness, gave it more than enough substance to carry the refreshing acidity that has enabled it to develop so beautifully. Rainer has made dry

Spätlese wines with much higher alcohol than this, though; the Scheurebe from the same vintage had a staggering 13.4 degrees of alcohol, but was still very fruity rather than heavy and alcoholic. For Rainer this kind of dry white wine is something almost unique to Germany. 'Because of our cool climate, and our white winemaking which seeks to preserve fruitiness at all costs, we are able to make white wines with high alcohol which don't taste heavy and oily. That can even be a problem some years in Burgundy, which also has a fairly cool climate, let alone in the New World.'

Modest sweetness and a good alcohol level also characterise the Auslese, Beerenauslese, and Trockenbeerenauslese dessert wines made at Weingut Lingenfelder. These have been a speciality since Rainer's father, Karl, took over the estate in 1952. Very fine examples indeed were made from Riesling and Scheurebe. 1985 and 1986 were also very good years for the production of these top wines in the Palatinate; in the former vintage the estate harvested a Scheurebe Trockenbeerenauslese, and in the latter year Riesling and Scheurebe Auslese wines.

The TBA is extraordinarily clean and fruity, rather than heavy and richly honeyed as these wines normally are, and was fermented through to 13 degrees of alcohol. The 1986 Scheurebe Auslese, which like the 1985 TBA comes from the great Freinsheimer Musikantenbuckel vineyard, has 12.5 degrees of alcohol and only 22 grams per litre of unfermented sugar; only 4 more grams per litre than the upper limit for a Halbtrocken wine. It has a magnificent dried peach/apricot richness, and very racy acidity. It is already a most exciting wine.

So, whilst Weingut Lingenfelder has certainly not renounced making sweeter wines like many producers in the Palatinate, they have worked towards a new balance for them. This style goes hand in hand with the dry white wine style, and the classical red wine style promoted by the estate. Where else in the world can one get such fine wines in three such distinct and highly developed styles from a single estate? This is surely one of the great virtues of Germany's wine producers.

Weingut Pfeffingen, Rheinpfalz

Karl Fuhrmann (owner and director),
Doris Eymael (owner and director),
Günther Eymael (owner and director).
Weingut Pfeffingen Fuhrmann–Eymael,
D 6702 Bad Dürkheim.
Tel: 06322 8607/5591.

11 hectares/27 acres.
60% Riesling, 15% Scheurebe, 10% Silvaner,
10% Müller-Thurgau, 5% Gewürztraminer.

Weingut Pfeffingen is yet another of the very top German estates which is virtually unknown in the UK. This is very perplexing, both because the estate has always produced a majority of its wines in the sweeter style, and because for decades they have specialised in the production of Beerenauslese, Trockenbeeren-auslese and Eiswein dessert wines. This would seem to be the ideal basis for a German estate to have been successful not just in North America (as Pfeffingen has been), but also in Britain. However, so far very little of Pfeffingen's superb Riesling and Scheurebe wines have made their way across the English Channel.

What makes the wines which come out of Karl Fuhrmann and the Eymaels' cellar so special is their combination of great elegance and the traditional Palatinate fullness of flavour. For some years now there has been a tendency in the region for the wines to be made much fresher and lighter than the rather plump, heavy style which has become associated with the region. Weingut Pfeffingen has certainly been a party to this movement, but whereas some producers have gone so far as to emasculate their wines, Weingut Pfeffingen's wines never lack regional character.

The estate's winemaking is a direct expression of the person-alities at the helm. Karl Fuhrmann, who is president of the Palatinate wine growers' association, is a typical Pfälzer in his warmth and relaxed manner. However, he is also rather more than this. He originally intended to study mathematics, but ended up marrying a local girl and taking over the family wine business. In spite of this there is something of the acuteness of a mathematician in the way he carefully weighs his words on anything connected with wine politics, and this precision is surely carried over into the estate's cellar. From the moment he took control of the estate, Karl Fuhrmann worked for the best possible qualities, and it is due to his single-minded determination that the estate has become acknowledged in Germany as one of the stars of the Palatinate.

Günther Eymael is much more reticent, reserved, and sparing with his words. He is virtually a foreigner in the region, having only come to the Palatinate when he married Karl Fuhrmann's daughter Doris. He originates from Ürzig on the Moselle (see Weingut Mönchhof, p. 123), and he and Doris met whilst whey were both studying at the Geisenheim viticultural and winemaking school. Since they both qualified, the estate now has three qualified winemakers on hand! Günther has undoubtedly brought something of a Moselle perspective to Weingut Pfeffingen, for there is a delicacy and floweriness of bouquet to all but the very richest of the estate's wines.

Part of the reason for the 'recent' success of Weingut Pfeffingen is that, from the purely practical point of view, it is a model small estate. All its vineyards are situated immediately around the elegant nineteenth-century estate house and tastefully integrated modern cellar buildings. This means that a vigilant eye can easily be kept on the condition of the grapes, so there is almost no precautionary spraying at the estate, only spraying in reaction to problems which are seen to be starting to develop. It also means that at harvest time every plot of vines can be picked at the optimum moment, and the grapes rapidly processed. As Karl Fuhrmann explained to me, 'This is a big problem for the big wine estates in our region. They have to run their harvests like commando operations simply because of the sheer quantities of grapes they have to deal with. However, rather than just sit back knowing that we have this advantage, we've tried to capitalise on it by doing a lot of selective picking.'

Selective harvesting means picking only bunches, parts of bunches, or individual berries at a particular stage of ripeness or over-ripeness. Such selections are often for grapes which have become infected with noble rot ('Edelfäule'), a type of *Botrytis* fungus which punctures the skin of the grapes, causing them to shrivel, and so concentrating the juice they contain. The *Botrytis* fungus also feeds on the water, sugar and tartaric acid in the grapes, but since it consumes more water than sugar and tartaric acid, the net effect of this is also a concentration of the juice. The chemical effects which it has on the pulp and juice within the grapes are very complex, and still imperfectly understood. However, several important processes are known to happen. The first is the rapid oxidation of many phenolic substances by the enzyme laccase which the fungus produces. This turns the berries and the resulting wine brown, or at the very least amber-tinged. Other changes occur which result in the finished wine having a glycerol content far higher than that of normal wines. All this glycerol makes the wine taste sweeter and richer, and gives it a thick, oily texture.

Weingut Pfeffingen take the selection of such botrytised grapes to an extreme matched only by the top châteaux of Sauternes, such as Château d'Yquem. It is rare that a vintage goes by at Weingut Pfeffingen without a single Riesling or Scheurebe Beerenauslese, Trockenbeerenauslese or Eiswein being harvested. Riesling is the grape variety traditionally used for wines of this type in Germany, but Karl Fuhrmann and Günther Eymael have had even greater success with the Scheurebe variety. They find that in late-harvested and botry-tised styles, it gives wines with an extra dimension of richness.

The Scheurebe variety was bred by Georg Scheu in 1916 at the Alzey viticultural research station, and is a crossing of Silvaner and Riesling. Trials were conducted with it at Alzey for many years, but in the end the results were rather disappointing. They were on the point of abandoning the variety as a lost cause when they were contacted by the owner of Weingut Annaberg in Bad Dürkheim. He planted Scheurebe in his vineyards, and in the great vintages soon after the war, 1947, 1949, and 1953, made stupendous Scheurebe Auslese wines.

It was shortly after Weingut Annaberg's dramatic first success with Scheurebe that Karl Fuhrmann was scanning about for something he could use to help build up his estate's reputation. It was therefore natural that he should choose to specialise in late-harvested and *Botrytis*-affected Scheurebe wines. The Pfeffingen estate has now made this style all its own, the best wines having a perfect marriage of great richness and brilliance which puts them amongst the world's great dessert wines. Although much ligher in alcohol than a fine Sauternes, they are yet more intense in flavour. However, whether it is such exceptional wines which even Weingut Pfeffingen can only produce in very small quantities, or the Riesling Kabinett wines which they can harvest every year, the estate's winemaking philosophy is basically the same.

Karl Fuhrmann explains this very simply. 'What you absolutely mustn't do is to start with your price list! To make great wines you need excellent vineyards, then you must cultivate them properly, harvest only the good grapes, carefully press them, and equally carefully make the wines. There are a great many wine producers who can do every stage of this well, except for one. As a result, everything which they have worked so hard for is lost, often in a matter of hours if their failing is in cellar work. We've worked hard to perfect every link in the chain, but you really have to be a perfectionist for that.'

Many aspects of Karl Fuhrmann's and Günther Eymael's methods are highly individual, and regarded as eccentric by some of their neighbours. For example, they fertilise the vineyards with pulverised volcanic rock, 'the idea for which we got from an Englishman who had done farming in an area of the Himalayan foothills where the fields were irrigated with glacial water rich in nutrients from volcanic rock'. Günther Eymael explained to me that, in contrast to many producers in the region, they are completely against trying to make up for deficiencies in the wine by various strategies in the cellar. 'Many growers think that they can make up for sloppy work at harvest time by letting the wines sit a long time on the lees – the dead yeast left at the bottom of a tank or cask of wine after fermentation – because they know the wine will gain in flavour from this. However, the wine is just as likely to pick up negative or "off" odours in this way as it is to acquire attractive flavours. We're completely against taking these risks, and we work to separate our wines from the yeast as quickly as is reasonably possible.'

From this point on in the winemaking process every wine at the estate is handled as an individual. However, as a general rule the Müller-Thurgau and Gewürztraminer wines are only held in tanks, and are bottled early. The Riesling and Scheurebe wines nearly all spend some time in old oak casks to develop their flavour and bouquet. Normally the estate does not hurry to bottle these wines. However, as a result of the incredible demand for dry Riesling wines on the German market some wines are bottled earlier than they consider ideal. With customers virtually beating on the door for dry wines it is difficult for them to do otherwise. I must say that these wines taste pretty good to me in spite of this!

As President of the Palatinate wine growers' association, Karl Fuhrmann has made his own estate stand as a shining example of his quality philosophy for the entire region. When he has talked to his members about reducing yields to obtain higher qualities he has been able to show how this works by example. This example has been one of the reasons why an ever-increasing number of growers in the Rheinpfalz have turned over to quality wine production, and the co-operatives have an increasingly quality-minded approach. More than this, though, Karl Fuhr-mann has been one of those who have raised winemaking from mere agricultural production to something greater. There is no hint of pretence when he says, 'I have never seen winemaking as purely a way of making money. Just look at our Scheurebe wines. The prices are quite good, but at this level the sales can't be rapid. In effect we have only invested money in these wines!'

Weingut Koehler-Ruprecht, Rheinpfalz

Bernd Philippi (owner and director).
Weingut Koehler-Ruprecht,
Weinstrasse 84,
D 6701 Kallstadt.
Tel: 06322 1829.

8.5 hectares/21 acres.
65% Riesling, 10% Spätburgunder (Pinot Noir), 8% Kerner,
5% Gewürztraminer, 5% Müller-Thurgau, 7% Muskateller,
Weissburgunder (Pinot Blanc), Huxelrebe, Scheurebe,
Silvaner, Dornfelder and St Laurent.

There cannot be another winemaker in the world who so enjoys wine, food, and travelling, who has quite such an irrepressible *joie de vivre*, as Bernd Philippi. What is remarkable is that far from this taking over from the serious job of making wine, it rather seems to underpin it. Bernd Philippi is a large, goatee-bearded man in his early forties, who everyone seems to agree is a 'great character'. This is also the right description for both types of Koehler-Ruprecht wines. I say both types, because on the one side Bernd Philippi makes extremely traditional Riesling, Gewürztraminer, Weissburgunder and Muskateller wines, and on the other there are some 'crazy' experimental wines quite as weird as anything that came out of California during the seventies.

There is hardly anyone in Germany who is more generous with tastings than Bernd, though for him this is not just fun or PR, but an essential learning experience. In May 1986 he staged an enormous tasting of Riesling Spätlese wines from his top vineyard site, the Kallstadter Saumagen, including every single vintage back to 1950, followed by four wines from the 1930s. While such a tasting would not have been possible in the north of Germany, where Spätlese wines can only be made once every two or three vintages, at Koehler-Ruprecht 50 per cent of the estate's entire production is of Spätlese grade wines.

The oldest wines in this tasting had been made as the majority of Koehler-Ruprecht wines are made today, that is, they are allowed to find their own harmony through fermentation with the natural yeasts which come into the cellars on the grapes. These wines were truly astounding, with an astonishing freshness and vigour for a region which is supposed to produce plump wines lacking the necessary structure for long ageing. The most amazing of this group of wines for me was the 1932 Kallstadter Saumagen Riesling Auslese. 1932 was a 'poor' vintage, and was totally forgotten after the two 'excellent' vintages of the thirties (1934 and 1937). One might expect a wine of this kind to be long dead. Red Bordeaux wines of this vintage would certainly be 'over the hill'. But no, the wine had the light, pale, gold-tinged colour normally indicative of a five- to ten-year-old wine. In bouquet and taste it was equally vital and almost youthful. It was dry, with a wonderfully refreshing acidity and a super peachy ripeness; an assertive wine, rather than elegant or flowery, but many-faceted. So much for vintage charts!

The 1985 Kallstadter Saumagen Riesling Spätlese Trocken and Auslese Trocken wines from Koehler-Ruprecht do not have quite the aggression that these wines must have had in their youth, but they too will confound the oft-repeated rule that German dry wines must be drunk young. They are typical of the 'new' Koehler-Ruprecht style that Bernd has worked towards since he started working in the family estate in 1969. This 'new' style means only a return to the estate's centuries-long tradition of dry winemaking.

This same seeming paradox is to be found in Weingut Koehler-Ruprecht's buildings, the larger part of which really do look as though they were only (re)built after the Thirty Years War, the fine half-timbered exterior beautifully decorated with painted carved wooden figures. Below ground is a newly expanded modern cellar, though this is filled with old wooden casks. This extension work will allow the estate to increase its storage of wines in cask and bottle from one and a half vintages to more than two complete vintages. This is essential to allow Bernd to mature his wines in the way he would like before putting them on the market. Already the estate's list goes back to wines from the 1973 vintage, and almost every vintage between that one and the last harvested is represented.

For Bernd Philippi, using wooden casks for the fermentation and maturation of his wines is not the result of a nostalgic attachment to old things, but an essential element of his wine-making. Without this Bernd feels that many of his wines might be too aggressive. 'It's very important not to hurry wines. I left the 1984 wines a really long time in cask, well over a year. This was necessary to make their hard acidity rounder and more harmonious. If I had made those wines in stainless steel tanks and bottled them early I think they would have needed many years in the bottle to be drinkable, and I don't think that they would ever have found the same harmony as they have as a result of being made traditionally.'

There is a point at which traditionalism ends for Bernd, though, and that point is Auslese wines. Up to this quality grade he makes his wines in the traditional manner. The other type of wine made by Koehler-Ruprecht is an extraordinary diversity of strange dessert wines: medium-dry Beerenauslese, red Eiswein, and Trockenbeerenauslese aged in new oak casks! There is nothing in Germany which can quite match these exotic creations, for although one or two dry Beerenauslese wines have been made in other regions they are little short of disgusting, while Bernd's dessert wines are at the least interesting, and at best of sensational quality.

'Interesting' can be a pejorative word as well as a positive one. The one case where I hover between these two uses of the term is with Bernd's Spätburgunder Beerenauslese Halbtrocken (a Kallstadter Kronenberg from the 1983 vintage). Its rich amber-copper colour, with a distinct pink tone, shows that it was made from red grapes. This wine showed very well in its youth, but already seems a little too alcoholic to be really well balanced. In comparison, the Spätburgunder Eiswein (a Kallstadter Saumagen from the same vintage) is a wonderful wine of great individuality and finesse. This is not the only red icewine to have been made in Germany, but it is easily the best. The colour is a deep rose red shading to garnet in the centre, and it has an intense, fragrant strawberry bouquet. The flavour is very similar, being exceptionally rich and luscious.

Bernd Philippi also makes conventional dessert wines, which can also be quite remarkable. The 1986 Riesling Trockenbeerenauslese has a staggering richness and a gigantic acidity level (17.5 grams per litre), which will make it virtually immortal. At present, its mouthfilling raisiny richness is almost too much to take. Next to it in the cellar sits a very different dessert wine maturing in two barriques. This is the joint creation of Bernd and Bernhard Breuer of Weingut Georg Breuer and Scholl & Hillebrand in the Rheingau (p. 64). It was made from a mixture of grape varieties, and has been 'tailored' to have roughly the same balance and structure as the wines of the top Sauternes Château d'Yquem.

Château d'Yquem does not normally give out analytical data as to what their wine is like at different stages of its development. Bernd and Bernhard virtually had to use undercover methods to get this information. Bernd is anxious to stress that 'we're not doing this as a gimmick though. I certainly wouldn't give a Riesling TBA this kind of treatment, because it's a complete wine just as it is. However, the late-harvested wines from non-traditional varieties really lack something as they are. We decided that there's nothing to lose from trying to give them a more complex character by using new oak. And I don't mean just a few weeks in the barriques. We're going to leave the wine there for at least a year! Of course then the oak flavour will be strong enough that we'll never get an AP number for it, and we'll have to sell it as Tafelwein!'

That Bernd is not worried about AP numbers and receiving the official blessing for his more unusual and experimental wines is typical of his relaxed approach to winemaking. During periods of the year when there is not much work to be done, he is as likely to be away in Madeira or California as at home enjoying the wines of Château Ducru-Beaucaillou, of which he has a remarkable collection. Clearly, a winemaker's life can be great fun.

Fürstlich Castell'sches Domänenamt, Franconia

Albrecht Fürst zu Castell-Castell (owner),
Eduard Krammer (cellarmaster).
Fürstlich Castell'sches Domänenamt,
Schlossplatz 5,
D 8711 Castell.
Tel: 09324 60170.

63.5 hectares/157 acres.
32% Müller-Thurgau, 24% Silvaner, 7.5% Kerner,
7.5% Bacchus, 6.5% Rieslaner, 5% Scheurebe, 4.5% Perle,
4% Carmina and Domina, 3% Spätburgunder (Pinot Noir),
6% other varieties.

There are very few wine producers in France who can prove that they have been continuously involved in wine growing for even a fraction as long as the great German aristocratic estates. Of these noble families, Graf Matuschka-Greiffenclau of Schloss Vollrads (p. 62) can trace his family's recorded involvement in winemaking back the furthest: to the year 1211. The family of the Prince of Castell-Castell in Franconia can only trace their involvement in wine growing back to 1258, but their family has been in Castell since soon after the turn of the first millennium, and their archive does contain details of every single vintage back into the sixteenth century! However, by that time they had already been growing wine, and managing substantial areas of farmland and forestry in the Steigerwald part of Franconia, for several centuries. Indeed, until the Bavarians invaded in 1806 after making a secret pact with Napoleon, Castell was not just an estate, but an independent principality.

This is something which quickly becomes apparent on entering Castell, which in spite of a population of a little over 500 people has a very large seventeenth-century castle, a baroque church almost large and grand enough to be a cathedral, and imposing government buildings of the same period. On entering the Schloss, the first of the marvellous collection of pictures which comes into view is an engraving showing the cutting of the first stone for the castle. 'This is the beginning of work on the new house,' one is told, though the 'new house' was completed in 1691! The town is also the headquarters of the Castell Bank, which, having been founded in 1774, is the oldest privately owned bank in Germany. In spite of all this grandeur many of Castell's residents keep pigs in their back yards, which gives one the feeling that it is only with some reluctance that Castell has moved roughly in the direction of the twentieth century.

This impression is quickly revealed to be false when one enters the cellars of the Fürst Castell wine estate buildings. These were completely modernised at the beginning of the 1970s, making the estate not just the largest privately owned wine producer of the region, but also among the most modern. Whilst a large number of wooden casks have been retained, there are also enough stainless steel tanks to hold an entire vintage of the white wines, and several large rotating stainless steel fermentation tanks for the substantial red wine production. Everything is spotless, and in perfect order.

Here in Franconia there is an uninterrupted tradition of dry wine production as a result of which the maximum unfermented sugar content for a dry wine here is four grams per litre, rather than nine in the rest of Germany. The Prince of Castell-Castell sums up his family estate's range of wine styles succinctly by saying, 'Here we have only dry wines, and Auslese. Only then do our wines have a pronounced sweetness, but even so the impression is of richness rather than of sugar. These wines should be savoured in small quantities, but the dry wines you must really drink.' The Prince himself has drunk two or three bottles of Castell wine every day of his long adult life, and though grey-haired looks the very model of good health at sixty-two years of age.

One could argue – and who knows, perhaps it is true – that Franconian wines are good for you because of their high mineral content. This is due to the very heavy soils in the Steigerwald area, which are largely of gypsum marl, a very heavy type of clay not unlike that found in the Côte d'Or area of Burgundy. The climate here is very continental, with hard winters, very warm summers, and early autumns. The combination of these factors makes for full-bodied wines rich in mineral extracts.

Another peculiarity of the region is the excellent wines it obtains from grape varieties which elsewhere give uninteresting wines. The classic example of this is the century-old Müller-Thurgau variety more usually associated with Liebfraumilch, which Castell pioneered in Franconia during the post-war years. In Castell, Müller-Thurgau makes quite substantial wines, which in years with good acidity go wonderfully with the kind of food for which Sancerre or lighter white Burgundies would normally be recommended as the vinous accompaniment.

Silvaner, the classic grape of Franconia, is still very important at the estate, though, and great efforts are made to produce not just typical earthy Silvaner QbA and Kabinett quality wines, but also to make wines of the very highest quality grades from this variety. In November 1983 the Castell estate harvested the first two icewines made in Franconia from Silvaner grapes grown in the Casteller Schlossberg vineyard. They are superb wines, the concentration of ripe fruit being quite staggering. The Silvaner Auslese, BA and TBA wines made from *Botrytis*-affected grapes are massive and magnificent, with quite as much sheer weight as the most powerful Sauternes.

Even more intense, though, and more elegant, are the Spätlese and higher Prädikat wines from the Rieslaner variety. Rieslaner is a crossing of Silvaner and Riesling, and it gives wines with a superb honeyed peachy richness, and enough acidity to age for decades. In time it will undoubtedly join the Silvaner as one of the region's classic grapes. The only problem with Rieslaner is the small quantity which it makes. At Castell it is only planted in the very best sites; even in the precipitous Schlossberg site on average it gives a mere 4000 litres per hectare.

Down at the foot of the Schlossberg are two more vineyard sites owned exclusively by the Prince of Castell-Castell, the Casteller Reitseig and Feuerbach. They lie in a bottom which is almost completely protected from wind by the surrounding hills. Here the soil is very deep and heavy. These factors make for ideal conditions for red grape varieties, and here too the Castell estate has a modern innovation which looks set to become a classic of the future: Carmina and Domina. These exceptional new varieties give red wines with a colour so deep that it is nearly opaque when a sample is drawn from cask. They look more like young red wines from the northern Rhône than anything German, and pure Carmina wines can taste remarkably like red Bordeaux.

The red wines at Castell are matured in oak casks on principle, but with the white wines how each is matured depends entirely on its character as assessed by cellarmaster Eduard Krammer. White wines with very aggressive acidity, such as the Rieslings which Castell has produced since the 1984 vintage, may be kept in wooden casks for well over a year, while the softer Müller-Thurgau wines will only ever see the inside of stainless steel tanks, and be bottled early. Herr Krammer has been with the estate for virtually his entire working life, and is nowhere more at home than in the extensive cellars. Here he nimbly nips from cask to cask, '. . . and now you must taste this wine, same grape variety, but next door vineyard, and then the Spätlese we picked there a bit later . . . yes, I'm not so happy with that one either, it lacks the typical varietal character which we always look for. That is partly a vintage question, though. Some years Traminer has that lovely full spiciness, and sometimes it doesn't, and nobody can say why . . .'

The fullest expression of varietal character, and wines with a marked taste from the soil on which the grapes grew, is the Castell hallmark. These are not the most elegant wines in Germany, but they are certainly amongst the most characterful.

The   same   style   characterises   the   wines   from   the

Erzeugergemeinschaft Steigerwald, a co-operative association of small growers whose wines are made in the estate's cellars to the same exacting standards. The Erzeugergemeinschaft produces fewer top Prädikat wines than the Castell estate, but the good side of this relationship between the area's small growers and the Prince of Castell-Castell's estate is that it means there is a larger quantity of well-made traditional-style Franconian wine available.

Freiherr von und zu Franckenstein'sches Rentamt Baden

Hubert Doll (owner and director).
Freiherr von und zu Franckenstein'sches
  Rentamt,
Weingartenstrasse 66,
D 7600 Offenburg.
Tel: 0781 34973.

13.4 hectares/33 acres.
30% Riesling, 20% Müller-Thurgau, 20% Spätburgunder
(Pinot Noir), 15% Grauburgunder (Pinot Gris),
10% Traminer, 5% Gewürztraminer, Kerner and Scheurebe.

While it is only recently that the white wines of Baden in general have started to lose their traditional heaviness, the Ortenau area which stretches from Baden-Baden southwards to just beyond Offenburg has long produced elegant Riesling wines. The rising star of the Ortenau is undoubtedly Hubert Doll, a rather reserved man in his thirties who originates from the famous wine village of Durbach near Offenburg. While he respects the Ortenau tradition of making sweet Auslese wines, his winemaking philosophy is directly opposed to this. 'I'm not against late-harvested wines at all, but I would rather ferment these dry. The northern regions of Germany have problems to produce good bone-dry wines, but here we have a combination of soil, climate and grape varieties which makes this easy. I feel that we should capitalise on this lucky position, and that the great majority of Ortenau Klingelberger, Traminer and Grauburgunder wines should be dry wines.'

'Klingelberger' sounds very strange to non-German ears, but

in fact it is just the local name for Riesling. Ortenau is the only part of Baden where Riesling is currently an important grape variety, though a little is being planted in many parts of the region at present. 'Grauburgunder' is a synonym for Ruländer, *Pinot Gris* which Herr Doll reintroduced into commercial use for dry Ruländer wines when he started to produce these in 1979. 'There was a big problem then, for when you said the word Ruländer to customers they immediately assumed that you were talking about a very sweet wine. I therefore looked in the wine law and found this synonym, which has since been adopted by thousands of growers. However, when I first presented a dry Ruländer at a competition as "Grauburgunder" I had to show the judges the relevant part of the wine law before they would even accept the wine as eligible for entry!'

In spite of its noble name, the one thing the Freiherr von und zu Franckenstein estate lacks is a fine schloss. The fine house in the centre of the Offenburg which the Franckenstein family used to own was sold off during the 1930s, and the estate is now based in a much more modern building near the outskirts of the town. The advantage of this is that they have enough space to store three entire harvests, one in cask and tank and two in bottle. That the cellar contains many more tanks than wooden casks is typical of Baden today; indeed there are many cellars in the region that have only stainless steel. Hubert Doll is not alone in thinking that the white wines of all parts of Baden need to be made in tanks in order to preserve every last spur of freshness, but he is unusual in bottling Riesling wines with so much acidity. This gives his wines an elegance like that of more full-bodied Rheingau wines. The flavour is, however, completely distinct.

The larger part of the Franckenstein vineyards is situated in the Abtsberg vineyard of Offenburg's attractively countrified suburb of Zell-Weierbach. Here the soil is of weathered red granite, which gives the Riesling wines a distinctive, full peachy-apricoty character, and the Grauburgunder wines a superb refined honey tone. I first visited the Franckenstein estate shortly after a trip to Alsace where I had tasted many of Domaine Zind-Humbrecht's great Alsace Grand Cru wines. Some of the best of these are from the Brand vineyard at Turkheim, which has a soil structure almost identical to that of the Abtsberg of Ortenau. That the Franckenstein Abtsberg wines have the same characteristic tones from the soil as Zind-Humbrecht's Brand wines says a lot about both estates' dedication to unmanipulative winemaking. There are of course differences between the wines of the two producers. Even the 1983 Grauburgunder Spätlese Trocken from Franckenstein with its 14 degrees of alcohol does not have quite the sheer power of Zind-Humbrecht's best Brand wines. On the other hand, the Franckenstein wines have a wonderful refinement in the bouquet which is rarely matched in Alsace.

To make such fine dry wines requires very careful handling of the grapes and grape must, for if they are pumped around too much, or fined too much, the resulting wine will be thin and will lack fruit. If that happens then the wine will not have enough body to carry the racy acidity, and what ought to be the animating component of the wine will become aggressive. The Franckenstein winemaking system is simple and elegant, the grapes being rapidly milled, then pressed. At this point the grape musts are left to settle overnight. Generally at this point German and other wine growers add bentonite powder to the must, which cleans it by causing fine solid particles to coagulate and fall out. However, Hubert Doll has virtually renounced this fining of the must as well as any fining of the wine. 'All these treatments take something out of the wine, so we try and avoid them at all costs. Bentonite is very aggressive to the fruit of a wine,' he says.

While the Franckenstein white wines are made in tanks to avoid the slightest oxidative influence, the red Spätburgunder wines are equally systematically aged in wooden casks in order that the wines do have a continuous slight contact with the air. In general these are old Halbstück casks, but some new oak casks are used, 'but only as an experiment at the moment. Red wines need the influence of oxygen during their youth to develop properly, but whether they should have an oak taste or not is another question entirely,' insists Herr Doll. For him the most important thing a red wine should have is an intense fruitiness, and it is because oak flavours tend to obscure this that he is so hesitant to go over to new oak barriques.

Another experiment the conclusion of which is still uncertain is Hubert Doll's use of the second or malolactic fermentation for his red wines. He feels the same doubts about this technique as about the use of new oak casks, yet it certainly had a very positive effect on the 1984 Spätburgunder. Without something to soften the acidity of this wine it would have been so hard as to be undrinkable. Having had malolactic fermentation, it is very mellow and Burgundian in style. However, it is certainly over-shadowed by the 1983 Spätburgunder Spätlese Trocken which did not have malolactic fermentation. That is still youthful, combining a rich fruitiness with a solid structure (13 degrees of alcohol). It shows just what can be achieved in the Zell-Weierbacher Abtsberg vineyard.

This series of undulating hillsides rising from Offenburg up to the edge of the Mooswald whose densely pine-covered slopes climb to 3000 feet above sea level look like model vineyards. The red granite soils give these hillsides a distinctive colour which enables those parts owned by the Franckenstein estate to be clearly differentiated, since they are green. This is necessary, though most local growers dismiss it as new-fangled nonsense, both to stop erosion and to combat the drought problem by improving water-retention.

Now that Herr Doll has leased the estate from the Freiherr von und zu Franckenstein, and has fully implemented his wine-making philosophy, I am sure that the wines of the Francken-stein estate will regularly be among the finest not only in the Ortenau, but in the whole of Baden. They are the perfect answer to those who say that only the Rhine and Moselle regions can produce wines of real elegance.

Weingut Graf Adelmann, Württemberg

Michael Graf Adelmann (owner and director).
Weingut Graf Adelmann,
Burg Schaubeck,
D 7141 Steinheim–Kleinbottwar.
Tel: 07148 6665.

15 hectares/37 acres.
22% Trollinger, 18.5% Riesling, 11% Traminer,
8.5% Ruländer (Pinot Gris), 6% Muskattrollinger,
5.5% Lemberger, 5.5% Muskateller, 5% Clevner,
5% Samtrot, 13% Urban, Dornfelder, Helfensteiner, Kerner,
Silvaner and Müller-Thurgau.

It is really astonishing how many of the German wine-producing regions produced significant quantities of red wines a century or more ago. Though there is currently a red wine revival in Germany, only one region has an uninterrupted tradition of producing full-bodied red wines of the highest quality: Württemberg. This region, centred on Stuttgart and Heilbronn to the east of the Odenwald, is dominated by co-operatives, some of which can produce very good quality wines. What are probably the finest wines of the region come from Michael Graf Adelmann's vineyards at Kleinbottwar and in the Neckar valley at Hoheneck. The only problem with these highly individual wines is that the demand for them on the German market is so hot that they are sold by allocation like the scarcest top-quality Burgundies.

The first reason for this success is that Michael's father, Raban Graf Adelmann, unlike the great majority of the region's wine growers, never pulled up the traditional red wine varieties to plant new high-yielding types. As a result they are the only producers in the region to still have the Urban variety, and one of only a handful to still have Muskattrollinger, Samtrot and Clevner vines in production. Undoubtedly the personality of the Adelmanns has also played a role in making their wines famous, for one could not wish to find someone more delightfully unaffected by success than Michael Graf Adelmann. In spite of the innumerable medals that the estate has won, and although they have the most expensive and rapidly sold out red wines in Germany, Michael is totally free of pretension. Though he has been running the estate for nearly ten years he still has an infectious interest in wines of all kinds.

This was perfectly demonstrated the first time I met Michael Graf Adelmann. We were both guests of the excellent Hotel Krautkrämmer in Münster for a Saint Emilion wine fair presented by the owners of the eleven 1er Grand Cru Classé Châteaux. It was only after we had critically discussed together with Monsieur Fournier of Château Canon the merits of the wines served with dinner on the first evening that I realised who I was sitting next to. Michael Graf Adelmann's first comment after we had been introduced was typically modest. 'But of course you realise we can't match these wines in Württemberg,' at which smiles appeared on the faces of several Saint Emilion château owners! 'Yes,' I replied rather politely, but quite honestly, 'though I think that you can produce red wines with enough body, and perhaps more elegance and perfume than the majority of Bordeaux wines.' Michael conceded this a little reluctantly, and the smiles slowly drifted from the faces of several of the Saint Emilion château owners.

In fact it is only in comparison with the heaviest French red wines that a Lemberger, Clevner, or Samtrot Spätlese Trocken from the Graf Adelmann estate fails a little in weight. Most German red wines are grown on light soils, because these warm up easily, making it easier to ripen the grapes. However, this means that the resulting wines are not heavy even if they have a lot of alcohol, since they do not have enormous amounts of mineral extracts from the soil. In contrast, the Kleinbottwar vineyards from which the Adelmann red wines come have much heavier loam and marl soils which give the wines much more substance, even when they do not have a very high alcohol content. Kleinbottwar's steep, south-facing vineyards have their problems, though, for as a result of their high altitude (210 to 340 metres) and the area's continental climate there is a real danger of spring frost severely damaging the vines' new growth. To counteract this the estate has installed a horrendously expensive system for pumping warm air into the vineyards where the most sensitive varieties (Lemberger and Samtrot) grow.

So, in spite of many advantages over the majority of German red wine producers, it is still not easy for Graf Adelmann to reach really high quality levels. Therefore the estate has long used a special label to identify their finest red and white wines from the more normal qualities. Since 1853 the normal quality wines from the estate have been sold under the designation 'Brüssele', which is a local corruption of the previous owners' family name, with an almost austerely elegant label featuring the family crest. The top wines are sold as 'Brüssele'r Spitze' (peak-quality Brüssele) with a wonderfully over-the-top traditional label which uses the pattern of a piece of antique lace as its background. As Michael Graf Adelmann says, 'Even I don't find it easy to read the Brüssele'r Spitze label, but it's so beautiful and unique that we decided not to make any changes to it at all.'

Changes have, however, been made in the estate's cellars down in the village of Kleinbottwar. Michael explained to me the

changes he has made to their winemaking over lunch at the family home, Burg Schaubeck. This is the nearest thing I have ever seen to a fairy-tale castle, and it is filled with museum-quality collections of Renaissance furniture, ivory carvings, paintings, watches and books. Surrounding it are delightful baroque and eighteenth-century English-style gardens. However, the Adelmann family self-deprecatingly refer to Burg Schaubeck as 'our medieval bunker'.

In spite of the impressive surroundings, lunch is always relaxed, the conversation flowing freely from family matters to anecdotes, and back to wine. 'Though I've installed some temperature-control equipment for fermenting the red wines, the biggest change I've made since taking control of the estate in 1978 is to start using new wooden casks for maturing the red wines. The 1985 Brüssele'r Spitze Lemberger Spätlese Trocken which we're drinking now shows exactly the wood character we want our red wines to have. They are aged in new Halbstück casks of Schwabian oak, because we feel that we should be using German oak, and not importing French character into our wines. The wines spend between 6 and 15 months in these casks, and as soon as the wine has gained an elegant oakiness we transfer it to a stainless steel tank. We really don't want to make woody wines, but rather to use the wood character to give the wines more complexity.'

That wine we drank with lunch, in spite of its youth, was a

supremely elegant red wine, powerful without being heavy, tannic, but not aggressively so. It will, like a fine red Burgundy, develop more and more perfume and mellow richness over the next five to ten years, and will last much longer than that. While Michael Graf Adelmann has learnt a great deal from his visits to the important red wine producing regions of France, and is very happy for people to know about this, for him it is more important to stress what is unique to Württemberg and to his family's estate. In Germany, for example, the Lemberger variety can only be found in Württemberg. It is a relatively new importation, having come to the region from Austria in the seventeenth century.

The most extreme example of a wine unique to Württemberg is the Urban or 'Schwarzurban' grape variety, which has been grown in Württemberg for many centuries and may even date back to the time of the first records of viticulture in Kleinbottwar (c. AD 950). This variety is related to the Trollinger, which is the commonest red variety in Württemberg. Urban wines are pale in colour like those of Trollinger, but are rather fuller, and have a more complex bitter almond, vanilla, and coriander toned flavour and bouquet. It seems typical of German wine production since the last war that the more interesting of these two vine varieties should have almost died out, while the lesser should have been more and more widely planted. The variety now remains only at the Adelmann estate. German wine bureaucracy seems typified by the fact that Weingut Graf Adelmann can only retain Urban as an 'experimental' variety!

Though the white wine varieties which are planted at Kleinbottwar and Hoheneck are common in Germany's vineyards, the wines which Riesling, Traminer, Ruländer, and Muskateller give here are quite different from those from other regions. Württemberg white wines are nearly always dry, broad and juicy, sometimes to the point of plumpness, but more often they are satisfyingly full and aromatic for German wines.

Because they are able to make wines of a sophistication far above the regional norm, but from the traditional regional varieties, Weingut Graf Adelmann have reached the point where their customers are frequently disappointed by finding that the wines they wanted to buy have long since been sold out. The estate is therefore founding a sister company, 'Schlosskellerei Graf Adelmann', which will make wines from bought-in grapes to expand the total quantity of wine they have available. So it should finally become possible to obtain the unique wines made by Michael Graf Adelmann outside Germany.

Directory of recommended producers

The wines of any country are extremely diverse, and a simple recommendation that a particular producer is 'good' means very little unless one knows something about the style of wines he or she produces. For the same reason, it is equally useless to classify or rank producers in classes, or on a numerical scale, because one is not comparing like with like in many instances, and questions of personal taste must influence the results. It should, however, be easy to tell who among those producers described in these pages I think makes really exciting wines simply by noting how much I have written about each. They are listed by region, then village or town, and the order in which they appear does not indicate any kind of ranking according to quality.

Often, a producer's wines mirror his or her character, and I always find it helpful to know something about the person, or people, behind the wines. Hence the personal details which pepper the text. Wine producers are very often interesting as personalities in their own right, and I do not think it would be going too far to say that it is very rare to find a dull or dour person who makes good wines. Certainly my experience in the German wine regions supports this assertion, for where else would the owner and director of a wine estate scale a flag-pole at three o'clock in the morning to the sound of Beethoven's Eroica Symphony? However, there are a great many cultured people in the wine business, as well as a great many characters. In Germany, at least, wine really is a part of culture.

Generally speaking, German wine producers are very welcoming and courteous to visitors. With the better-known estates it is advisable to make an appointment when planning a visit (they can sometimes be put under a lot of pressure by visitors), but smaller, less renowned growers and co-operatives can usually be dropped in on without any problem. A great many Ger-

Elbling: upper Moselle grape best in sekt

mans speak at least some English, and their generosity can sometimes be overwhelming. A word of warning: since German wines are generally low in alcohol, many Germans drink the samples poured at wine tastings, and some producers can be offended if visitors do not join them in doing this. It is always possible to ask for a spittoon, but this should be done diplomatically.

When visiting Germany as mentioned before it should not be forgotten that there are more Michelin starred restaurants there than in any other European country except France. A few restaurants of particular interest are mentioned in the following pages, but there are many, many more, especially in Baden.

Lastly, even though nearly a hundred producers are listed and described in this directory, many others who are also of note have had to be left out. Even if an entire book of this size had been devoted to one or two of the regions, there might still have been a problem of this kind. The mere fact of exclusion from this directory should certainly not be taken as a recommendation not to drink the wines of a particular producer.

Mosel-Saar-Ruwer

As the contemporary name for this region suggests, it is in fact composed of several regions each with a quite distinct character. It is only by breaking this sprawling region's 12,750 hectares/ 31,490 acres of vineyards up into these 'sub-regions' that a proper picture of the region can be gained.

From where the Moselle river crosses the Luxemburg border to Konz near the city of Trier is the Upper Moselle, or Ober Mosel. Since records have been kept, the ancient Elbling grape variety has been dominant here. It produces a straightforward but very satisfying dry wine, which is rarely made at a quality grade higher than Qualitätswein. It can be made into excellent sparkling wines (as at the Schloss Thorn estate), which is probably the best vinous product the region can offer. The region also boasts one of Germany's top restaurants, Hubert Scheid in Wasserliech.

Winding, or perhaps one should say snaking, northwards to Konz is the Moselle's most important tributary, the Saar. The Saar is a little world unto itself, and very picturesque in the eighteenth-century meaning of the word, which implied a certain severity or austerity. The Saar is open to the wind, and therefore significantly cooler than other parts of the region. However, it has some of the best and most precipitous vineyard sites in Germany, the Scharzhofberg, Kanzemer Altenberg, Saarburger Rausch, Schodener Saarfeilser Marienberg, Ockfener Bockstein, Wiltinger Braune Kupp, and Ayler Kupp being the most important. These produce steely, slaty wines, which in good vintages have the greatest possible elegance. In poor vintages they are only for those hardened to high-acidity wines. Saarburg has a little tourism, and the one top restaurant on the Saar: the Burg.

Just the other side of Trier, again on the south side of the Moselle, is the much smaller tributary of the Ruwer, which is really no more than a stream. The Ruwer valley looks much more gentle than the Saar, with hillsides of an almost English roundness. The wines are similarly less assertive than those of the Saar, with a distinctive, delicate herbal-flowery bouquet; like Saar wines they have plenty of acidity, but it is much less pointed. There are several very great vineyard sites: Maximin Grünhaus, Eitelsbacher Karthäuserhofberg, and Kaseler Nies'chen, and in a neighbouring valley Avelsbacher Altenberg.

The vineyards along the Moselle from Schweich near Trier roughly down to Riel (in the Koblenz direction) comprise the Middle Moselle, the heart of which has a reputation for fine wines which goes back at least to Napoleonic times. This central area runs from Trittenheim to Erden. The vineyard classification of 1804 which the Napoleonic regime undertook placed Brauneberg alone in class 1, with Piesport, Wehlen, Graach, Zeltingen, Erden and Lösnich in class 2. Certainly it is these villages, together with Trittenheim, Bernkastel and Ürzig, which today produce most of the great Moselle Riesling wines. However, even here there are virtually unknown vineyards like Wintricher Ohligsberg, Kestener Paulinshofberg, Kinheimer Hubertuslay, Kröver Steffansberg, and Wolfer Goldgrübe, with the potential to equal the famous names. The wines of the Middle Moselle are the most full-bodied of the Mosel-Saar-Ruwer, and the best have a wonderful combination of mouthfilling rich fruitiness and elegant acidity, often with a distinct slatiness.

118

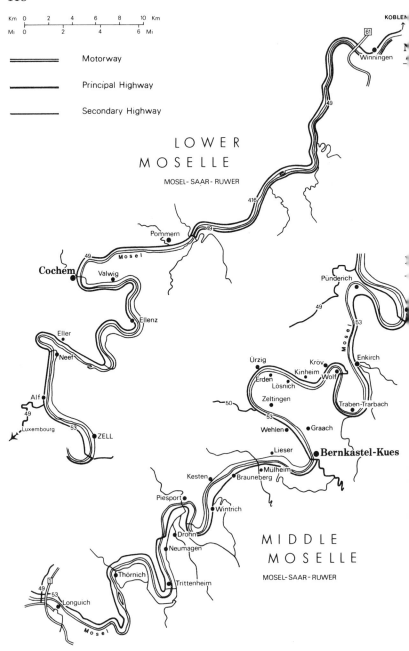

Km 0   2   4   6   8   10 Km
Mi 0   2   4   6 Mi

════════ Motorway

──────── Principal Highway

──────── Secondary Highway

LOWER
MOSELLE
MOSEL- SAAR - RUWER

KOBLEN

Winningen

Pommern

Cochem
Valwig

Ellenz

Eller
Neef

Alf

Luxembourg

ZELL

Pünderich

Enkirch

Ürzig
Kröv
Kinheim
Erden
Lösnich
Wolf
Zeltingen
Traben-Trarbach

Wehlen
Graach

Lieser
Bernkastel-Kues

Mülheim
Kesten
Brauneberg
Piesport
Wintrich

Drohn
Neumagen

MIDDLE
MOSELLE
MOSEL-SAAR- RUWER

Thörnich
Trittenheim

Longuich

Mosel

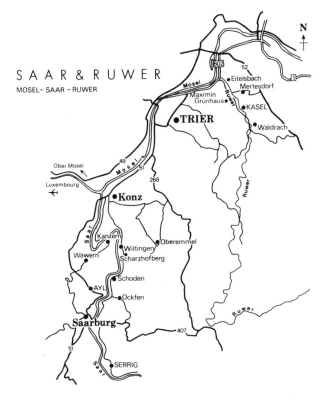

The Moselle, Saar and Ruwer valleys

The one drawback of the Middle Moselle is that places like Bernkastel and Kröv become packed with tourists during the summer months. Because the majority of these tourists are not wealthy people there are few really good restaurants or hotels in the area. However, despite this it is well worth visiting the region, because the scenery could hardly be more dramatic, every southward-facing steep hillside along the river being covered with vines. The Middle Moselle's problem is that some of the north-facing slopes and flat land near the river have also been planted with vines in recent decades. These give inferior or even disgusting wines. They would also look better with the fruit trees which used to be planted there.

From Reil downstream to the Rhine at Koblenz is the Lower Moselle, which is generally much more rugged than the Middle Moselle, and not blessed with such a good climate. Here, once again, the valley becomes open to the wind in many places. The main thing which has held the area back is the lack of larger estates that could build up a reputation for the top vineyards and the region as a whole. There are, however, a few really top vineyards, principally the Pündericher Marienburg, Eller Calmont, Ellenzer Ruberberger Domherrenberg, Pommerner Sonnenuhr, Winninger Hamm and Uhlen. The wines of this area generally do not have quite the ripeness of the Middle Moselle wines from top vineyards. Like the wines of the Saar, they can have phenomenal elegance in the best vintages, though.

The whole region is a bit of a rural backwater, and most attractive.

Weingut Freiherr von Landenberg

Marie-Luise Trimborn von Landenberg (director),
Nelly Freifrau Trimborn von Landenberg (owner and
director).
Weingut–Schlosskellerei Freiherr von Landenberg,
Moselweinstrasse 60,
D 5591 Ediger–Eller/Mosel.
Tel: 02675 277.

10 hectares/24.5 acres.
95% Riesling, 5% other varieties.

While the Landenberg estate produces many attractively flowery Riesling wines from its vineyards in Eller and Ediger, those from the Eller Calmont are more than one class above the majority of wines from this area of the Lower Moselle valley. With a 65 per cent inclination at its steepest point, the Calmont is the steepest cultivated vineyard in the whole of Germany, and probably the entire world. It is composed of a towering south-facing 'wall' of tiny terraces, among which are many small springs. Some of the Moselle's top vineyard sites can become too dry in really hot years, with the result that the wines are a bit heavy and flabby. The Calmont never has this problem, owing to these springs, and in vintages like 1983 its wines have the perfect combination of richness and refreshing acidity, with a delicate earthiness reminiscent of the wines from Erden on the Middle Moselle.

Marie-Luise Trimborn von Landenberg has only recently returned to the estate after completing her studies in viticulture and oenology. Her engagement in the estate gives reason to hope that the slightly erratic quality of the Landenberg wines will be improved upon, and that the great Calmont wines will gain the international fame they deserve. In the last few years the proportion of dry and medium-dry wines has slowly increased, but the majority of the estate's wines are made with some sweetness.

Weingut Erbhof Stein

Dr Ulrich Stein (owner and director).
Weingut Erbhof Stein,
D 5581 St Aldegrund/Mosel.
Tel: 06542 2979.

Dr Ulrich Stein,
Haus Waldfrieden,
D 5584 Alf/Mosel.
Tel: 06542 2608.

3 hectares/7.5 acres.
90% Riesling, 5% Spätburgunder, 5% other varieties.

Discovering Dr Ulrich Stein and his wines was one of the biggest surprises I have ever had while visiting the German wine regions.

Dr Ulrich Stein is one of the wine world's great free spirits and innovators, an artist whose medium is the technical possibilities of winemaking. As soon as he has an exciting idea for a wine he attempts it, often only looking to see if the result can be legally sold after the wine is already bottled. A classic example of this are the dessert wines of 'Beerenauslese' and 'Trockenbeeren-auslese' quality that he has made during the last few vintages. Rather than risk losing the grapes out in the vineyard as a result of bad weather, Dr Stein has harvested fully ripe clean grapes, taken them home, laid them on trays and then infected them with *Botrytis*. Thus he can press them at precisely the right point to get the balance he is looking for in the wine. Techniques akin to this are widely practised in California, but in order not to get into trouble with the wine control authorities the corks for the few dozen bottles of these wines produced each year have to be stamped with the words 'Nur Für Uns' (only for us, i.e. for home consumption).

Much more commercial, but no less at odds with the current German wine law, are the 'Stein Wein' selection. These are all QbA wines, but produced from grape musts with easily enough sugar to be made into Kabinett or even Spätlese wines. Sugar is added so that they can have an alcohol content which will enable them to make more successful dry wines. Dr Stein is a dry wine fan, but believes that to make a good dry wine a dry Moselle Riesling must have a minimum of about 10° of alcohol. A three-star system is used to rate the quality of these wines. The results of the first vintage, the 1986 'Stein Wein' selection, were very impressive.

The general approach to the making of the Erbhof Stein wines is generally less extreme, but they too are full of surprises, and the best wines are superb.

Weingut Erben Stephan Ehlen

Stephan Ehlen (owner and director).
Weingut Erben Stephan Ehlen,
Hauptstrasse 21,
D 5553 Lösnich/Mosel.
Tel: 06532 2388.

2.5 hectares/6 acres.
75% Riesling, 17% Kerner, 8% Müller-Thurgau.

Stephan Ehlen is one of the great unknown winemakers of the Middle Moselle valley. Nobody produces better wines from the Erdener Treppchen vineyard than Stephan Ehlen, though a couple of other producers match him in some vintages. Though well into his forties, Herr Ehlen is unmarried and lives with his considerably more aged mother in a slightly dour-looking house in the somewhat nondescript village of Lösnich. Whilst Stephan Ehlen does the great majority of the vineyard and cellar work himself, during the harvest his mother joins him, operating his incongruously hyper-modern 'Howard' (pneumatic) press, whilst he is out in the vineyards with the pickers.

The quantity of wine produced is small, and this enables Herr Ehlen to make each barrel of wine completely individually. The winemaking is uncompromisingly traditional, or almost so, for sometimes Kabinett quality wines have to be bottled a few weeks before the ideal moment to satisfy the great demand for them from the US and Japan! Otherwise the wines benefit from many months of slow maturation in the very cool, exceedingly humid, cellars under Hauptstrasse 21 and its pretty garden. Because he is so committed to making the very finest wines, and has no interest in promoting himself, it seems unlikely that Stephan Ehlen will ever become famous. However, at the least, his Erdener Treppchen wines should be put on connoisseurs' lists of wines to be actively sought out.

Weingut Mönchhof

Robert Eymael Snr (owner),
Robert Eymael Jr (director).
Weingut Mönchhof–Robert Eymael,
D 5564 Ürzig/Mosel.
Tel: 06532 2116.

5.1 hectares/12.5 acres.
100% Riesling.

It is very sad that almost solely because of the difficulty of pronouncing its name the great Ürziger Würzgarten vineyard is virtually unknown in Britain, and even in the USA its fame is much less than that of the top vineyards of Wehlen, Graach, or Bernkastel. However, at Erden and Ürzig there is a unique combination of perfect south-southwesterly exposure and *red sandstone* sub-soil. Of all the Moselle estates, Weingut Mönchhof's Ürziger Würzgarten wines are the most classic expression of this character. Their full earthiness, spicy tones, and exotic fruit flavours (in ripe vintages) are not what most people expect from the Moselle, and hence they are often underrated. Robert Eymael Jr finds that even some German wine writers do not understand their wines. 'We don't want to produce wines which have the aggressive acidity which is currently what the German writers want to find everywhere, but wines which are full of the special character which the soil and microclimate here at Ürzig and Erden give them.'

The Mönchhof wines have as much character as the magnificent Renaissance mansion which houses the estate, and is now one of the stars of the German TV soap-opera 'Mosellebrücke'. The style of the Mönchhof wines has subtly shifted since the involvement of the new generation in the estate, with the wines now a little fresher and the overall quality even better than before. More dry wines are being made, but the selection of the grapes which will be used for these is strict, so even in years when the acidity is naturally high, such as 1984, the dry wines are beautifully balanced.

The focus of Robert Eymael Snr's and Jr's work, though, is the making of really fine Spätlese and Auslese wines with some sweetness. Though these wines can be astonishingly rich, only the Goldkapsel Auslese and the Beerenauslese wines are really sweet in taste. The necessary sugar levels for these late-harvested wines are easier to obtain here than in most parts of the Middle Moselle, and it is a poor vintage at Mönchhof which brings no Spätlese wines. The harvesting is not easy, because all the vineyards are very steep, and there is a sheer drop (no handrail!) from those above the cliffs around the Erdener Prälat vineyard. The best vintages here are those which have autumn-ripened, such as 1987, 1985, 1979 or 1975.

Robert Eymael Jr is still young, and great things can be expected from Weingut Mönchhof as he becomes more established there.

Weingut E. Christoffel-Berres

Otto Christoffel (director),
Elizabeth Christoffel-Berres (owner).
Weingut E. Christoffel-Berres,
Geschwister Berres,
Zehnthofstrasse,
D 5564 Ürzig/Mosel.
Tel: 06532 2225.

2 hectares/5 acres.
100% Riesling.

Otto Christoffel is one of the great characters of the Middle
Moselle valley, but he is also the producer of some fine sweeter
Rieslings. He always states his winemaking philosophy very
clearly. 'I only want to own vines in the top vineyard sites,
because you have more success there, and lesser vineyards only
cost you money. I therefore have only Riesling vines on their
original rootstocks in very steep vineyards in the sites of which
my family, and my wife's family, have always been amongst the
owners. Because we have such really top-class vineyards, and
they are in excellent condition, we never deacidify the wines at
all, and we never sweeten them up with Süssreserve.'

This clear line really is reflected in the wines, which are always
full of character, rich and mouthfilling, even at Kabinett quality.
Some people feel that the wines of Ürzig and Erden lack a little
elegance, but it could also be argued that a Spätlese or Auslese
from these sites will be more complex, longer and fuller in
flavour. This is really a matter of personal taste. Certainly these
qualities enable this corner of the Mosel to make some good
dry wines. These are not an important part of the estate's
production, but they are always a delight.

One of the things which deeply saddens Otto Christoffel is the
way in which the 1971 wine law extended the area of vineyard
whose wines could bear the famous Ürziger Würzgarten and
Erdener Prälat names. He feels that 'each of the original,
smaller, vineyards really did give wines with a slightly different
character, and that's why all these names developed. I'd still like
to get these back, and have the great Erdener Prälat vineyard
reduced to its original area. It's probably the best site on the

Moselle, in terms of the potential for making great wines, but now several small growers who own a few vines in the extended Prälat are selling barrels of wine under this name.' Otto Christoffel certainly cares for the Erdener Prälat, and his wines from this vineyard site can be quite superb.

Weingut Joh. Jos. Prüm

Dr Manfred Prüm (owner and director).
Weingut Joh. Jos. Prüm,
Uferallee 19,
D 5550 Bernkastel–Wehlen/Mosel.
Tel: 06531 3091.

14 hectares/34.5 acres.
99% Riesling, 1% other varieties.

Dr Manfred Prüm produces some of the greatest Riesling wines not just on the Moselle, but in the whole of Germany. However, his wines are easy to misjudge in their youth, because they are made in an extremely uncompromising style. Even the Auslese wines from Joh. Jos. Prüm estate often have a vigorous 'Spritz' of (naturally retained) carbon dioxide, which together with their powerful acidity can make them aggressive in their first year. However, this also gives them a *very* long life. While the majority of wines from Dr Manfred Prüm's top vineyard site, the world-famous Wehlener Sonnenuhr, have a wonderful silky elegance from an early age, the Joh. Jos. Prüm Wehlener Sonnenuhr wines only develop this after many years, but then they have the greatest possible finesse.

Dr Manfred Prüm is not easily approachable, but once he is convinced that those in front of him know about, and appreciate, wine then there could hardly be a more generous host. Rather than try and push the latest vintage on guests, he is anxious to demonstrate how fine his wines are when they have been aged for a few years. Even a Kabinett wine from the Joh. Jos. Prüm estate can take as much as five years in bottle to reach its peak, and can live for decades beyond this. These are, perhaps, the wines Dr Manfred Prüm enjoys most, though he has also produced some excellent dry wines in the last few years (for the German market).

What has made the estate famous, though, is the selectively picked late-harvested wines which they pioneered in the Moselle from the 1920 and 1921 vintages (these wines are still fascinating). These can taste wonderful in their youth, but are never at their best until they have been in the bottle for *at least* a decade. The prices may seem high, but the hundreds of man-hours needed just to pick the grapes are not counted when the price is fixed. Neither is the extremely stringent cellar work, which combines traditional techniques with modern technology. All the wines are made individually in Füder or Halbfüder casks, and are never bottled before the early summer after the vintage. Some wines are aged in cask for up to three years, but this never results in them having even the slightest whiff of oxidation.

Dr Manfred Prüm and his charming wife Amei live for their wines, and even the briefest meeting with them leaves the impression that producing the highest qualities is a matter of honour, and a source of constant delight, for them.

Weingut Heribert Kerpen

Martin Kerpen (owner and director),
Hanna Kerpen (owner).
Weingut Heribert Kerpen,
Hauptstrasse 77 and Uferallee 6,
D 5550 Bernkastel–Wehlen/Mosel.
Tel: 06531 6868.

2.5 hectares/6 acres.
100% Riesling.

There has recently been a meteoric rise in the reputation of Weingut Heribert Kerpen, which is undoubtedly due to the increasing involvement of the new generation of the Kerpen family in running the estate. Martin Kerpen, who is only now starting to work full-time at the estate, had to make the estate's wines in several small rented cellars around Wehlen until the Kerpen family recently purchased a large house on the Uferallee. Here he has installed his 'antique' hydraulic basket press and its computer control equipment; a bizarre combination of the mechanical and electronic.

While Weingut Heribert Kerpen does not produce a big

proportion of dry wines, the level of unfermented sugar in all their wines is very modest. Many of the wines have a 'Spritz' of carbon dioxide, as a result of the very careful handling of the wines and the generally early bottling (always before the following harvest). Martin Kerpen seeks to produce wines of great elegance, which will show very well when they are placed on the market but also have considerable ageing potential.

With their new cellar, and the estate's style now clearly established, Weingut Heribert Kerpen will undoubtedly produce many worthy followers to their excellent 1983, 1985, and 1986 wines.

Weingut S. A. Prüm Erben, S. A. Prüm

Raimund Prüm (owner and director).
Weingut S. A. Prüm Erben, S. A. Prüm,
Uferallee 25–6,
D 5550 Bernkastel–Wehlen/Mosel.
Tel: 06531 3110.

6 hectares/15 acres.
100% Riesling.

The Prüm family have been winegrowers in the Moselle valley since the twelfth century. As a result of the division of the family vineyards when they were passed from one generation to the next, there are now numerous Prüm estates. Those bearing the Prüm name today could hardly be more different in appearance and character. Raimund Prüm looks nothing like any of the other members of his extensive family, being very tall and red-headed. He also has a highly idiosyncratic approach to running his estate. Whilst most Moselle estates are moving over to early bottling of their wines, Raimund Prüm is experimenting with more extended cask ageing of the kind which was normal before the Second World War. But Raimund is also no extreme traditionalist, for at the same time he has also been experimenting with radical new vine training and pruning systems.

Perhaps Raimund Prüm's most revolutionary move has been the packaging he has developed for his QbA wines. Like many other VDP estates in the region, he has been selling his QbA wines from the 1985 and later vintages under the estate name (without any vineyard designation), but instead of using a variation on the estate's normal label for these wines he has had an entirely new ultra-modern label specially designed. In contrast, the label for the Prädikat wines is ultra-traditional, being based on a turn-of-the-century design. Eighty per cent of the wines sold under both these labels are dry or medium-dry. Any sweetness in the S. A. Prüm wines is entirely natural, never being the result of Süssreserve being added to the wines.

Weingut S. A. Prüm is not, perhaps, the most consistent of the top Middle Moselle estates, but the majority of the wines are very classic Moselle Rieslings, and the best wines are really outstanding. In their youth the best Prädikat wines are not as aggressive as those from Weingut Joh. Jos. Prüm, but also need long ageing to show their considerable best.

Weingut J. Lauerburg

Karl-Heinz Lauerburg (owner and director),
Patrick Lauerburg (director).
Weingut J. Lauerburg,
Graacher Strasse 24,
D 5550 Bernkastel/Mosel.
Tel: 06531 2481.

4 hectares/10 acres.
100% Riesling.

The Lauerburg family are unique among the top Middle Moselle estates, being possessed of an extremely independent spirit. It would be most unwise to turn up at their austere early eighteenth-century house on the Graacher Strasse expecting to be immediately welcomed in for a tasting, though they can be met more casually in their shop in Bernkastel's medieval marketplace. This shop is itself remarkable, being the only building in the centre of Bernkastel not over-restored to the point of kitsch for the benefit of tourists.

The Lauerburg family own vineyards in all the important sites of Bernkastel, and make Bernkastel wines of a most uncompromising kind. These are always austere in their youth, and even the QbA wines are much better after a couple of years ageing in bottle. If any criticism can be made of the Lauerburg estate, it is that their more modest quality wines are perhaps too steely. The higher quality wines, from Spätlese upwards, are really fine, and for exactly the same reason that the more ordinary qualities can be a little problematic: they retain all their considerable natural acidity.

To some extent the Lauerburg style is a product of their unique cellars, which are built on five levels, the cask cellars being cut deep into the slate hillside of the Doctorberg. Here the wines ferment very slowly indeed, often retaining a lot of carbon dioxide. The lesser wines are sometimes made in stainless steel tanks, and all the wines which have finished maturing in cask are stored in such tanks prior to bottling. The press and other cellar equipment is very modern. Because of the many levels of the cellars, the wines are only pumped once, at bottling, otherwise being moved by force of gravity. Like the Lauerburg family themselves, the Lauerburg wines can be difficult to approach, but are always full of character.

Wegeler-Deinhard

Norbert Kreuzberger (director),
Deinhard & Co. (owners).
Wegeler-Deinhard
(Gutsverwaltung Deinhard),
Marterthal,
D 5550 Bernkastel-Kues/Mosel.
Tel: 06531 2493.

24.5 hectares/60.5 acres.
97% Riesling, 3% other varieties.

The Deinhard estate is one of the largest privately owned wine estates on the Moselle, having been built up through purchase and long-term leases since the turn of the century. The estate is managed by Norbert Kreuzberger, who worked as cellarmaster for Weingut St Johannishof (pp. 42–6) before joining Deinhard in 1973. Herr Kreuzberger is a conservative Moselaner who normally wears kneebreeches, and whose speech is always somewhat coloured by the local dialect. His knowledge of the Middle Moselle vineyards is excellent, and a great deal of money is being put into consolidating and rationalising these.

If the wines from Deinhard's Moselle estate have been a bit erratic – some superb racy wines with great class, the majority very good and typical, and some slightly flat, over-sweet wines – then the problem lies with the winemaking, or to be more precise with the pressures put on it. Deinhard have long concentrated on exporting their wines, and some of their export markets still prefer really sweet wines. With taste around the world tending in the direction of dryness it is not surprising to find that the proportion of well-balanced wines from Deinhard's Moselle estate has been steadily increasing lately. As a result the largest owners of the world-famous Wehlener Sonnenuhr vineyard seem to be better fulfilling the role such a position gives them the opportunity of playing: that of regional flagship.

Weingut Dr H. Thanisch

Sofia Knabben-Spier (director),
Weingut Wwe Dr H. Thanisch,
Saarallee 31,
D 5550 Bernkastel-Kues/Mosel.
Tel: 06531 2282.

6.5 hectares/16 acres.
100% Riesling.

Two historical factors and some great wines conspired to build up the stratospheric reputation which the Thanisch estate once enjoyed. The historical factors were the work of Dr Hugo Thanisch during the latter part of the last century, and the fact that the estate was, together with Deinhard and Lauerburg, one of the original owners of the Bernkasteler Doctor vineyard. The legendary wines began with the 1921 Bernkasteler Doctor Riesling Trockenbeerenauslese, the first wine of this quality grade to be harvested on the Middle Moselle.

Unfortunately difficult times came for the estate at the beginning of the 1980s, the end result of which was the estate's division (the Müller-Burggraef family also use the Thanisch label, but make their wines elsewhere). The wines from this period were erratic, and occasionally poor. Those made by the Müller-Burggraef family (*no* VDP eagle on the label!) were, and remain, miserable. When wines are made in barrels in the

traditional Moselle manner, it is necessary to work very carefully. However, in the last few years there has been a sharp upturn,
both in the quality of the *Thanisch* wines, and in the reputation
of the estate. The charming young Sofia Knabben-Spier, who
has run the estate since 1983, has done much to change the lax
cellar regime which had developed. With a new cellarmaster
from the 1987 vintage it can be realistically hoped that the
Thanisch estate will shortly be one of the great names of the
Middle Moselle once again.

Weingut Max Ferd. Richter

Dr Dirk Richter (owner and director),
Horst Richter (owner).
Weingut–Weinkellerei Max Ferd. Richter,
D 5556 Mülheim/Mosel.
Tel: 06534 704.

15 hectares/37 acres.
90% Riesling, 10% other varieties.

Dr Dirk Richter's best Moselle Riesling are among the best-
value fine white wines in Europe. Why so many wine drinkers
are willing to pay three or more times as much for white
Burgundies as for a Max Ferd. Richter Riesling Spätlese of
equivalent elegance and complexity is completely beyond my
comprehension. Indeed, even the Richter estate's most
straightforward wine, 'Dr Richter's Riesling' (a QbA wine
sold without vineyard designation), is of very good quality,
with classic Moselle Riesling character. This is the perfect
introduction to the region's wines.

Though the Richters buy in wines which they sell under a
second label (they are one of the best 'négociants' on the
Moselle), their estate wines are made very individually, and
single barrels of wine are regularly bottled separately if they
have a special character. Dr Richter feels that this individuality is
an essential aspect of the Moselle's wines, and must be preserved. 'Think of Château Mouton Rothschild in Bordeaux,' he
says. 'Each year they produce about a quarter of a million bottles
of one wine. This is a very high-class wine, but at the same time it
is a mass-produced product compared with a fine Moselle Ries-

ling, of which there are only a few hundred or a thousand bottles.'

The extreme of Weingut Max Ferd. Richter's high-quality wine production is the icewines they have made from Riesling grapes grown in the Mülheimer Helenenkloster vineyard since 1961. As a result of nearly three decades' experience, the estate is one of the specialists in icewine production.

Weingut Milz Laurentiushof

Karl Josef Milz (owner and director).
Weingut Milz Laurentiushof,
D 5559 Trittenheim/Mosel.
Tel: 06507 2300.

7.5 hectares/18.5 acres.
90% Riesling, 10% Müller-Thurgau.

The Milz family have been winegrowers in Trittenheim since 1608, and without doubt the best wines from Trittenheim's vineyards produced today come from their estate. Most of all the wines from their three monopole vineyards, the Lieterchen and Felsenkopf on opposite sides of the village, and the Neumagener Nüsswingert are often of very high quality. Perhaps because of microclimatic factors, every few years a vintage occurs which seems to favour this corner of the Moselle particularly, as happened in 1981 when the estate produced the best wines in the entire region.

The Milz wines are all made traditionally in Füder casks in the vaulted cellars under the estate house in the middle of the small town of Trittenheim. Because the town sits in the middle of one of the Moselle's most dramatic and picturesque bends, there are wonderful views of the vineyards from almost every street corner in Trittenheim. To see the area best one should take the road up from the town on to the Hunsrück. Here Josef Milz has positioned his new house on the perfect view-point high above the river. From here he can survey his vineyards, and point out with some pride just how perfectly the best of them are placed.

The Milz estate's wines are made predominantly in the sweet and medium-dry styles.

Weingut Reichsgraf von Kesselstatt

Annegret Reh (director),
Bernhard Keiper (cellarmaster).
Weingut Reichsgraf von Kesselstatt,
Liebfrauenstrasse 10,
D 5500 Trier/Mosel.
Tel: 0651 75101.

c. 80 hectares/200 acres.
100% Riesling.

It is difficult to put a precise figure on the vineyard area of the Kesselstatt estate at the moment, because the estate is in the process of being slimmed down to nearer 60 hectares/150 acres in size. 'We still make our wines traditionally in wooden casks, but with the present scale of production the cellarmaster is a little over-stretched. I would rather have a little less wine, and a yet better standard of quality. This is also obviously easier to sell,' director Annegret Reh explains.

In the last few years the other large Trier-based estates have not often been able to match the very best wines from Weingut Reichsgraf von Kesselstatt. This is particularly true of the wines from their monopole vineyard, the 'Josephshöf' in Graach. This is the only 'château'-style property in the Middle Moselle valley, the 6 hectares/15 acres of vineyards surrounding the Josephshof building with its baroque chapel. It is sad to see the Josephshof itself in a rather dilapidated state at present, but the vineyards are in excellent condition. More than most wines from the Bernkastel–Graach–Wehlen area, these are wines which develop slowly. In their youth they are concentrated and firm, but do not have much charm or floweriness. After four or five years ageing, though, they have a superb richness of flavour.

The Josephshof is one of four self-sufficient estates which make up Kesselstatt (though all pressing and winemaking is done centrally in Trier), the others being the 'Domklausenhof' in Piesport on the Moselle, the 'St Irminenhof' in Kasel on the Ruwer, and the 'Oberemmeler Abteihof' on the Saar. Some excellent wines come from each of these collections of vineyards, and, partly in consequence of the sheer quantity of wine which Kesselstatt makes each year, also some more ordinary ones.

From the 1988 vintage all these wines will be made in the cellars of Schloss Marienlay, outside Trier. The Reh family which owns Kesselstatt also owns or has an interest in several other Moselle wine concerns, which form the 'Günther Reh Group'.

Bischöfliche Weingüter

Wolfgang Richter (director).
Verwaltung der Bischöflichen Weingüter,
Gervasiusstrasse 1,
D 5500 Trier/Mosel.
Tel: 0651 43441.

105.5 hectares/261 acres.
96% Riesling, 4% experimental varieties.

Since Wolfgang Richter's arrival in 1981, Bischofliche Weingüter, which is an amalgamation of the church-owned Bischöfliches Priesterseminar, Hohe Domkirche, and Bischöfliches Konvikt estates, has made big strides forward. Before 1981 there were too many non-traditional grape varieties in their vineyards on the Ruwer, and all the wines were made in a rather soft style which often did not bring out very well the special, characteristic flavours of each vineyard.

Wolfgang Richter is an extremely energetic and affable man, who enjoys nothing more than to taste and talk about wine with visitors, and is really the best possible company at wine tastings. He has no interest in making a heavy sales pitch, or in enumerating his personal achievements. The wines do this for him. A small majority of these are now made dry and medium-dry, usually with real success. The sweetness of the 'normal'-style wines has also been reduced, much to their benefit, and the Bischöfliche Weingüter wines seem more classic and elegant with each year that passes.

Friedrich-Wilhelm-Gymnasium

Benedikt Engel (director).
Weingut Stiftung Friedrich-Wilhelm-Gymasnium,
Weberbach 75,
D 5500 Trier/Mosel.
Tel: 0651 73849.

45 hectares/111 acres.
85% Riesling, 13% Müller-Thurgau, 2% other varieties.

The Friedrich-Wilhelm-Gymnasium has maintained a very clear style for many years, their wines almost invariably being light, elegant Moselle and Saar Rieslings with a really flowery bouquet. If the wines of many Moselle estates need to be aged for many years before they open out, the Friedrich-Wilhelm-Gymnasium wines often have charm from the moment they come on to the market. This is not to say that they will not age well, as many examples have shown.

The estate director, Benedikt Engel, is as charming as the wines he makes, and gives everyone who meets him the impression of great integrity, and of having an unshakeable commitment to maintaining the winemaking philosophy the Friedrich-Wilhelm-Gymnasium has built up over decades. Perhaps even Karl Marx, who was educated at the school after whom the estate is named and who took a great interest in the plight of the Moselle wine growers, would approve of the Friedrich-Wilhelm-Gymnasium's very dependable quality and fair prices.

All the estate's wines are fermented and matured in wooden casks, and the best introduction to their style is probably the wines from their monopole vineyard on the Saar, the Falkensteiner Hofberg.

Vereinigte Hospitien

Dr Hans Pileram (director),
Hermann Hochschied (assistant director).
Vereinigte Hospitien,
Krahmenufer 19,
D 5500 Trier/Mosel.
Tel: 0651 468210/468211.

55 hectares/132.5 acres.
91% Riesling, 9% other varieties.

Nearly half the Vereinigte Hospitien's vineyards are on the Saar, and it is these wines which are generally their best. They are classic steely Saar wines, but with more delicacy than is often the case. Vereinigte Hospitien work particularly hard to make the finest possible wine from the Wiltinger Hölle and Seeriger

Schloss Saarfelser Schlossberg vineyards, the latter only failing to have a reputation as one of the best vineyards on the Saar because of its all but unpronounceable name.

Although the Vereinigte Hospitien has 'only' been in existence since the Napoleonic occupation, when all the charitable foundations of the Abbey of St Irmin were amalgamated, its buildings go back much further. One section of the cellars is partly of Roman origin, originally having been built as a warehouse by the Emperor Constantine (who ruled from AD 306 to 336). Other parts of the Vereinigte Hospitien's buildings date from various intervening periods, so a visit to the estate for the architectural feast, as well as the fine wine, is an essential part of a tour of the Moselle. The foundation still cares for about six hundred people, being largely financed by its vineyards and forests.

Weingut Egon Müller-Scharzhof

Egon Müller Snr (owner and director),
Egon Müller Jr (director),
Horst Frank (cellarmaster).
Weingut Egon Müller-Scharzhof,
Scharzhof,
D 5511 Wiltingen.
Tel: 06501 17232.

8.5 hectares/21 acres.
95% Riesling, 5% other varieties.

The large mansion with its outbuildings at the foot of the massive 'wall' of the precipitous Scharzhofberg vineyard is some distance from the nearest village. It retains something of a monastic atmosphere from its clerical past, tastings of the young wines taking place in the often ice-cold hallway around a small marble table with more than a hint of ritual. This is just as much a part of the distinctive Egon Müller style as the often astonishing perfection of their best Scharzhofberger wines, which have great refinement as well as the classic steeliness of the Saar. Though this vineyard has been famous since at least the eighteenth century, and growers were consequently allowed to continue selling its wines without a village name after the 1971 wine law was passed, it is the Egon Müller estate which has made it world-famous during the decades since the Second World War.

The estate is renowned for the comparative frequency with which it produces high Prädikat wines. The secret of how Egon Müller was, for example, able to make Riesling wines of Beerenauslese quality in 1979 and 1986, when nobody else on the Saar or Ruwer succeeded in doing so, is their extremely selective harvesting techniques. Because they have over twenty acres of vineyards all close together they are in the ideal position to make such selections – a great quantity of grapes to choose from – but that does not make this work easy. 'Either I or my father have to be out with the pickers the entire time we are harvesting,' Egon Müller Jr insists, 'otherwise we couldn't be sure of getting these top wines. You have to point out to the pickers again and again exactly the kind of grapes you want them to pick.'

There is also a very rigorous selection of the grape must and of the Füder casks of wine at Scharzhof. In 1984, for example, 80 per cent was sold away in bulk without the Egon Müller name, and the remaining QbA wines were sold under the Le Gallais label. Weingut Le Gallais is a separate estate joint-owned and managed by Egon Müller. Its vineyards are exclusively in Willtingen, and its wines are made in the cellar at Scharzhof. Only Prädikat wines, that is wines of Kabinett quality upwards, are sold under the turn-of-the-century Weingut Egon Müller-Scharzhof label. The cellar is remarkably primitive for such a top estate, but Herr Frank's extremely conservative and unmanipulative cellar work is infinitely more important than the fact that the estate has not got the latest model of press (in fact an old hydraulic basket press is retained for the top wines). As at the majority of top Moselle, Saar, and Ruwer estates, any sweetness which the wines have comes from the grape must.

The estate's speciality is Eiswein, the systematic making of which was pioneered by Egon Müller Snr during the 1960s and 70s. The 1983 Eiswein must hold the world record for the highest price for an 'en primeur' wine, having sold for the equivalent of £400 per bottle at the Grosser Ring (VDP) auction in 1984! More normal qualities from the estate are thankfully much less expensive. Indeed, considering its fully justified reputation as one of the finest white wine producers in the world, the wines are almost cheap.

Weingut von Hövel

Eberhard von Kunow (owner and director).
Weingut von Hövel,
Agritiusstrasse 5–6,
D 5501 Konz–Oberemmel.
Tel: 06501 2408.

12.5 hectares/31 acres.
95% Riesling, 3% Weissburgunder (Pinot Blanc),
2% Müller-Thurgau.

A tasting with the gregarious Eberhard von Kunow is always great fun, as well as being an opportunity to taste some really elegant first-class Saar wines. In particular, it is always a delight to taste the Weingut von Hövel wines which Eberhard von Kunow himself most likes to drink. 'Yes,' he says with great conviction, 'we make some nice dry wines which I enjoy with meals sometimes, and the Auslese wines are always exciting to taste, but what I get the most pleasure out of are the Kabinett wines made in the traditional style. The only sad thing is that most people think you've got to drink them young, whereas they are almost always better after three, four, or many more years of ageing.' The 1977 Kabinett wines, for example, are only just coming to their peak.

During the last few years the quality of the Weingut von Hövel's Kabinetts, as well as of their bone-dry Riesling and Weissburgunder wines, and the luscious Auslese and icewines, has been getting better and better. The estate is now certainly amongst the very best producers on the Saar, and without doubt offers the best value for money in the region too. Eberhard von Kunow runs a very tight ship at Weingut von Hövel together with his wife, and also works as auctioneer for the Moselle, Saar, and Ruwer section of the VDP, the 'Grosser Ring'.

It is not just with the quality of their best wines that Weingut von Hövel are close to matching the great Egon Müller estate. Their new label (featuring a turn-of-the-century print of the house) is as beautiful as the Müller label, and their hallway is also nearly as cold as that at the Scharzhof!

Weingüter Dr Fischer

Hans H. Fischer (owner and director).
Weingüter Dr Fischer,
Bocksteinhof
D 5511 Ockfen.
Tel: 06581 2150

Weingüter Dr Fischer,
D 5511 Wawern.
Tel: 06581 16859

23 hectares/57 acres.
98% Riesling, 2% other varieties.

The most important vineyards of Weingüter Dr Fischer give wines with markedly different characteristics. The Ockfener Bockstein is undoubtedly one of the top vineyards on the Saar, but more than most vineyards it needs a good vintage to yield wines which show why it has gained a special reputation. Sadly the Fischer estate is the only one in the pretty village of Ockfen currently producing wines worthy to carry the Bockstein name on the label. Weingüter Dr Fischer Ockfener Bockstein Spätlese, or higher Prädikat wines, have a wonderful racy acidity which scintillates on the tongue. They are at the same time light yet very concentrated wines. However, a Bockstein wine from a vintage in which the grapes did not fully ripen can be very aggressive. Because the estate's wines are normally bottled very early, Hans Fischer rightly recommends that his wines be given time to show their best. This is particularly true of the fine but very steely dry wines.

In less than excellent vintages the rather fuller, earthier wines from the Wawerener Herrenberg vineyard are more rounded and harmonious. Then it is possible to understand why the wines of this vineyard used to attain some of the highest prices at the Trier wine auctions at the beginning of the century. At that time it was in the ownership of the Lintz family, who sold the Wawern estate to Dr Fischer in 1964. However, the Lintz family has not quite given up wine production. The youngest generation of the Lintz family, Christian Pies-Lintz, is planting vineyards in Martinborough, New Zealand.

Weingut Forstmeister Geltz Zilliken

Hans-Joachim Zilliken (owner and director).
Weingut Forstmeister Geltz Zilliken,
Heckingstrasse 20,
D 5510 Saarburg.
Tel: 06581 2456.

8.5 hectares/21 acres.
90% Riesling, 10% Müller-Thurgau.

The rapidly rising star of the Saar is undoubtedly the Zilliken estate in Saarburg. Though the estate has always had a good name from the time it was established by the Royal Prussian Forestry Officer Ferdinand Geltz (1851–1925), it is since Hans-Joachim Zilliken took over in 1976 that its international reputation has soared. The estate has all the necessary prerequisites for producing the finest quality Saar wines; in particular, parcels of some of the best Saar vineyards, and an exceptionally deep cellar with an unchanging temperature of 9°C and 100 per cent humidity. Here the estate's wines are fermented and matured exclusively in Füder and smaller old oak casks in the traditional manner.

The Zilliken wines are almost never deacidified even to the slightest degree, and are always tremendously racy. Sometimes the dry wines, which are often fermented through to bone-dryness, can be a bit aggressive as a result of their high acidity. However, the Halbtrocken and (very slightly) sweeter wines are always very good. The best wines in this style are sensational, having the finest possible differentiation of subtly nuanced flavours. In top vintages like 1976 and 1983 the Zilliken wines have the perfect combination of tremendous concentration and excellent acidity structure.

Like many of the VDP estates on the Moselle, Hans-Joachim Zilliken now sells his QbA wines under the estate name, but he is anxious to point out that this does not imply any compromise in the winemaking. 'These are individual vineyard wines, which have received the same degree of care as the Prädikat wines. However, since the majority come from the less well-known vineyards, we make it easier for customers by simply leaving off the vineyard names.' Wines which do not meet the estate's

minimum standard are sold away. Unknown to Hans-Joachim Zilliken, I was once able to taste some of these declassified wines at H. Sichel Söhne in Alzey (p. 15), where their clean, elegant fruitiness stood out among dozens of samples from other producers in the region. Even these rejected wines are better than what many small growers on the Saar sell in bottle.

Zilliken has for some years also been an icewine specialist, and has managed to make at least one such wine in almost every recent vintage. Since the 1985 vintage he has also used the icewine technique in order to harvest Spätlese and Auslese wines when a normal harvest would yield musts with the bare minimum sugar levels to make these Prädikats. These wines have a fabulous brilliance, but need a *long* time to develop after bottling. A Zilliken Eiswein is virtually immortal, and should be approached with caution if drunk at less than ten years of age; these wines have a phenomenal acidity content as well as phenomenal concentration!

Weingut Schloss Saarstein

Christian Ebert (owner and director),
Dieter Ebert (owner and director).
Weingut Schloss Saarstein,
D 5512 Serrig.
Tel: 06581 2324.

11 hectares/27 acres.
92% Riesling, 8% Müller-Thurgau and Kerner.

Schloss Saarstein is the only 'château'-style estate on the Saar,
the Ebert family being the exclusive owners of the vineyards
bearing the Saarstein name which surround the nineteenth-
century schloss, perched on a hill just outside the small town of
Serrig. The estate came into the ownership of the Ebert family in
1956, since which time they have done an enormous amount of
work on the house, the cellars, and, most of all, the vineyards.
Their system of vineyard cultivation, which involves putting an
enormous amount of humus into the soil, is unique in the region.
It means that even in difficult vintages their wines are never thin
and angular, but always filled out by a very high level of mineral
extracts.

The estate concentrates on Riesling QbA and Kabinett wines,
with quite a large proportion of these being made dry and
medium-dry. These are perhaps the most harmonious dry wines
produced on the Saar. Although the Eberts produce good
quantities of Spätlese and Auslese wines when a fine vintage like
1983 comes along, Christian Ebert prefers the high Prädikat
wines which are the result of very strict selection of the grapes,
such as the amazing 1985 Auslese of which only 240 litres could
be made. It is a wine with real power.

Weingutsverwaltung Karthäuserhof

Christoph Tyrell (owner and director),
Ludwig Breiling (cellarmaster).
Rautenstrausch'sche Weingutsverwaltung Karthäuserhof,
Karthäuserhof,
D 5500 Trier–Eitelsbach.
Tel: 0651 5121.

18.5 hectares/44.5 acres.
90% Riesling, 10% other varieties.

By the time Christoph Tyrell started working at his family estate
in the spring of the 1984 vintage, the famous Karthäuserhof
estate had fallen into disrepute and was in some financial
trouble. Since that time Christoph and Graciela Tyrell have
made rapid and continuous progress in rebuilding the reputation

of Karthäuserhof as one of the two great estates in the tiny Ruwer valley. The unexcelled quality of the 1986 vintage Karth-äuserhof wines and Christoph Tyrell's complete takeover of ownership of the estate in April 1987 set the seal on the new regime's dedicated work.

RIESLING
HALBTROCKEN
A. P. Nr. 3 561 303 - 7 - 87
Qualitätswein b. A.

ERZEUGERABFÜLLUNG
RAUTENSTRAUCH'SCHE
WEINGUTSVERWALTUNG
KARTHÄUSERHOF
5500 TRIER-EITELSBACH
Product of Germany

1986er EITELSBACHER KARTHÄUSERHOFBERG
750 ml

The Karthäuserhofberg is a very steep vineyard on the eastern side of the Ruwer, at the foot of which nestle the medieval buildings used by the Carthusian monks who worked the vineyards from 1335 until Napoleon's arrival in the region, and the elegant nineteenth-century estate buildings which the Tyrell family put up after buying the estate in 1811. Every third row of vines has recently been pulled out, which improves the exposure of the vines and grapes to sun and air and enables the majority of the vineyard work to be done using caterpillar tractors. The estate now uses no insecticides, preferring pheromones which prevent insect pests from reproducing.

Under the estate buildings is the vaulted stone cellar where the wines are made in a combination of tanks and wooden casks. The wines sold under the estate's name are 100 per cent Riesling, the other varieties being sold off as grape must. There is little deacidification of the grape must or wine. If fermentation is stopped artificially this is done using refrigeration, and the final (low or very low) level of sweetness in the wines is adjusted by blending together different barrels and tanks. The result of this is that the wines are both fresher and more elegant than under Christoph's father. The estate also makes a high proportion of dry and medium-dry wines now. These can sometimes be a little hard for non-German palates, but others are a revelation and have begun to sell on the export markets. The finest wines have a highly seductive cassis/ripe peach tone.

The commitment of Christoph and Graciela Tyrell and Ludwig Breiling is surely set to bear great fruit during the coming years.

Weingut Karlsmühle

Peter Geiben (owner and director).
Weingut Karlsmühle,
D 5501 Mertesdorf/Ruwer.
Tel: 0651 52035.

8 hectares/20 acres.
80% Riesling, 20% other varieties.

Weingut Karlsmühle wines have changed dramatically during the last few years. Peter Geiben, the new young owner and director, has dramatically decreased the proportion of sweeter wines at the estate, is making all the wines with much more pronounced fruity acidity, and has had a radically new and much more attractive modern label designed. The new regime at Karlsmühle probably requires a few more years to be further refined, but already the majority of the wines are of excellent quality. The new Karlsmühle wines are steely Rieslings with the classic delicately herbal-flowery character of the Ruwer.

The Ahr and Mittel Rhein

The Ahr and Mittel Rhein areas are the second and third smallest of the German wine-growing regions at 450 hectares/ 1110 acres and 786 hectares/1940 acres in extent. Little of their wine is exported, the majority of Ahr wines being drunk in the Bonn–Koblenz area and the greater part of the Middle Rhine wines being sold to sparkling wine companies or to tourists.

The Middle Rhine is situated in the Rhine gorge which has inspired so many German and English poets and many nineteenth-century romantic painters. The reason why there are so many castles here is nothing to do with the picturesque nature of the scenery, though; because of the narrowness of this part of the Rhine valley, it was easy to extract tolls from commercial shipping using the river. There certainly are some excellent vineyard sites here, particularly at Boppard, St Goarshausen, and Bacharach, and the potential to make high-class Riesling wines somewhat in the style of the Moselle. However, the region has little reputation and this makes it difficult for the growers to get the prices needed to make high-class wine production worth while. The good growers here are few and far between.

The little Ahr valley, which runs westwards from the Rhine a little to the south of Bonn, has similar slate and weathered volcanic soils to the Middle Rhine, and perhaps an even higher proportion of steeply sloping vineyards where the grapes of the classic vine varieties can fully ripen. It has an easy market for its very limited production of wines though, and prices here are consequently much higher than in the Middle Rhine. Although the most important grape variety here is Spätburgunder, the region is probably best suited to Riesling. However, both really good Riesling and Spätburgunder red wines are a rarity here.

Any visitor to either of these regions should be aware that they are real tourists spots, and can be particularly full of people at weekends during the summer. For this reason the price of meals and hotels can be quite as steep as the vineyards.

Weingut J. J. Adeneuer

Max and Frank Adeneuer (owners and directors).
Weingut J. J. Adeneuer,
Max Planck-Strasse 8,
D 5483 Bad Neuenahr–Ahrweiler.
Tel: 02641 34473.

6 hectares/15 acres.
75% Spätburgunder (Pinot Noir), 20% Portugieser,
5% Dornfelder.

The Ahr is the second smallest of the German wine-producing regions, and as a result of its proximity to the West German capital, Bonn, has a ready home market for its wines. Unfortunately this means that there are very few producers in the region who try hard to produce the best possible wines, because they simply do not need to in order to sell their wines for good prices! Max and Frank Adeneuer's wines are exceptions in this puddle of mediocrity, and are amongst the few Ahr red wines which are acceptable to international taste.

Whereas most Ahr red wines are presumptuous rosés, the Adeneuers' wines are deep in colour and rich in flavour. They have a fair amount of acidity compared to, say, most French red wines, but this is not aggressive since it has been softened by a second, or malolactic, fermentation. Also unlike the majority of their neighbours the Adeneuer estate produces almost no sweet wines, Max and Frank feeling that sweetness and red wine simply do not go together. Their best wines are the Spätburgunders from the Gärkammer vineyard, which is probably the best site in the region. It faces due south, is very steep, and has a weathered slate soil (like that in most of the Moselle vineyards). The Adeneuer's regularly get a whole degree more of potential alcohol here than anywhere else in the region. Even in average vintages they usually make at least one Gärkammer wine with 12 degrees of naturally achieved alcohol.

Because of healthy domestic demand their wines are not cheap.

Weingut Toni Jost–Hahnenhof

Peter Jost (owner and director).
Weingut Toni Jost–Hahnenhof,
Oberstrasse 14,
D 6533 Bacharach.
Tel: 06743 1216.

10 hectares/24.5 acres.
70% Riesling, 10% Müller-Thurgau, 8% Spätburgunder
(Pinot Noir), 12% other varieties.

Peter Jost makes some of the most elegant Middle Rhine Riesling wines from his 3.5 hectares of vineyards in the Bacharacher Hahn site. Indeed, they are comparable in style and ageing potential to the best wines of Lorch in the Rheingau just across the river. All his Rieslings and Spätburgunder wines (from vineyards at Walluf in the Rheingau) are made in wooden casks, but the other varieties are made in stainless steel tanks and bottled early in order to retain as much freshness as possible. He also makes fine dry Riesling Sekt (Extra Brut).

Deinhard

Manfred Völpel (director of winemaking).
Deinhard & Co.,
Deinhardplatz,
D 5400 Koblenz.
Tel: 0261 1040.

As well as having estates in three regions of Germany (see the directory sections on the Moselle, Rheingau, and Rheinpfalz), Deinhard also produce blended regional wines, and a great deal of sparkling wine or Sekt. Their Sekt production is described here, because their most important Sekt for the export markets, Deinhard Lila Imperial, is produced from Middle-Rhine Riesling wines. To these is added a small amount of wine from Deinhard's three estates, to add depth. The result is a very clean, elegant sparkling wine with a slaty Riesling aroma. The vintage Lila Imperial has a touch more depth, and is firmer. It can develop for at least a decade in bottle, and is much better than the majority of cheaper champagnes.

Lila Imperial, along with Deinhard's other sparkling wines, is made at a large modern plant in the Koblenz suburb of Wallersheim. Here sparkling wines are made by the tank method, because with a total production of about 40 million bottles per year, the champagne method would take up too much space and be too time-consuming. However, Deinhard's de luxe Sekts, one of which is made from top-quality wines from each of their three estates, are 'Méthode Champenoise'. For these relatively small quantities of very high quality wine it is more than worth the extra labour needed to produce the sparkle through a second fermentation in the bottle rather than in a tank. Best of these de luxe Sekts is the Bernkasteler Doctor from the Middle Moselle, which has great finesse. As Manfred Völpel says, 'This shows what you can do in Germany in the sparkling wine field, if you select high quality base wines and don't cut any corners in the Sekt-making process.'

Nahe

The Nahe is one of the larger tributaries of the Rhine, joining it at Bingen. The region's 4600 hectares/11,360 acres of vineyards

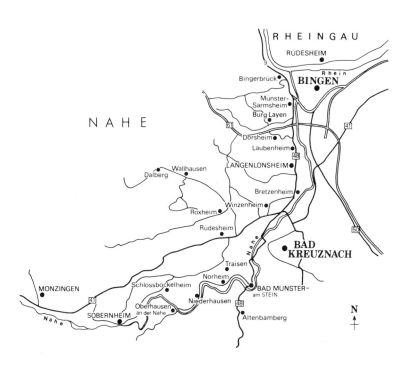

RHEINGAU

RUDESHEIM

Bingerbruck • **BINGEN**

NAHE

Munster-Sarmsheim

Burg Layen

Dorsheim

Laubenheim

LANGENLONSHEIM

Wallhausen

Dalberg

Bretzenheim

Winzenheim

Roxheim

Rudesheim

BAD KREUZNACH

Traisen

Norheim

MONZINGEN

Schlossbockelheim

BAD MÜNSTER-am STEIN

Oberhausen an der Nahe

Niederhausen

SOBERNHEIM

Altenbamberg

N

Km	0	2	4	6	8	10	Km		Motorway
Mi	0		2		4		6	Mi	Principal Highway
									Secondary Highway

The Nahe

are largely between Bingen and the large spa town of Bad
Kreuznach, the remainder being scattered along the Nahe valley
upstream from Bad Kreuznach and along its small tributaries.
Unlike the somewhat smaller neighbouring Rheingau, the Nahe
has a blurred and rather weak image as a region. A few of the
best-known producers here are better known than the region as a
whole.

＊The wines of the Bingen–Bad Kreuznach area are quite
different from those of the Upper Nahe, being fuller and more
powerful. This area makes excellent dry wines. The wines made
from the vineyards between Bad Kreuznach and Monzingen at
the western edge of the region have a character similar to those
of the Middle Moselle: light, racy, and often very refined. The
scenery is also distinctly different in the two areas, the Lower
Nahe consisting of a series of rolling ridges of hills, the Upper
Nahe valley and its tributaries being narrow and rocky, with
many porphyry cliffs of varying sizes.

The Nahe does not have a single traditional grape variety,
Riesling, Silvaner, and Müller-Thurgau being of roughly equal
importance. The new regional 'Nahesteiner' wine is a blend of
these varieties.＊The best wines, generally speaking, are the
Rieslings, which can be as fine as those of the Rheingau or
Moselle.＊

Weingut Bürgermeister Willi Schweinhardt

Wilhelm Schweinhardt (owner and director).
Weingut Bürgermeister Willi Schweinhardt,
Heddesheimer Strasse 1,
D 6536 Langenlonsheim/Nahe.
Tel: 06704 1276.

25 hectares/62 acres.
34% Riesling, 5.5% Scheurebe, 12.5% Müller-Thurgau,
8% Kerner, 2.5% Weissburgunder (Pinot Blanc),
10% Grauburgunder (Pinot Gris), 5% Spätburgunder (Pinot
Noir) and Portugieser, 2.5% Gewürztraminer, 20% other
varieties.

In contrast to the majority of German wine growers, Wilhelm
Schweinhardt is an unreserved modernist when it comes to

A classic white wine cellar: Wilhelm Haag, owner and director of Weingut Fritz Haag in Brauneberg on the Moselle, tastes one of his best wines of the great 1985 vintage from the barrel in his cellar under the Dusemonder Hof (*Courtesy of Weingut Fritz Haag*)

The beautifully preserved medieval buildings of Maximin Grünhaus in the Ruwer valley seen from its best vineyard, the steep slate-soil Abtsberg. The Riesling wines from this vineyard are among the most refined of those produced in the valleys of the Moselle and its tributaries, the Saar and the Ruwer (*Courtesy of Carl von Schubert*)

A classic red wine cellar: Rainer Lingenfelder, winemaker for Weingut Lingenfelder in Grosskarlbach in the Palatinate, draws a sample of one of his superb *barrique*-aged Spätburgunder (Pinot Noir) red wines. The barrels come from Château Grand Puy Lacoste in Bordeaux (*Courtesy of Weingut Lingenfelder*)

The baroque home of the Staatsweingut Meersburg on the northern shore of Lake Constance. The lower bay window in the centre of the palace on the left marks the office of Herr Häussermann, the estate's director. Because of the view from here across the lake to the Alps, it has been described as 'the most beautiful office in Germany' by some of his colleagues (*Stuart Pigott*)

A ripe bunch of Scheurebe grapes, in the Palatinate region, just beginning to be affected by noble rot or *Edelfäule*. This fungus causes the grapes to shrivel, concentrating the juice they contain. The result is a dessert wine of great intensity and complexity of flavour (*Stuart Pigott*)

A neighbouring bunch with the botrytis infection fully developed. Note the crumpled looking berries. Although the grapes look ugly, their juice will be extremely sweet and fruity (*Stuart Pigott*)

Heinrich (left) and Bernhard Breuer, owners of Weingut Georg Breuer in Rüdesheim, in the Rheingau, in their private cellar where their Charta Rheingau Riesling wines rub shoulders with top clarets, Burgundies, old champagne, and many other goodies (*Courtesy of Scholl & Hillebrand*)

The Village of Ürzig on the Middle Moselle with (left to right) the Ürzigen Wunzganten, Endenen Prälab and Erdener Treppchen vineyard sites (*Stuart Pigott*)

Hans Hermann Eser of Weingut Johannishof in Johannisberg in the Rheingau with the developing grapes of the 1987 vintage in the excellent Geisenheimer Kläuserweg vineyard. The high training of the vines is a system of Herr Eser's invention (*Stuart Pigott*)

Ernst Loosen, owner of Weingut St Johannishof, in Bernkastel on the Moselle
(*Stuart Pigott*)

selling his wines, using the most modern computer mail shot and cable TV methods. Beneath his amiable manner is an extremely sharp businessman and a thoughtful winemaker.

Herr Schweinhardt produces many good conventional dry and sweeter wines from the classic grape varieties. The Kabinett wines are sometimes a little light, but also immediately attractive. The Spätlese and Auslese wines are much more serious. The estate's most recent innovation is Auslese wines with a level of sweetness just above the legally defined upper limit for medium-dry wines. Different labels are used to distinguish between the sweeter wines (the traditional yellow label with the Schweinhardt coat of arms), and the dry wines (white background with line drawing of the estate house).

Weingut Paul Anheuser

Rudolf Peter Anheuser (owner and director).
Weingut Paul Anheuser,
Stromberger Strasse 15–19,
D 6550 Bad Kreuznach/Nahe.
Tel: 0671 28748.

76 hectares/188 acres.
70% Riesling, 7% Müller-Thurgau, 7% Ruländer (Pinot
Gris), 7% Kerner, 2% Weissburgunder (Pinot Blanc),
2% Spätburgunder (Pinot Noir), 2% Scheurebe, 3% other
varieties.

Of all the larger top wine estates in Germany, Weingut Paul Anheuser is one of the most under-valued. This is, perhaps, because they do not have an aristocratic title, and because they do have a very individual style that is not everybody's taste.

Rudolf Anheuser is a tall, heavily built man, who gives the impression of having principles as solid as he is physically. He is completely committed to quality, and to making wines in his own way regardless of whether that happens to be in vogue. Until he took over the estate from his father in 1964 they had, apart from naturally sweet Auslese, never made a wine with sweetness! While Herr Anheuser changed that, he has never made really sweet QbA, Kabinett or Spätlese wines. The most distinctive element of his winemaking style is a period of contact with the skins for the grape pulp and juice before pressing, which is extremely rare in Germany. He believes that the juice extracts many flavouring substances from the skins which makes the resulting wine more complex. This skin contact also means that his wines have a very attractive, pale primrose-yellow colour. All the Anheuser wines are fermented and matured in Stück and Doppelstück old oak casks (new wood having been rejected outright after several experiments) in the massive vaulted cellars under the press house. These are chilled down to 4–5°C so that the wines ferment slowly, and consequently they do not lose any of their finer flavours.

Weingut Paul Anheuser's Rieslings are excellent, quite full wines, which always have a very distinctive character from the soil of whichever vineyard they came. The Weissburgunder wines, which are always made in a drier style, are also excellent. Not every vintage favours the vineyards of Bad Kreuznach, but when vintages come which bring good ripeness and a lively acidity, as was the case in 1975 and 1985, these wines can be very fine.

Prinz zu Salm-Dalberg'sches Weingut

Michael Prince Salm-Salm (owner and director),
Daniel Chaventré (cellarmaster).
Prinz zu Salm-Dalberg'sches Weingut,
Schloss Wallhausen,
D 6551 Wallhausen/Nahe.
Tel: 06706 289.

10 hectares/25 acres.
60% Riesling, 15% Müller-Thurgau, 10% Spätburgunder (Pinot Noir), 5% Scheurebe, 5% Silvaner, 5% Kerner.

Michael Prince Salm-Salm's estate has been in his family's ownership for almost 850 years, and is certainly one of the oldest German wine producers (the earliest records of the Wallhausen vineyards date from 1200 and 1217). One of the first recorded members of the family, Hermann I, was chosen king of Germany in 1081. The fifth prince, Ludwig Otto, almost became king of England, but the House of Hanover's religious persuasion was more acceptable. Prince Karl-Theodor was Lord High Chancellor of Germany at the beginning of the last century, and until recently the present Prince Salm has been director of the Castell estate in Franconia (pp. 102–106). Enough history for a whole German wine region!

Michael Prince Salm-Salm is very jovial and open, with an infectious enthusiasm for good wine. While very keen to present his own wines, he is also a committed unofficial 'ambassador' for fine-quality German wines as a whole. Now that he has moved back to Wallhausen his increased engagement in the estate should be of great assistance to his French cellarmaster, Daniel Chaventré. While the wines are presently a little rustic, like this area of the Nahe, they are absolutely pure varietal wines with a lot of character. Generally the wines ferment out by themselves in the ancient cellars under Schloss Wallhausen, and are bottled with whatever sweetness they naturally retain.

When planning a visit to the Nahe, the excellent small restaurant in the ground floor of the Schloss, the 'Wein-Cabinet' run by Ingrid and Daniel Chaventré, should not be missed.

Weingut Hans Crusius & Sohn

Hans Crusius (owner and director),
Dr Peter Crusius (owner and director).
Weingut Hans Crusius & Sohn,
Hauptstrasse 2,
D 6551 Traisen/Nahe.
Tel: 0671 33953.

12.5 hectares/31 acres.
70% Riesling, 13% Müller-Thurgau, 7% Kerner,
7% Weissburgunder (Pinot Blanc), 3% Spätburgunder
(Pinot Noir).

I am far from being the first wine writer to praise the wines of the Crusius estate in the Nahe. About the excellence of their wines I am in complete agreement with Hugh Johnson, Ian Jamieson, and other colleagues. However, the style of the Crusius wines has subtly changed since the last reports on their wines appeared. They have now adopted a policy of making their dry wines (nearly a quarter of their production) with a little touch of unfermented sweetness to round the pronounced acidity, and they have reduced the level of sweetness in their traditional sweeter-style wines to near the lower limit which the law sets.

This move was Peter Crusius's idea, but typically there was agreement between him and his father on this point. While there is active, and often bitter, conflict between the generations at many German wine estates, the Crusius wines are the product of the best possible creative co-operation between father and son. The visitor quickly senses this from the remarkably easy, open atmosphere at the estate. Neither Peter nor Hans Crusius ever tries to cut into what the other says, and they listen attentively to any comments made.

What distinguishes their best wines from the majority of those made on the Nahe is a combination of the exceptionally fine vineyards they own, and the care with which these are cultivated, and with which the resulting wines are made. The most impressive of their vineyards is the Traiser Bastei, a narrow strip of porphyry at the base of the massive Rotenfels cliffs (at over 600 feet in height, the highest inland cliffs in northern Europe). Facing almost due south under this massive heat reservoir, the vineyard produces wines with great ripeness and a distinctive, almost indescribable taste from the soil. Also with a special soil, south-facing, and situated under cliffs, though of less awe-inspiring dimensions, is the Schlossböckelheimer Felsenberg vineyard, of which the Crusius family have owned a large piece almost since the founding of the estate in the sixteenth century. The soil here is melaphyry, another kind of rock of volcanic origin, which weathers to a very rich soil. The wines from these vineyards are made in a conservative manner, the great majority being fermented and matured in old wooden casks in the estate's slightly cramped cellars.

Visiting an estate like that of Hans and Dr Peter Crusius gives one faith that, in spite of the contemporary trend towards the wines from different regions and countries tasting the same, there will always be available at least some wines of great individuality.

Staatliche Weinbaudomänen
Niederhausen-Schlossböckelheim

Dr Werner Hofäcker (director).
Verwaltung der Staatlichen Weinbaudomänen
Niederhausen-Schlossböckelheim,
D 6551 Oberhausen/Nahe.
Tel: 06758 6215.

45 hectares/111 acres.
90% Riesling, 8% Müller-Thurgau, 2% other varieties.

Of all the state wine domaines in Germany the finest, and the one which has most impressively fulfilled its task of developing high-quality wine production in its region, is the Verwaltung der Staatlichen Weinbaudomänen at Niederhausen-Schlossböckelheim. The Nahe State Domaine was created largely out of rocky scrub land on the Upper Nahe in the first years of this century, using convict labour. Inside the door of the estate buildings are several dramatic photographs showing this work under way. The most important result of this is visible through the windows or from the entrance; the towering amphitheatre of terraces which make up the Kupfergrübe vineyard.

This vineyard produces wines of incomparable concentration and raciness, the best of which need decades to develop fully. The best 1983 Auslese from this vineyard, for example, did not evolve at all during the first four years of its life! While the Kupfergrübe shines in the good and great vintages, the Niederhauser Hermannsberg gives very fine wines almost every year, and Hermannsberg wines from supposedly 'lesser' vintages are often quite stunning. Most accessible and flowery of the Niederhausen wines are those from the Hermannshöhle, which have a wonderful juicy fruitiness that makes them delicious from two or three years of age. The estate's vineyards on the lower Nahe were only added in 1953, and give rather fuller, more earthy wines, which are often vinified dry, being much better suited to this style than the nervier wines from the Niederhausen-Schlossböckelheim area.

It was during the many years when the now-retired (but consulting) cellarmaster, Karl-Heinz Sattelmeyer, was in charge of the winemaking that the estate's reputation soared up, and up, and up. He established the style of the estate, with winemaking in the Moselle style; i.e. any unfermented sweetness in the wines being the result of the fermentation stopping by itself, or being artificially stopped. All the wines are made in wooden casks, the majority being bottled ready for the annual June VDP auction in Bad Kreuznach. The first signs are that Dr Hofäcker has found a new cellarmaster who will be able at least to maintain the long-established quality standards.

Rheingau and Hessische Bergstrasse

The Rheingau is, in spite of its modest size (3,000 hectares/7,410 acres), the most famous of the German wine-producing regions. This is because it has the longest history of *quality* wine production, going back to the twelfth century, and because since the sale of wines in bottle became normal practice during the eighteenth century the Rheingau has been the most consistent producer of fine Riesling wines. It must be added that the many noble estates in the region have undoubtedly helped its image during this period, and continue to do so today.

In spite of the subtle diversity of its wines, due to the 286 soil

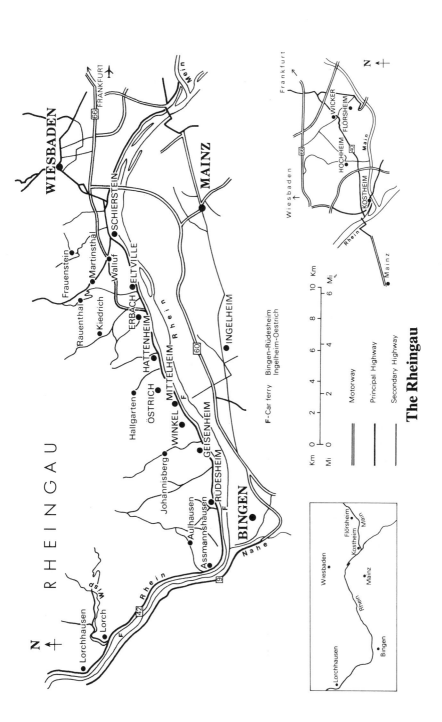

The Rheingau

N

RHEINGAU

WIESBADEN

MAINZ

BINGEN

FRANKFURT

66

60

Frauenstein
Martinsthal
SCHIERSTEIN
Walluf
Rauenthal
Kiedrich
ERBACH
ELTVILLE
HATTENHEIM
INGELHEIM
Hallgarten
ÖSTRICH
MITTELHEIM
WINKEL
GEISENHEIM
Johannisberg
RÜDESHEIM
Aulhausen
Assmannshausen
Nahe
Lorchhausen
Lorch
Rhein
42

F-Car ferry   Bingen-Rüdesheim
                   Ingelheim-Oestrich

| Km 0 | 2 | 4 | 6 | 8 | 10 Km |
| Mi 0 | | 2 | 4 | 6 Mi |

Motorway

Principal Highway

Secondary Highway

Frankfurt
N
WICKER
FLÖRSHEIM
HOCHHEIM
66
40
Wiesbaden
KOSTHEIM
Rhein
Mainz

Wiesbaden
Flörsheim
Main
Kostheim
Mainz
Rhein
Lorchhausen
Bingen

types in the region, the main body of the Rheingau, between Rüdesheim and Wiesbaden, produces Riesling wines with a strong family resemblance. They are quite powerful, yet elegant wines with a delicate and often complex earthiness. Though analytically the level of acidity in Rheingau Rieslings is generally lower than that of wines from the Middle Moselle, it is just as prominent in taste. Generally speaking, the wines from the gently sloping vineyards near the river are rather fuller and softer in character than the racy, more elegant wines from the vineyards on the higher and more steeply sloping ground back from the river and at Rüdesheim.

The Riesling wines of the area northwards from Rüdesheim to Lorch are lighter and cleaner, and often marked by slatiness or flintiness. In many ways they are comparable to those of the Middle Rhine. The village of Assmannshausen in this area is famous for red wines from the Spätburgunder grape, though their fame has tended to make them over-priced. The tourism it has brought has resulted in a great hotel and restaurant, however, the Krone. The other top restaurants of the region are the Alte Villa (in the valley of the Wisper), the Graues Haus in Winkel, and Boris in Walluf.

In contrast to the northern end of the Rheingau, the wines from Hochheim between Wiesbaden and Frankfurt are much fuller than those from the central area of the Rheingau, often having a strong earthiness. The word Hock derives from the name Hochheim, first having been used just for the wines of this town, then for Rheingau wines as a whole, and finally for any Rhine wines. Queen Victoria's famous remark 'A bottle of Hock keeps off the doc[tor]', and the English royal family's healthy consumption of fine Rheingau wines from that time up to the present day, has done much for the image and fame of Rheingau wines.

The one thing which the visitor to this most attractive region should beware of is Rüdesheim in the summer. The town is very touristic during this season, and should be approached only by those aware of what they are letting themselves in for. In the town the best restaurant is probably the Rüdesheimer Schloss, but it, like the rest of the town, is noisy. On the other hand there are many sites in the region which *must not* be missed, particularly the medieval abbey of Kloster Eberbach, whose monks established the region as an important wine producer, and the beautiful Gothic church in Kiedrich.

Hessische Bergstrasse is the smallest of the German wine regions with only 388 hectares/960 acres of vineyards. Since little is produced, little gets exported. However, because the region lacks a reputation, very good value can be had here.

Weingut Graf von Kanitz

Carl Albrecht Graf von Kanitz (owner),
Gernot Boos (director).
Weingut Graf von Kanitz,
Rheinstrasse, 49,
D 6223 Lorch.
Tel: 06726 346.

17 hectares/42 acres.
91% Riesling, 4% Müller-Thurgau, 3% Ehrenfelser,
2% Gewürztraminer.

Lorch, tucked at the end of the Rheingau where the Rhine runs northwards after its massive right-angle bend at the Rüdesheimer Berg, is often regarded as the 'rump of the Rheingau'. This is unfortunate, for some of the region's finest wines come from here. The Lorch vineyards have a completely different range of soil types from the majority of the Rheingau, with a lot of slate and quartzite mixed with some loam. The vineyards, being along the eastern side of the Rhine gorge, are also much steeper than the majority of the region's gently rolling hillsides. As a result, Riesling wines from Lorch are altogether more delicate and flowery than those from the majority of the Rheingau, having something of the flintiness of fine Moselle wines. Though they do not lack acidity, this is never as aggressive as it can be in the middle Rheingau.

The most important estate in Lorch is undoubtedly that of Graf von Kanitz. Although it has only been in the possession of this particular noble family for sixty years, the estate dates back to the thirteenth century, and the estate house is perhaps the finest example of Renaissance architecture on the middle part of the Rhine. In its cellars the Kanitz wines are made, both in tanks and wooden casks, depending on the character of each individual wine. (There is an excellent wine bar here too.) The character which each wine has derived from the particular soil and microclimate of the vineyard it came from is lovingly preserved at the Kanitz estate, and every wine tastes subtly different from the others of the same quality grade and vintage.

Gernot Boos, the director, strongly believes that if Riesling wines are made as serious wines with ageing potential they should not be put on the market too young. As a result none of the Kanitz wines go onto the list before they are two years old, and the list contains Kabinett and QbA wines going back nearly ten years (all still very fresh!). These qualities fermented to dryness are the normal products of the estate, and these wines are always delightful, sometimes having a stunning raciness. Those from Lorcher Krone and Kapelleneberg are the roundest, the wines from Lorcher Schlossberg and Pfaffenwies the most slaty, and the wines from the Lorcher Bodental-Steinberg complex, richest in mineral extract.

All the Graf von Kanitz wines are organically produced. They are the only large estate in Germany whose entire production is made in this way.

Weingut Troitzsch

Otto Troitzsch (owner),
Dieter Pusinelli (director).
Weingut Troitzsch,
Haus Schöneck,
Bächergrund 12,
D 6223 Lorch.
Tel: 06726 9481.

3 hectares/7.5 acres.
50% Riesling, 50% Silvaner, Müller-Thurgau,
Weissburgunder (Pinot Blanc), Spätburgunder (Pinot Noir),
Scheurebe, Gewürztraminer and Ehrenfelser.

Tucked away among the vineyards to the south of Lorch, Haus Schöneck, which houses the Troitzsch estate, enjoys one of the most delightful positions in the entire Rheingau. Otto Troitzsch, now well into his seventies but still active, is undoubtedly the most extreme traditionalist in the entire Rheingau, never having made a single wine with any detectable sweetness since taking over the small estate in 1945. From the late fifties, and right through the sixties when the sweet wine vogue was at its height, Otto Troitzsch struggled to sell his wines. In spite of this, he never wavered for a moment, sticking almost stubbornly to the style he believed to be correct for the wines of his area. Then, when the taste pendulum in Germany swung back towards dry wines during the seventies he was discovered. Now almost all the estate's small production is sold to little more than a hundred private customers! Often they have to be rationed, as yields are small and the quantity of each individual wine very limited.

The small cellar under the rather dour, nineteenth-century brick house is cramped, and equipped with the barest minimum of cellar technology. Otto Troitzsch's son-in-law is now making the wines, sticking to precisely the same winemaking methods that the estate has used for more than four decades. The fruits of this work are wines with great character, many-faceted rather than elegant, and full of extract. All the Troitzsch wines are better when they have been mellowed a little by ageing in bottle.

Klosterkellerei Sankt Hildegard

Klosterkellerei Sankt Hildegard,
Abtei St Hildegard,
Postfach 1320,
D 6220 Rüdesheim.
Tel: 06722 3088.

3.1 hectares/7.5 acres.
100% Riesling.

The convent of St Hildegard makes really traditional Riesling wines from the vineyards on the eastern side of Rüdesheim. Apart from the Bischofsberg, none of their vineyards are really first-class, yet such is the conscientiousness of the nuns' cultivation of their vineyards, and of the estate's winemaking, that the products of their work are often of excellent quality. While the convent has a shop where the wines can be bought, it is not possible to visit the cellars, no wines not on the present list can be tasted, nor is it possible to discover much about how the wines are made. For once all this seems irrelevant. The majority of the

St Hildegard wines are medium-dry, and none are either really sweet or poor in quality.

Schloss Johannisberg

Wolfgang Schleicher (director),
Wolfgang Heinrich (cellarmaster).
Schloss Johannisberg,
D 6222 Geisenheim–Johannisberg.
Tel: 06722 8012/8028/8029.

35 hectares/86.5 acres.
100% Riesling.

Schloss Johannisberg is the only Rheingau estate which is also the exclusive owner of a great vineyard site bearing its own name. The steep, south-facing slope directly in front of the neo-classical schloss is certainly one of the best vineyard sites in the entire Rheingau. The extent of the total vineyard area, which extends around this slope on three sides, is great enough for many selected harvest wines to be made, and the very first Spätlese and Auslese wines were made here in 1775 and 1787 respectively. Although Auslese wines were picked in 1983 and 1985 these were not considered up to the estate's minimum standard for this Prädikat, so they were blended with Spätlese wines and sold as such. (The resulting wines are wonderful.)

The baroque cellar beneath the schloss is certainly the most beautiful cask cellar in Germany, and is also perfect from the practical point of view, having a constant low temperature and high humidity. Here the estate's wines are all fermented and matured in wooden casks in the traditional manner. Dry wines have been made since the early seventies, but are only now becoming a really important part of the estate's production. The estate went through a few difficult years during the late seventies and early eighties, as a result of a partial change of ownership (Fürst von Metternich sold 50 per cent of the estate to the Oetker industrial group in 1978), and the retirement of the previous cellarmaster, Josef Staab. While some of the wines from this period were still up to scratch, the wines made from the 1984 vintage onwards have once again been first-class.

There is no way around the fact that the wines of Schloss

Johannisberg are expensive, certainly the most expensive in the region, but when one tastes a fifteen-year-old QbA or Kabinett that is still beautifully fresh, with a scintillatingly brilliant acidity, one tends to forget all about this. Though the estate works very hard for the highest Prädikat wines, Beerenauslese, Trockenbeerenauslese and Eiswein are still rarities here. They are absolutely astounding wines; the stuff legends are made of!

Landgräflich Hessisches Weingut

Karl-Heinrich Glock (director),
Karl Klein (cellarmaster).
Landgräflich Hessisches Weingut,
Grund 1,
D 6222 Geisenheim–Johannisberg.
Tel: 06722 8172.

40 hectares/99 acres.
85% Riesling, 8% Müller-Thurgau, 2% Scheurebe, 5% other varieties.

As a result of considerable vineyard purchases, Landgräflich Hessisches Weingut (Princes of Hessen Foundation) has become one of the largest in the Rheingau. The estate's wines are always correct and of dependable quality, and represent good value for money in a region where it is possible to pay a high price for unexciting wines. In recent years Landgräflich Hessisches Weingut have made particularly good wines from the 1983 vintage, and their wines from the best vineyards in the Johannisberg–Winkel area are always really fine. If a criticism has to be made it is that the wines of lower quality grades, and from the less well-known vineyards, have a tendency to be a little samey. As the estate's winemaker, Herr Klein, has decades of experience behind him, this would appear to be the result of an error of policy somewhere.

Landgräflich Hessisches Weingut's best wines show that a 500-year-old castle is not needed in order to make good wines. From outside, the cellars and offices look like light industrial units. Their unique speciality, for the Rheingau, is wines from the Scheurebe grape variety (grown in the Winkeler Dachsberg vineyard). In a good vintage these can be stunning, and in a poor vintage are best avoided, such is the fickle nature of this grape variety.

Wegeler-Deinhard

Norbert Holderrieth (director).
Wegeler-Deinhard,
(Gutsverwaltung Geheimrat J. Wegeler Erben),
Freidensplatz 9,
D 6227 Oestrich–Winkel.
Tel: 06723 3071.

55 hectares/136 acres.
95% Riesling, 2% Scheurebe, 1.5% Müller-Thurgau,
1% Ruländer (Pinot Gris), 0.5% Gewürztraminer.

Norbert Holderrieth manages Deinhard's estate in Rheingau, one of the largest privately owned estates in the region, with great professionalism. He also oversees the management of the two other Deinhard estates in the Moselle (p. 130), and in the Rheinpfalz (p. 204). Herr Holderrieth's commitment to quality is complete, and his approach to winemaking pragmatic. In general the wines at the Wegeler-Deinhard estate in Oestrich are made with the aim of retaining as much fresh fruitiness as possible, and many never see anything but the inside of a stainless steel tank as a result. However, where necessary, wines are matured in wooden casks, sometimes for many months. This applies particularly to the estate's recently created special de luxe Cuvée 'Geheimrat J', a blend of the best Riesling Spätlese Trocken wines produced at the estate. It was produced in 1983, 1985, and 1986, and sold out rapidly despite its high price. This idea is now being copied by a number of other estates around Germany.

The estate is a committed member of the Charta, having produced Charta wines from the first vintage from the formation of the association (1983). In general, drier wines are an increasingly important part of the estate's production, but the large vineyard area also allows many selected harvest wines to be made. For example, whereas most growers in the Rheingau made wines up to Spätlese grade from the 1983 vintage, Wegeler-Deinhard made wines up to Beerenauslese quality!

Herr Holderrieth also made another in the long series of extremely fine icewines to come out of the estate.

Weingut Riedel

Wolfgang Riedel (owner and director).
Weingut J. Riedel,
Taunusstrasse 1,
D 6227 Hallgarten.
Tel: 06723 3511.

3.5 hectares/8.5 acres.
100% Riesling.

Wolfgang Riedel is probably the most enthusiastic wine producer in the entire Rheingau. As soon as one is introduced to him, he immediately starts a long and passionate exposition of his winemaking philosophy, which is for wines fermented out to dryness in tanks. The wines he makes in this style are very masculine, firm, and racy, but full of flavour. In spite of his opposition to sweeter wines as 'the products of manipulation', he makes some excellent wines in this style that knock spots off the products of the other growers based in Hallgarten.

Hallgarten's wine production is dominated by two co-operatives, whose wines are not poor but are rarely exciting. This has meant that the name of Hallgarten is barely known in comparison to, say, Hattenheim, which is full of estates producing high-quality wines. Only two well-known estates have substantial vineyard holdings in Hallgarten: Fürst Löwenstein and Deinhard. This makes it difficult for a producer like Wolfgang Riedel to acquire the excellent reputation he undoubtedly deserves.

Schloss Schönborn

Robert Englert (director),
Klaus Hermann (assistant director).
Domänenweingut Schloss Schönborn,
Hauptstrasse 53,
D 6228 Eltville–Hattenheim.
Tel: 06723 2007.

45 hectares/110 acres.
88% Riesling, 6% Spätburgunder (Pinot Noir),
6% Müller-Thurgau, Weissburgunder (Pinot Blanc) and
Auxerrois.

The Schloss Schönborn estate has been somewhat slimmed down lately, and new staff have been brought in, after several very difficult years when the winemaking was erratic and the quality of the Schönborn wines was sometimes below what the many excellent vineyards in the estate's possession make possible. The result has been a very rapid transformation, with some good wines made in 1985, and the very best collection of wines in the Rheingau from the 1986 vintage.

The director, Robert Englert, is a remarkable character. For him every wine is like a woman; this one still a pretty young girl, the next a middle-aged woman of strong character and with plenty of determination (sexism, or just an amusing idiosyncrasy?). A native of Württemberg, a region with a strong red wine tradition, Robert Englert has done a great deal for the Spätburgunder wines which Schloss Schönborn make; these can sometimes be as good as fine red Burgundy.

The new generation at the estate is Klaus Hermann, a young and extremely enthusiastic Geisenheim graduate whose work has had much to do with the dramatically improved wines coming out of the estate in the last few years. A larger proportion of dry wines is now being made, including wines from the estate's very best vineyards. These wines are of stunning quality. Anyone doubting whether German dry wines can be truly great should taste a Spätlese Trocken from Schloss Schönborn.

The estate continues to make 'traditional' sweeter-style wines, and those from the Erbacher Marcobrunn and Hattenheimer Pfaffenberg (a Schönborn Monopole) vineyards are among the finest wines of this style produced in the region. The wines from the Schönborn vineyards in Hochheim, which used to be made in a separate cellar there, are now also made in the extensive Hattenheim cellars, and are all the better for this. Here the estate's wines are fermented and matured almost exclusively in wooden Stück casks, in the most traditional manner.

Georg Müller Stiftung

Roland Brossman (director).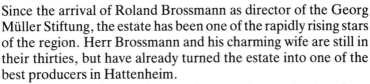
Georg Müller Stiftung Hattenheim
(Weingut der Stadt Eltville),
Erbacher Strasse 7–9,
D 6228 Eltville–Hattenheim.
Tel: 06723 2020.

11 hectares/27 acres.
90% Riesling, 10% other varieties.

Since the arrival of Roland Brossmann as director of the Georg Müller Stiftung, the estate has been one of the rapidly rising stars of the region. Herr Brossmann and his charming wife are still in their thirties, but have already turned the estate into one of the best producers in Hattenheim.

In average and poor vintages the estate's superb wines from the Nussbrunnen and Wisselbrunnen sites are much riper than those from the other Hattenheim vineyards. The wines from the Hattenheimer Schützenhaus and Engelmannsberg vineyards in such difficult years are really steely, but in good vintages they too can be excellent, having the necessary acidity structure to age for decades. Like many estate directors today, Herr Brossmann does not do severe selections of the grapes in order to make Spätlese and Auslese wines. He attaches more importance to making wines with the right balance of ripe fruitiness and acidity, and only makes higher Prädikat wines when a good quantity can be produced. The Georg Müller Stiftung wines are made both in tanks and in wooden casks.

Great things should be expected from the estate in the near future.

Weingut Balthasar Ress

Stefan Ress (owner and director).
Weingut–Weinkellerei Balthasar Ress,
D 6228 Eltville–Hattenheim.
Tel: 06723 3011.

23 hectares/56.5 acres.
84.5% Riesling, 7% Spätburgunder (Pinot Noir),

3.5% Ehrenfelser, 5% Müller-Thurgau, Scheurebe and Reichensteiner.

Stefan Ress is one of the most active promoters of Rheingau wines, so much so that some people say that he does not give his wines enough attention: surely this ought to be taken as a compliment, such has been the lethargy of most German wine producers in telling the world about their fine wines during recent years. However, it is certainly untrue, for in every one of the last half-dozen vintages the Balthasar Ress estate has produced some superb wines, and I have never tasted a really disappointing wine under the estate's label.

Stefan Ress is a firm believer in reductive winemaking, that is keeping the wine completely away from the influence of oxygen during its fermentation and subsequent maturation. He consequently has almost no wooden casks in his cellar, and a great many small stainless steel and fibreglass tanks. Along with Schloss Vollrads and Fürst Löwenstein, his estate is certainly one of the masters of this style of winemaking in the Rheingau. The result of his approach to winemaking is that his wines are tremendously clean and crisp, retaining their initial youthful freshness for a very long time.

Each year since 1979 Stefan Ress has engaged an artist to create a special artist label for a selected wine of particular note from the last vintage. These artist-label wines are available as limited editions at three different price levels, the luxury version including a beautifully framed signed printing of the label on hand-made paper. Each label has been completely different from the others, though there has been a clear tendency towards a more and more complete integration of the bottle and capsule into the artist's conception, to create an art object, rather than a bottle with a picture stuck to it. In 1986 Stefan Ress organised an exhibition of the six artist-label wines produced to date at the Soho Gallery 54 in New York. He plans to take his ever-expanding collection of works to Japan, and then to Britain.

Stefan Ress is also an enthusiastic, completely committed member of the Charta association.

Weingut von Oetinger

Eberhard von Oetinger (owner),
Christoph von Oetinger (director).
Weingut Eberhard Ritter und Edler von Oetinger,
Maximilianshof,
Rheinalle 2,
D 6228 Eltville–Erbach.
Tel: 06123 62648.

7.5 hectares/18.5 acres.
80% Riesling, 10% Müller-Thurgau, 6% Spätburgunder
(Pinot Noir), 4% Ruländer (Pinot Gris).

The Maximilianshof 'Gutsausschank', or wine bar, is the best in the middle Rheingau, whether one sits out in the gardens or in the art-nouveau-style interior. The Oetinger wines also have a very distinctive style, and are made by a highly idiosyncratic version of traditional methods. Though their acidity can be really high, the Oetinger wines are never raw, but racy and powerful. Almost all their wines, apart from the Spätlese and Auslese, are made dry or medium-dry. Unlike the great majority of Rheingau growers, they ensure that any sweetness in the Oetinger wines results from the fermentation being stopped in their temperature controlled fermentation cellar. All the Riesling and Spätburgunder wines are matured in wooden casks, sometimes for well over a year.

Best of all, but in very short supply, are the Erbacher Marcobrunn wines which show just why this vineyard has gained a special reputation. These wines are the perfect combination of complexity and power. Like all the Oetinger wines, they need many years of ageing to show their considerable best. Christoph von Oetinger, who is in the process of taking the estate over from his father, is determined to stick to the estate's unique philosophy and methods, 'Today all too many producers just make wines exactly as they were taught at Geisenheim or one of the other winemaking schools, by rote as it were. We've got our own way of doing things, and I think that this gives our wines a special character. I'd like to think that in many respects we are closer to the region's traditions than most producers here, many of whom systematically deacidify their wines, and don't bother to mature them in wooden casks.'

Schloss Reinhartshausen

Dr Karl-Heinz Zerbe (director).
Administration Schloss Reinhartshausen,
Hauptstrasse 35,
D 6228 Eltville–Erbach.
Tel: 06123 4009.

70 hectares/173 acres.
80% Riesling, 5% Weissburgunder (Pinot Blanc) and
Chardonnay, 5% Spätburgunder (Pinot Noir), 2% Traminer,
8% Kerner, Müller-Thurgau and Ehrenfelser.

Schloss Reinhartshausen is one of the best-known Rheingau estates outside Germany. Unfortunately most of their best wines are sold within Germany, since these are bottled as dry wines, and are therefore not even considered by the majority of non-German buyers.

While the estate's experiments with Chardonnay have attracted a lot of interest, they seem to have distracted the estate a little from what should be its principal business: the making of great Riesling wines which are the traditional product of the region. There is also a tendency for the estate to sometimes play around a bit too much with very long cask ageing, and with gimmicky marketing ideas. On the plus side, the estate's wine-making seems to have been sharpened up quite a bit recently. In spite of not having a clear enough strategy in the cellar or on the marketing side, the best Schloss Reinhartshausen wines can still be impressive.

Weingut Dr R. Weil

Robert Weil (owner),
Wilhelm Weil (director).
Weingut Dr R. Weil,
Mühlberg 5,
D 6229 Kiedrich.
Tel: 06123 2308.

18 hectares/46.5 acres.
94% Riesling, 4% Spätburgunder (Pinot Noir),
2% Müller-Thurgau.

The Dr Weil estate is one of the best in the entire Rheingau, and without doubt is currently the best producer in Kiedrich, and of wines from the great Kiedricher Gräfenberg vineyard. This is as it was a hundred years ago, when the estate's best private customer was the Kaiser. He regularly served their wines at dinner alongside the finest clarets and champagnes.

The estate has a remarkable cellar, with enough space to make a whole harvest either in steel tanks or in wooden casks! In fact the wines are all fermented in tanks, and as at the Oetinger estate any sweetness in them is the result of the fermentation being stopped, though here this is done with pressure (from the carbon dioxide gas produced by the fermenting wines). As a result, nearly all the wines retain a 'Spritz' of carbon dioxide, which makes the estate's wines very fresh and lively and helps to preserve them for a very long time. Nearly all the wines are matured in wooden casks for several months.

The estate is now being run by Wilhelm Weil, who found control of the estate thrust upon him the day he left the Geisenheim viticultural and winemaking school in 1986, when his father was very suddenly taken seriously ill. He is keen to continue with the style his father established, making medium-dry and traditional-style wines (with a very modest level of sweetness). Wilhelm is also keen to continue working to make the best possible QbA wines, since these are the normal product of the Kiedrich vineyards which lie far back from, and high above, the Rhine. However, when a really good vintage comes, of which 1985 was the latest, then the late-harvested Spätlese wines from the Gräfenberg can be unexcelled in the entire region.

Interestingly, the wonderful ornately half-timbered estate house in its beautiful park-like gardens was built by an Englishman, Baron Sutton, in the middle of the last century.

Weingut Hans Hulbert

Adam Hulbert (owner and director).
Weingut Hans Hulbert,
Friedrichstrasse 59,
D 6228 Eltville.
Tel: 06123 2910.

7 hectares/17 acres.
84% Riesling, 8% Spätburgunder (Pinot Noir),
6% Müller-Thurgau, 2% other varieties.

The Rheingau is quite a compact region, and as a result of its fame is very well explored. It was therefore a real delight to stumble upon a genuine discovery in the form of Adam Hulbert's estate in Eltville. Adam Hulbert is a tall, bearded man, reserved yet very warm, and of scrupulous honesty. Unlike many estates in the Rheingau, when the word Riesling appears on the label, then what is in the bottle really is 100 per cent Riesling. He also has respect for the comments of customers and visitors, adding his own honest, and often critical, comments after theirs. It is such self-criticism that has caused Adam Hulbert to make numerous changes to the estate's winemaking since he took over in 1968, and visiting him today one feels that the process of evolution is still under way.

The Hulbert estate looks from the outside as though it is no more than a large suburban home, and the cellars are a working place where no concessions to tourism have been made; visitors have to pick their way carefully between the casks, tanks, pumps and other machines. However, the wines are classical Rheingau Rieslings, always completely clean and clear, with a pronounced acidity. In recent years deacidification of the wines has been virtually abandoned, making them even racier.

Adam Hulbert takes many risks in pursuit of Spätlese and Auslese wines, since there is a family tradition for making them. Some of the finest, the most beautifully fresh and elegant 1959, 1964, and 1971 Rheingau wines I have tasted, have come from Weingut Hulbert. What makes a visit to this estate such a delight, is not just the wines though, but also the extraordinarily friendly welcome which Adam and Doreen Hulbert give all their visitors. They are the good people behind a good estate, which is sadly little-known.

Weingut J. Fischer Erben

Fraulein Helga Fischer (owner and director).
Weingut J. Fischer Erben,
Weinhohle,
D 6228 Eltville.
Tel: 06123 2858.

7.5 hectares/18.5 acres.
95% Riesling, 5% other varieties.

It is difficult to tell exactly how old Fräulein Fischer is, but she must be at least seventy. In spite of this she does almost all the estate's vineyard work herself! It really fills one with faith in life to meet a woman of Fräulein Fischer's age with such seemingly unflagging energy for her work. The estate's wines, while rarely scaling the greatest heights, are very classic Rheingau Rieslings with as much vigour as Fräulein Fischer herself. When the estate does make a Spätlese or Auslese, these wines can be absolutely sensational. The best 1967 German wine I ever tasted was from the Fischer estate, and it was still full of life at twenty years of age. The estate's normal products are Kabinett wines of all levels of sweetness, except sticky sweet. The drier wines from the estate are very good, though their acidity is uncompromising. All the wines are made traditionally, the dry wines being fermented out to as near complete dryness as they will go.

Verwaltung der Staatsweingüter Eltville

Dr Hans Ambrosi (director).
Verwaltung der Staatsweingüter Eltville,
Schwalbacher Strasse 56–62,
D 6228 Eltville.
Tel: 06123 61055.

157 hectares/388 acres.
85% Riesling, 10% Spätburgunder (Pinot Noir), 5% other
varieties.

The State Wine Domaine in Eltville is in fact an amalgamation of the seven state-owned Rheingau estates: in Assmannshausen, Rüdesheim, Hattenheim, Steinberg, Rauenthal, Eltville and

Hochheim. Though the façade of the estate buildings dates from 1911, the winemaking facilities are extremely modern and very extensive. The great majority of the State Domaine's wines are fermented and matured in stainless steel tanks, but some wooden casks are retained for the top wines. In spite of having excellent vineyards and well equipped cellars, the State Domaine's wines were often very disappointing during the years from the last enlargement of the cellar facilities (1976) until the 1984 vintage, from which time there has been a steady improvement in quality and a distinct change of style.

Though the majority (70 per cent) of the State Domaine's wines are still made in the sweeter style, their sweetness is right on the lower limit which the law sets for this style. As a result, the really racy wines from the estate's great monopole vineyard, the Steinberg, and its extensive holdings in Rauenthal *taste* dry or virtually dry, even if the words Trocken or Halbtrocken do not appear on the label. These vineyards undoubtedly yield the estate's finest wines, wines with a nerviness and piquancy quite different from the rather richer, lightly earthy wines of the vineyards close to the Rhine. The sweeping slopes of the Rauenthaler Berg and the Steinberg suggest that they must yield wines of an altogether austerer, firmer style than those from the gentle countryside around Eltville, Erbach and Hattenheim only a couple of miles away.

In fine vintages, like 1983, 1976, or 1971, the Rauenthal and Steinberg wines are among the greatest in the Rheingau, because they then have an extra spur of acidity together with the richness common to all wines from such vintages. After five or more years of bottle age they then show a remarkable spicy complexity, with flint, and even gunpowder tones. The recent change of winemaking policy at the state domaine means that wines capable of developing this character are once again being produced.

Dr Ambrosi, a middle-aged man of Romanian extraction, has very strong opinions which are saved from being dogma by his sharp, wry wit. Perhaps his major contribution to the State Domaine has been the development of icewine production on an almost industrial scale. Barely a vintage has gone by during the last twenty years without the estate harvesting at least one icewine. Whereas most estates would be very happy to harvest as little as 500 litres of such wine in an ideal vintage, the Rheingau State Domaine harvested virtually four times that quantity in 1984, a vintage many considered completely unsuitable for icewines! This, indeed, is the problem with these wines; icewine harvesting concentrates whatever is in the grapes, and if this is unripe, then the resulting wine is a concentration of unripeness. . . . In ripe vintages with clean grapes the result is altogether better, but this is not accepted by Dr Ambrosi, who actually favours the State Domaine's icewines from the unripe vintages over those from the ripe years!

Reuter & Sturm

Helmut Sturm (director).
Reuter & Sturm GmbH,
Hauptstrasse 12a,
D 6229 Walluf.
Tel: 06123 72565/73367.

The quality of the sparkling wines which Helmut Sturm makes is demonstrated by the number of top Rheingau estates that bring wines to him to be turned into Sekt. These include Freiherr Langwerth von Simmern, Landgraf von Hessen, the Staatsweingut Assmannshausen, and Weingut Hulbert. However, the best sparkling wines he produces are the small range of super de luxe Sekts sold under the 'Reuter & Sturm Classic' label. These are completely hand-made products, even the corking being done manually using tools over a century old.

Very few non-champagne sparkling wines have the finesse and elegance of a Reuter & Sturm Brut or Extra Brut Riesling Sekt, a fact which Helmut Sturm puts down not only to this hand-making, 'which really does make a difference to the quality', but also to the extremely rigorous selection of the base wines. These are selected in the early spring, when the new vintage's wines are clear enough to taste. Helmut Sturm then tours many small estates and several co-operatives in the Rheingau looking for Riesling and Spätburgunder wines with the right harmony. 'The reason why German sparkling wines were of such generally poor quality,' he insists, 'is not because we lack the potential for making fine sparkling wines – quite the opposite – but because only the poorest wines were turned into Sekt. Our policy is the opposite to this, and we only work with wines which are ideal to make Sekt with. Given this I don't think it's surprising that the end result is good.' It certainly is very good, but all that hand labour means that it is not cheap either.

Geheimrat Aschrott

Holger Schwab (director).
Geheimrat Aschrott'sche Erben
*   Weingutsverwaltung,*
Kirchstrasse 38,
D 6203 Hochheim am Main.
Tel: 06146 2207.

20 hectares/49.5 acres.
95% Riesling, 2% Spätburgunder (Pinot Noir),
2% Müller-Thurgau, 1% Gewürztraminer.

In spite of being technically a part of the Rheingau, and thus a Rhine region, Hochheim lies close to the Main river, slightly to the east and south of Wiesbaden. Hochheim's wines have a very different character from those of the rest of the Rheingau, principally on account of the much heavier soils. In this respect, the wines from the Hölle and Domdechaney vineyards are the quintessential wines of the area, since here the earthiness and smokiness typical of Hochheim wines are most pronounced. When these wines are correctly made, which means with a concern to preserve their freshness, then they develop very slowly into wines of great power and complexity.

Of all the Hochheim estates, the one which most often succeeds in the balancing act of making wines which have the fullness of flavour Hochheimers should have without letting them become crude or heavy is Geheimrat Aschrott. This estate, tucked away among the narrow streets of the beautifully preserved old town, is owned by a group of six Englishmen, several of whom now live in Australia. It has been managed since 1949 by the Schwab family. Holger Schwab is a slightly reserved, serious man who needs a little time to open out, much as his wines do. Virtually all the estate's wines are made in wooden casks, but he always bottles them very early.

When an excellent vintage for the area comes, like 1971, 1979, or 1986, the wines can have a bouquet so strong that it literally leaps up from the glass as the wine is poured. Herr Schwab makes a good proportion of the Aschrott wines dry and medium-dry, and these are never thin or weak.

Domdechant Werner'sches Weingut

Dr Franz Werner Michel (owner).
Domdechant Werner'sches Weingut,
Rathausstrasse 30,
D 6203 Hochheim.
Tel: 06146 2008.

12 hectares/30 acres.
95% Riesling, 3% Spätburgunder (Pinot Noir),
2% Ehrenfelser.

Dr Michel's estate owns vineyards in virtually all the same sites as Geheimrat Aschrott, whose cellars are only a few streets away. In both these cellars the wines are fermented and matured in wooden casks. Yet there is a very clear difference between the wines of these two producers, who at first glance would appear to be nearly identical. This is a particularly fine example of how the smallest differences in winemaking can turn nearly identical batches of grape must into quite different wines in the cellars of neighbouring estates. Since the 1984 vintage the Domdechant wines have become much firmer and fresher, and are now consistently leaner and more racy than those of Geheimrat Aschrott. This has pluses and minuses, for although the Dom-dechant wines clearly have the potential for very long ageing, they do not have as much of the rich fruitiness and earthiness associated with Hochheim wines. However, Dr Michel's estate particularly shines in average or difficult vintages like 1984 and 1987, when excellent wines were made.

Staatsweingut Bergstrasse

Heinrich Hillenbrand (director).
Staatsweingut Bergstrasse,
Grieselstrasse 34–36,
D 6140 Bensheim.
Tel: 06251 3107.

31.5 hectares/77.5 acres.
66% Riesling, 11% Müller-Thurgau, 7% Ruländer (Pinot
Gris), 4% Weissburgunder (Pinot Blanc),
2.5% Spätburgunder (Pinot Noir), 2.5% Gewürztraminer,
7% Scheurebe, Huxerebe and other varieties.

Members of the Hillenbrand family have run the Bergstrasse
State Domaine since 1904, and their continuous commitment
has meant that the estate has consistently made good wines for
many decades. The style of the wines is a little broader and
juicier than that of the Rheingau State Domaine (with which
they share common marketing and sales departments), as a result of the generally heavier soils here. The Bergstrasse State
Domaine's wines are fermented exclusively in old wooden casks.
Quite a large proportion of the wines are made in drier styles,
and, as at the Rheingau Staatsweingüter, icewines are a regularly made speciality. They can be quite superb.

Rheinhessen

It is difficult to talk about Rheinhessen as a region. It is really
more of an *area*, a 25,000 hectare/61,750 acre expanse of
vineyards (and agricultural land) sitting in the middle of the
western side of Germany. The majority of this great swathe of
vineyards produces cheap Liebfraumilch, Bereich Nierstein,
and Niersteiner Gutes Domtal QbA wines, most of which are
bland and rather characterless. However, that part of Rheinhessen close to the Rhine on the eastern side of the region is
altogether different. Friedel Bohn of Weingut Anton Balbach
has founded the Rhine Terrace (Rhein Terrasse) Association,
devoted to giving this part of Rheinhessen a clearer, more
distinct identity. Their area certainly produces the larger part of
the finer wines from the classic grape varieties in Rheinhessen
(the remainder come from the Bingen–Ingelheim area). What
the region as a whole needs is exactly this kind of focus where
high qualities are seen to be produced, so that Rheinhessen's
reputation as a bulk wine-producing area can be overcome.

Unfortunately, rather few growers in the Rhine Terrace area
produce the fine qualities which are possible here. There ought
to be a huge difference between a Niersteiner Gutes Domtal

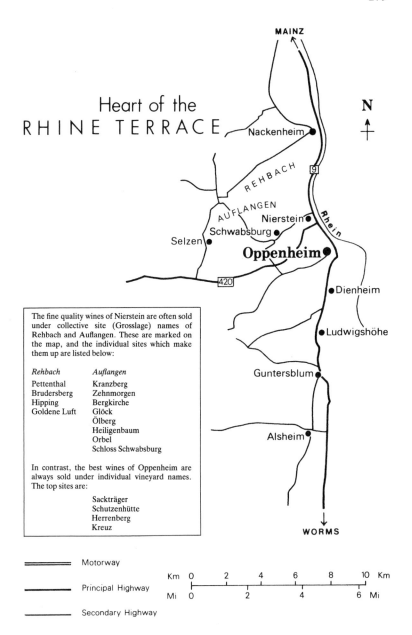

Heart of the
RHINE TERRACE

MAINZ

N

Nackenheim

REHBACH

AUFLANGEN

Nierstein
Schwabsburg
Selzen
Oppenheim

420

Dienheim

Ludwigshöhe

Guntersblum

Alsheim

WORMS

Rhein

9

The fine quality wines of Nierstein are often sold under collective site (Grosslage) names of Rehbach and Auflangen. These are marked on the map, and the individual sites which make them up are listed below:

Rehbach	*Auflangen*
Pettenthal	Kranzberg
Brudersberg	Zehnmorgen
Hipping	Bergkirche
Goldene Luft	Glöck
	Ölberg
	Heiligenbaum
	Orbel
	Schloss Schwabsburg

In contrast, the best wines of Oppenheim are always sold under individual vineyard names. The top sites are:

Sackträger
Schutzenhütte
Herrenberg
Kreuz

══════ Motorway

━━━━━ Principal Highway

───── Secondary Highway

Km 0   2   4   6   8   10 Km

Mi 0   2   4   6 Mi

The Rhine Terrace area of Rheinhessen

blended wine, and a single vineyard Riesling wine from Nierstein. Such a real Niersteiner, or a wine from one of the
neighbouring villages which also have good vineyards, *can* be
every bit as good as a fine Rheingau wine. Sadly, however, there
is often only a small difference in quality which does not justify
the price differential. The fact is that the commercialisation of
the lesser wines of the region under the famous names of
Nierstein, Oppenheim, and Bingen has made it hardly worth
while for estates or co-operatives to bother making top-quality
wines, because there is little to distinguish them from the mass-
produced wines when they reach the shelf. Those who, in spite of
this, produce superb wines deserve the highest praise for doing
so against all commercial odds.

This is a region where the younger generation (though some of
them are well over thirty years of age) are making a big impact. It
is they who are finally pulling the region round after the degen-
eration of recent decades. This even applies to some of the better
parts of the hinterland of Rheinhessen, from where some excellent wines are beginning to emerge. These already ought to give
the more sluggish producers in Nierstein something to worry
about!

The key to Rheinhessen's future must be with Riesling in the
best vineyard sites, Silvaner and the Pinot grape varieties in the
second-class sites, Müller-Thurgau in the third. The great
acreage of the new vine crossings should be pulled up, and only a
part of it replanted with these varieties. 'RS', the Rheinhessen
dry Silvaner which numerous estates and co-operatives in the
region produce, and sell under a very modern common label, is a
most important part of the process of re-establishing a regional
identity. All the signs are that the region is on the way up again,
though this is a painful experience for many.

Well-made Rheinhessen wines from the classic grape varieties
are almost never as firm and austere as Rheingau wines, normally being a little broader and earthier. However, at their best
the Rieslings can have real refinement and complexity, and
great ageing potential. The Silvaner wines, which should be
bone-dry to show their best, have a neutral, chalky character,
which is very satisfying. The Weissburgunder wines can also be
really first-class, dry, rich and powerful.

Weingut Villa Sachsen, Rheinhessen

Heinz Brandstetter (cellarmaster).
Weingut Villa Sachsen,
Mainzer Strasse 184,
D 6530 Bingen.
Tel: 06721 70231.

30 hectares/74 acres.
65% Riesling, 10% Kerner, 10% Silvaner,
15% Müller-Thurgau, Weissburgunder (Pinot Blanc) and
Ruländer (Pinot Gris).

The Villa Sachsen estate, situated in a magnificent romantic-style early nineteenth-century villa directly across the Rhine from Rüdesheim, is perhaps the only producer who realises the potential of the great Binger Scharlachberg vineyard. Owing to the exceptional exposure of this steeply sloping site, and the estate's reduction of yields to less than half the average for Rheinhessen, they are able to harvest some QmP grade wines virtually every vintage. What makes this success story remarkable is that they are owned by the giant Nestlé company, and are a small cog in an industrial empire; something normally guaranteed to wreck a fine wine estate.

Herr Brandstetter is an ardent traditionalist, and almost all the wines are fermented and matured in wooden casks. The wines are handled very little, and often have a slight sparkle of carbon dioxide. Herr Brandstetter is convinced that this is a good sign, saying, 'if you've handled a wine so carefully that it still retains some CO_2 from the fermentation, then it will also retain all the finer aroma compounds too. This is something not widely understood, and some colleagues mistakenly think that we put CO_2 into the wines in order to keep them fresh!'

While the Villa Sachsen wines range from bone-dry Riesling Kabinetts to lusciously sweet Beerenauslese and Trockenbeerenauslese (made in 1976, 1979, 1983, 1985, and 1986!), and even includes organically produced wines, their most important product is Binger Scharlachberg Riesling Kabinett. This is normally made medium-dry, and is ideally suited to drinking with fine cuisine, particularly with river fish. The estate is proof that the Nierstein–Oppenheim area of Rheinhessen does not have a monopoly on elegant Riesling wines in this region.

Weingut Schloss Westerhaus

Dr Heinz von Opel (owner),
Otto Guthier (director).
Weingut Irmgard von Opel Schloss
  Westerhaus,
D 6507 Ingelheim am Rhein.
Tel: 06130 6674.

13 hectares/32 acres.
51% Riesling, 12% Müller-Thurgau, 20% Spätburgunder
(Pinot Noir), 5% Gewürztraminer, 12% Weissburgunder
(Pinot Blanc), Chardonnay and Ruländer (Pinot Gris).

Since Otto Guthier arrived at Schloss Westerhaus in 1982 immediately after completing his studies at the Geisenheim viti-

cultural and winemaking school, he has steadily pulled the estate up from a fairly run-down condition to the point where it is now being recognised as one of the best estates in the entire region. This is all the more remarkable when you see the estate's vineyards, the majority of which are *east*-facing. This is hardly the ideal exposure in such a northerly climate. On the positive side, these vineyards do greatly benefit from the proximity of the Rhine, just a few miles to the north; from the tasting room at Schloss Westerhaus is a fine view of the Rheingau.

Otto Guthier and Dr von Opel, who also owns and directs the largest lead capsule factory in Germany, could hardly be more committed to the estate, and work closely together. In the last few years yields have been reduced, and much more selective picking has been done. The result of the latter work was that in 1986, not a vintage of remarkable quality in the more northerly Rhine regions, Schloss Westerhaus harvested *six* different Beerenauslese wines! The press-house work has also been greatly sharpened up, with the grapes being processed much more quickly than in the past. The exception to this are the Gewürztraminer and Ruländer grapes, which are given some skin contact after being milled, to extract a fuller flavour. Each grape variety is dealt with individually, so that all the estate's wines are 100 per cent varietals.

Otto Guthier is very keen that virtually all the estate's wines should ferment and mature in wood. However, great care is taken to work very cleanly, and the wines are ready for bottling by Christmas. They are then stored in cask or tank until they reach exactly the right point of development for bottling. Experiments with new-oak ageing for the red wines are under way, but this is being approached with some caution. Schloss Westerhaus is undoubtedly an estate to watch in the next years.

Weingut Gunderloch-Usinger

Friedrich Hasselbach (director),
Agnes Hasselbach-Usinger (owner and director).
Weingut Gunderloch-Usinger,
Carl-Gunderloch-Platz 1,
D 6506 Nackenheim.
Tel: 06135 2341.

11.5 hectares/28.5 acres.
70% Riesling, 20% Silvaner, 5% Müller-Thurgau,
5% Ruländer (Pinot Gris), Kerner, Scheurebe and Huxelrebe.

Weingut Gunderloch-Usinger is one of the rapidly rising stars of the Rhine Terrace area of Rheinhessen which stretches from Bodenheim, just south of Mainz, to Osthofen, just north of Worms. Their Riesling wines from the Rothenberg, and Silvaner wines from the Engelsberg in Nackenheim, are absolutely classic examples of the combination of fullness and elegance which the wines from these varieties can achieve here.

The young couple who run the estate, Fritz and Agnes Hasselbach, are extremely modest about the quality of their wines, to the point where both seem surprised and a little overwhelmed when their wines are praised. They are completely without pretention, and have a pleasingly direct approach to winemaking. Their minimum standards for each of the Prädikat levels are extremely stringent, and are way above the legal minima. The yield from their vineyards is also small, with the classic varieties giving an average of only 45 hectolitres per hectare (1800 litres per acre)! There is exceptionally little handling or treatment of the wines, and when Süssreserve is added in order to give the wines some sweetness, this has always been made from their own grapes, and is from the same vine variety as the wine to which it is added.

There is no deacidification of the Gunderloch-Usinger wines, Fritz Hasselbach feeling that 'in our region it is often having a little bit more acidity, rather than a little bit more ripeness, that makes the difference between a good and a great vintage. Therefore, it would really be silly to take away any of the acidity. However, we have recognised that in order to round off the slightly higher acidity our wines now have, to harmonise them, they must mature a little longer in cask than was once the case. As a result, we rarely bottle any wines before the middle of May now.' Such care in balancing the different elements of the winemaking process is essential to the production of really fine wines.

The estate's speciality, of which they are undoubtedly the masters for the Rhine regions, is Ruländer. In Germany this is normally a rather plump, heavy, sweet wine, but the Hasselbach's have created a new style. Their Ruländer is dry, is an Auslese Trocken almost every vintage, and has exactly the delicate pink blush, and refined flowery-honey bouquet of the greatest Tokay–Pinot Gris wines from Alsace, save that it is perhaps even finer!

Weingut Heinrich Braun

Peter H. Braun (owner and director).
Weingut Heinrich Braun,
Neugasse 9,
D 6505 Nierstein.
Tel: 06133 5130.

18 hectares/44.5 acres.
60% Riesling, 20% Müller-Thurgau, 5% Silvaner,
5% Ruländer (Pinot Gris), 3% Gewürztraminer, 7% other
varieties.

Peter Braun produces some of the finest dry Riesling wines in Germany, the best of which is an extraordinary Spätlese Trocken from the Pettenthal vineyard. The reason why this wine is particularly interesting is that the Riesling vines planted here are a Moselle type (in fact a clone from Leiwen on the Middle Moselle), and this gives the wine a remarkable floweriness quite unlike the normal character of Riesling wines produced on the red slate soils in this vineyard.

Peter Braun is an extremely energetic, but also slightly disorganised man, and one gets a feeling that the slightly erratic quality of his wines is ultimately caused by his personality. None the less, in every style from bone-dry Kabinett to rich, sweet Auslese the estate produces some really first-class traditionally made Riesling and Silvaner wines. In the cellar, which has recently received a much-needed clean up and reorganisation, tanks are used as well as wooden casks, and since the 1985 vintage several wines each year have been made in new oak casks (Limousin oak). The oak flavour in these 'barrique' wines, which are sold in a special bottle, is very pronounced.

The estate's cellars are also used by the Gräflich Wolff-Metternich'sches Weingut, an estate which is owned by Peter Braun's wife. These wines are made in a very similar way to those from the Heinrich Braun estate, and are of comparably high quality.

Weingut Gustav Gessert

Kraft Gessert (owner and director),
Peter Gessert (director).
Weingut Gustav Gessert,
Wörrstadter Strasse 84,
D 6505 Nierstein.
Tel: 06133 5642.

10 hectares/24.5 acres.
50% Riesling, 20% Silvaner, 20% Müller-Thurgau,
5% Kerner, 5% other varieties.

The modern buildings which house the family estate that Kraft and Peter Gessert run suggest that they are newcomers to the Nierstein area. Nothing could be further from the truth, the family having documentary proof that they have been involved in viticulture in the Nierstein area for over 300 years. The reason for the new buildings was that the cellars they originally had in the centre of town were very cramped, and they felt it was important to gain enough space to work easily. They now have enough cask and tank space to be able to decide which type of vessel any particular wine ought to be made in; an ideal position.

The Gessert Rieslings are quite full, typical Rhine Terrace wines, with plenty of fruit and extract. Though the majority of them are still made in the sweeter style, Peter Gessert is working hard to bring their clients round to dry wines, so that the proportion of these can be increased. Certainly if the wines of this area are to be drunk young, then the subtle minerally tones which make the best Nierstein wines so complex are more apparent in the dry-style wines. The excellent dry Rieslings and Silvaners from the Gessert estate are a little leaner and firmer in style than the sweeter wines, which can sometimes be quite soft. Altogether, the Gesserts produce wines of a very dependable quality, the best of which, sweet and dry, are really fine.

Weingut Anton Balbach

Friedel Bohn (director).
Weingut Bürgermeister Anton Balbach,
Mainzer Strasse 64,
D 6505 Nierstein.
Tel: 06133 5585.

18 hectares/44.5 acres.
80% Riesling, 10% Müller-Thurgau, 5% Silvaner,
5% Kerner.

It was completely in character that I should first have met Friedel Bohn at the Hyatt Regency Hotel in San Francisco. Herr Bohn travels extraordinarily widely selling his wines, and promoting the 'Rhine Terrace', which he invented (see p. 178). This is an excellent concept, for the wines of this area are distinctly different from, and generally finer than, those from the hinterland of Rheinhessen. He is now the president of the Rhine Terrace Association, which is doing more and more to make the area known throughout Germany and abroad.

For some years the Balbach wines have been made almost exclusively in stainless steel tanks, Friedel Bohn being a fan of very fresh wines with a 'Spritz' of carbon dioxide. The majority of his wines are in the sweeter style, and these can be very sweet, sometimes to the point where the Riesling character is a little smothered. The dry wines from the Balbach estate are very full, masculine wines, with a lot of character.

Weingut Kapellenhof

Volker Schätzel (owner),
Thomas Schätzel (director).
Weingut Kapellenhof,
Ökonomierat Schätzel Erben,
D 6501 Selzen.
Tel: 06737 204.

15 hectares/37 acres.
30% Riesling, 20% Silvaner, 18% Müller-Thurgau,
7% Kerner, 7% Ehrenfelser, 7% Portugieser and Dornfelder,
6% Ruländer (Pinot Gris) and Gewürztraminer,
5% Scheurebe.

It is indeed rare to find a wine producer in Rheinhessen, a region which is renowned in Germany and around the world for producing sweet wines, who is a specialist in dry wines. However, for some years Volker and Thomas Schätzel have produced predominantly medium-dry and dry wines. In particular, their Silvaner wines, which come from vines of a special very old clone of this variety, are extremely fine, Silvaner wines with real finesse.

These, and their equally fine Rieslings, are always made in wooden casks ranging from 300 to 2400 litres in size. The complete clarity and freshness of their wines speaks volumes for the care taken with cellar work at the estate. With Thomas Schätzel only having been back at the estate after completing his studies since 1984, there is every reason to hope for even better things from this already fine estate in the future.

Weingut Louis Guntrum

Hanns-Joachim Louis Guntrum (owner and director),
Lorenz Guntrum (owner and director).
Weingut Louis Guntrum,
Rheinallee 62,
D 6505 Nierstein.
Tel: 06133 5101.

67.5 hectares/166.5 acres.
28% Riesling, 25% Müller-Thurgau, 14% Silvaner,
9% Scheurebe, 7% Kerner, 4% Ruländer (Pinot Gris),
3% Gewürztraminer, 10% other varieties.

Hanns-Joachim Louis Guntrum is without doubt the most active international promoter of fine Rheinhessen wines, and an enthusiastic champion of fine German wines altogether. With the greatest possible charm he dismisses the official promotion of German wines as 'hopeless', and goes his own way. His words are in no sense empty, for the Guntrum wines from the traditional grape varieties are excellent, and those from the new crossings are usually most attractive too (quite an achievement in itself).

In particular, Hajo, as his contacts around the world are asked to call him, has done an enormous amount to awaken wine drinkers in many countries to an awareness of how fine German

dry wines are, and how admirably they complement a wide
variety of dishes. At the head of his range of dry wines is the
'Guntrum Dry', a bone-dry Müller-Thurgau which offers a
modestly priced easy introduction to drier German wines. Consistently good as this wine has been since the concept was
developed, the Spätlese and Auslese Trocken wines produced
by the estate are more than a class better. So far, such powerful
dry wines have been produced from Riesling, Silvaner, Gewürztraminer, and Kerner, and all have been impressive.

This is not to say that the sweeter-style wines are ignored by
the estate, rather that Hajo feels that the traditional dry style
must be revived to complement the wines which those outside
Germany have long enjoyed. The finest sweeter wines from the
estate are undoubtedly the Rieslings from the Sackträger, and
Guntrum's monopole Schutzenhütte vineyard. A vertical tasting
of wines from this vineyard undertaken at the top of the Schutzenhütte, a small observation tower at the edge of the partially
ruined Oppenheim town walls, demonstrated just how consistent a quality this top site gives.

To distinguish his very best wines, dry, medium-dry and
sweet, Hajo has developed 'Guntrum Classic'. This is a special
range packaged in the very long traditional flute bottle of the
Rhine regions. The standard of these is very high.

Weingut Bürgermeister Carl Koch Erben

Klaus Stieh-Koch (owner and director),
Carl-Hermann Stieh-Koch (owner and director).
Weingut Bürgermeister Carl Koch Erben,
Wormser Strasse 62,
D 6504 Oppenheim.
Tel: 06133 2326.

11 hectares/27 acres.
40% Riesling, 20% Silvaner, 10% Müller-Thurgau,
30% Weissburgunder (Pinot Blanc), Ruländer (Pinot Gris),
Spätburgunder (Pinot Noir), Scheurebe and Kerner.

Thankfully, the Carl Koch estate has begun to attract some
attention outside Germany, but considering that it produces
some of the very best Oppenheim wines it is still far too little
known. With the increasing involvement of the new generation

of the Koch family, Carl-Hermann, recently the quality of the best wines has reached the highest level. This fact has not, perhaps, received the acknowledgement it deserves, on account of the current vogue around the world for light, very fresh wines. The wines from Oppenheim are full-bodied, big wines, almost the opposite of what the average wine drinker today is supposed to be seeking. However, they are wines of great character, packed with fruit.

The Koch estate is housed in a most remarkable building which can only be described as a 'semi-schloss', and which has a distinctly fairy-tale quality to it. The building has been added to at several points over the centuries, though part of it dates back to the early Middle Ages. It is tacked onto a remnant of the Oppenheim town wall, directly in front of which is a small patch of Silvaner vines. Above this is the garden, which is of a formal design, that has 'relaxed' over the years. The estate is worth a visit just to see this.

Carl-Hermann Koch is a little shy, or perhaps it is simply that he would rather be down in the cellar with the wines. He is certainly an extremely conscientious winemaker. He wishes that it was still possible for them to be able to wait to bottle all the wines until immediately before the next harvest, as was once the case. Today the demand for their Kabinett wines is so great that this is no longer possible, but Carl insists that if he thinks the best wines need a year's cask maturation then they get it. The same applies to bottle maturation, the higher Prädikat wines only becoming available when they drink well.

Though Carl's first love is the Riesling wines, the estate is rapidly developing dry Weissburgunder into a speciality. Grown on the heavy chalky soils of Oppenheim it gives wines with the same kind of power – 13 degrees of naturally achieved alcohol! – and richness as top white Burgundies.

Weingut P. J. Valckenberg

Wilhelm Steifensand (director).
Weingut P. J. Valckenberg,
Weckerlingplatz 1,
D 6520 Worms.
Tel: 06241 6871.

4 hectares/10 acres.
80% Riesling, 20% Gewürztraminer, Weissburgunder (Pinot Blanc) and Ehrenfelser.

The Wormser Liebfrauenstift-Kirchenstück vineyard, now rather incongruously surrounded by the suburban and industrial development of Worms, was the original Liebfraumilch vineyard. Liebfraumilch production has long since grown to such an enormous degree that this vineyard has been given a different name to distinguish its wines from the blended regional wines bearing the Liebfraumilch name.

The largest owner of this site is the Valckenberg family, who own and run one of the most important wine exporting houses in Germany. Wilhelm Steifensand, whose principal duties in the family firm are those of export director, has taken a special interest in these wines. They are now of very good quality, particularly considering that though this vineyard benefits from the proximity of the Rhine, it is not one of the top sites of the region. The Rieslings are elegant wines with a marked acidity and a firm fruitiness. The best are capable of developing for some years in bottle. A good proportion are made in the drier styles, and with considerable success.

Rheinpfalz

The Rheinpfalz, or Palatinate as it is more commonly called in English, is, like Rheinhessen, a large, sprawling region. However, it has an area identified with fine quality which has not been sullied by crude commercialisation. This is the Middle Haardt (Mittel Haardt) area centred around the famous wine villages of Wachenheim, Forst, and Deidesheim. These certainly are not the only parts of the region where high-quality wines are produced, but that at least part of the region has a long tradition for quality does much for the reputation of the region as a whole.

The landscape of the Palatinate is very similar to that of Burgundy and is geologically and climatically a continuation of Alsace. The vineyards are mostly situated on the lower slopes of the eastern side of the Haardt mountains which run roughly north–south; the landscape looking almost identical to the Côte d'Or in Burgundy. Like the Alsatian vineyards, those of the

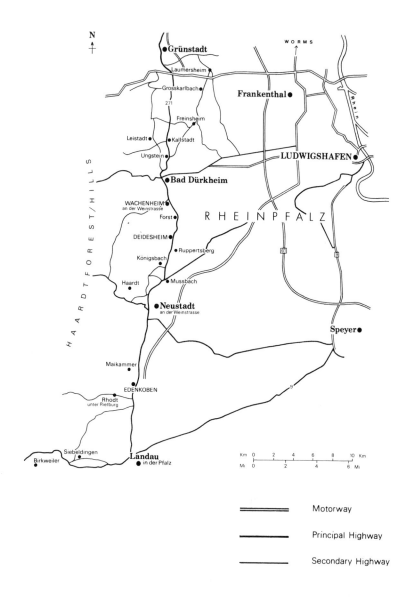

N

W O R M S

●Grünstadt

Laumersheim

Grosskarlbach●

271

Freinsheim

Frankenthal ●

Leistadt ●

● Kallstadt

Ungstein ●

LUDWIGSHAFEN ●

● Bad Dürkheim

WACHENHEIM
an der Weinstrasse

Forst ●

R H E I N P F A L Z

DEIDESHEIM ●

● Ruppertsberg

Königsbach
●

Haardt
● Mussbach

● Neustadt
an der Weinstrasse

Speyer●

H A A R D T   F O R E S T / H I L L S

Maikammer
●

EDENKOBEN

9

Rhodt
unter Rietburg

Siebeldingen
●

Birkweiler
●

Landau
● in der Pfalz

Km 0   2   4   6   8   10 Km
Mi 0   2   4   6 Mi

═══════════   Motorway

───────────   Principal Highway

───────────   Secondary Highway

The Rheinpfalz

Palatinate receive a great amount of sunshine, and comparatively little rain. The Palatinate even has many of the same grape varieties as those which dominate Alsace's and Burgundy's production: Riesling, Gewürztraminer, Weissburgunder, Ruländer, and Spätburgunder.

The difference between the Palatinate and the larger part of these French regions is the soil, which is generally light and sandy, or of limestone, in the Palatinate. There are some areas where the soil is so open that erosion is a big problem, and terracing is necessary to help prevent this. The advantages of such light soils are great though, since heavy rain drains through them quickly rather than sitting in the soil long enough to enter the vines' roots and end up swelling the grapes. They also warm up rapidly, and it is a poor vintage in the Rheinpfalz which does not produce any Riesling Spätlese wines in the best vineyards.

This extra ripeness and the softer acidity which goes with it means that the Palatinate makes excellent full-bodied dry wines. If the present trend continues, then by 1990 the great majority of the region's wines will be made in drier styles. That is to say that the region will have returned to its traditional style. Palatinate Rieslings make much better bone-dry wines than those from the Rheingau generally do (though with a somewhat similar set of flavours, if a little more filled out, forthright and flowery). The best of them are every bit as good as the very finest Alsace Rieslings, having a little less sheer power but generally more finesse.

The region also makes excellent dry wines from Gewürztraminer, Weissburgunder, Muskateller, Silvaner, and Blauer Portugieser among the traditional grape varieties. Of the new crossings, Scheurebe makes some of the greatest dessert wines of Silv.X Ries the world, and Kerner and Müller-Thurgau good medium-dry and sweeter quaffing wines. This means that although the region is associated primarily with the Riesling, it offers a wide palate of wines.

The Palatinate is famous for very hearty food like Saumagen, which is the stomach of a sheep stuffed with pork, potatoes, and spices. However, while this traditional *Pfälzer Kuche* is still very widely available, during the last few years an incredible number of top-quality restaurants have opened in the region. Zur Kanne (owned by Weingut Dr Bürklin-Wolf) in Deidesheim, and the

Haardter Schloss in Neustadt-Haardt are probably the best of these. I think the finest restaurants of the region, though, are those which reinterpret the classic cuisine of the region, and Wein Castell in Kallstadt (owned by Weingut Koehler-Ruprecht, p. 98) is the best in this class by a street.

The Palatinate is a wonderful place to relax in, with dozens and dozens of beautiful old villages along the Weinstrasse which runs through the region. While more and more good quality and fine wine is coming out of the region, it still *generally* has very high yields. Although the second largest of the German wine regions with 22,850 hectares/56,440 acres of vineyards, its total production is still the highest in Germany by a significant margin. At least things are moving quickly in the right direction on this score, though.

Weingut Knipser–Johannishof

Werner Knipser (owner and director).
Weingut Knipser–Johannishof,
D 6711 Laumersheim.
Tel: 0638 742.

15 hectares/37 acres.
25% Riesling, 25% Spätburgunder (Pinot Noir), Portugieser and Dornfelder, 15% Scheurebe, 35% Gewürztraminer, Grauburgunder (Pinot Gris), Ehrenfelser and other varieties.

Werner Knipser, a close friend of Dr Ulrich Stein from the Moselle valley (p. 121), shares the latter's technical inventiveness. Werner Knipser's most innovative wines are his reds from Portugieser and Spätburgunder, and his new-oak-aged Grauburgunder. Portugieser is a variety which is widely cultivated in the middle part of the Palatinate, giving a rather pale, soft wine just about acceptable to international taste as a red wine rather than a rosé. By reducing the normally high yield easily achieved with this variety, by fermenting the wine long on the skins, and then ageing it for a year and a half in small wooden casks, Herr Knipser has produced a rich red wine of considerable power (12.5 degrees of alcohol!)

There is quite a story behind the barrique-aged Grauburgunder Spätlese Trocken which Weingut Knipser–Johannishof produced from the 1985 vintage. The intention was that this wine should have a little touch of oakiness. However, during the wine's maturation in barriques made of Vosges oak it suddenly started taking on a strong oakiness. Realising that this might already make it ineligible for an AP number on the ground of non-typicality, Werner Knipser quickly bottled the wine. Immediately after bottling the oakiness disappeared, so a bottle of the wine was raced to the AP number testing station, where it easily passed. The wine's oakiness has since returned.

Weingut Knipser–Johannishof also produces very fine Riesling and Scheurebe wines, in both dry and medium-dry styles. Herr Knipser makes no bones about the fact that he prefers to make these wines in steel tanks. Top Prädikat wines are also a speciality, and there is quite a range of Beerenauslese, Trockenbeerenauslese, and Eiswein. The best of these are of stunning quality. Werner Knipser is a very good host, with a lot of fascinating ideas about winemaking. It is difficult to make a brief visit to his estate!

Weingut Gg Henninger IV

Georg Henninger (owner and director),
Walter Henninger (owner and director).
Weingut Gg Henninger IV,
Weinstrasse 93,
D 6701 Kallstadt.
Tel: 06322 2277.

6.5 hectares/16 acres.
50% Riesling, 12% Silvaner, 10% Spätburgunder (Pinot Noir), 10% Gewürztraminer, 9% Scheurebe,
9% Grauburgunder (Pinot Gris) and Weissburgunder (Pinot Blanc).

Georg and Walter Henninger have an absolutely clear vision of the kind of wines they want to be producing; bone-dry, high in alcohol, with a racy acidity. Their wines are all fully fermented out to dryness, and never have Süssreserve added to them for sweetening. The alcohol content of their best Riesling wines goes as high as 13 or more degrees without any sugar having been added to build this up! While Riesling wines can have a high alcohol level without becoming heavy in the way that Chardonnay wines often do, 14 degrees of alcohol is probably at, or fractionally over, the upper limit for Riesling wines if they are to retain some elegance. The alcohol level of the majority of the Henninger wines is a more reasonable 10 to 11.5 degrees.

This is all a big change from the seventies when the great majority of the Henninger wines were made in the sweeter style. However, the high quality and individuality of wines produced in the uncompromising style is even better than under the previous regime. As well as being purists in the cellar, the Henningers are also purists in the vineyard, using no chemical fertilisers, and pruning hard to get a harvest which even in poorer vintages is largely of Prädikat-quality wines.

Weingut Eduard Schuster

Detlev Schuster (owner and director).
Weingut Eduard Schuster,
Neugasse 21,
D 6701 Kallstadt.
Tel: 06322 8011.

15 hectares/37 acres.
41% Riesling, 22% Silvaner, 6% Müller-Thurgau,
6% Scheurebe, 2% Gewürztraminer, 23% Siegerrebe,
Ehrenfelser, Muskateller and other varieties.

Although Detlev Schuster produces some very nice Riesling wines, what sets his estate somewhat apart from those of his neighbours is his Silvaner wines. Silvaner is one of the traditional grape varieties of the Palatinate, but is little grown here now. (The only regions in which Silvaner remains an important variety are Rheinhessen and Franconia.) Detlev Schuster's enthusiasm for the variety is such that he has planted it in his best site, the Kallstadter Saumagen, which is one of the finest vineyards in the entire Palatinate. From these vines he produces both bone-dry and sweet wines up to Spätlese quality level which have a depth and complexity quite exceptional for the variety.

Herr Schuster is not quite a typical Pfälzer, being a little more serious and business-minded than is usual here. As a result his cellar is very well organised, the numerous wooden casks and steel tanks all in pristine condition, and every surface so clean one could eat off it. The wines Herr Schuster produces here are all correct, having been made with great attention to detail. If there are fewer really top wines than at some estates in the area, this is because Herr Schuster does not set so much store by the selective harvesting of the grapes. In marked contrast to the Koehler-Ruprecht estate (pp. 98–102) around the corner, where only Prädikat wines are produced, Detlev Schuster makes large quantities of QbA wines. Nearly all his bone-dry (Trocken) wines are QbAs.

Weingut Karl Schaefer

Bernhard Lehmeyer (director),
Dr Wolf Fleischmann (owner and director).
Weingut Karl Schaefer,
Weinstrasse Sud 30,
D 6702 Bad Dürkheim.
Tel: 06322 2138.

17 hectares/42 acres.
71% Riesling, 7% Müller-Thurgau, 5% Silvaner, 3% Kerner, 14% Gewürztraminer, Muskateller, Spätburgunder (Pinot Noir), Scheurebe and other varieties.

The Schaefer estate has a unique style amongst the top producers of the Mittel Haardt area of the Palatinate. Their wines have a degree of refinement and polish rarely to be found outside the Moselle valley or Rheingau regions. For those who find the wines of the Palatinate generally a bit too heavy, or a little too extrovert in flavour, the Schaefer wines will probably be very suitable. In terms of style these wines stand at the opposite extreme to the powerful, assertive Rieslings of Weingut Georg Siben (p. 201).

What gives the Schaefer wines their special character is their long maturation in old wooden casks, normally between nine months and a year. However, the influence of the air on the wine during this period is very slow, because the cellar is kept very cool using refrigeration equipment. The results of this are particularly clear if one tastes the dry wines. Dry (Trocken) Rieslings are normally at least a little aggressive until they have been

198   DIRECTORY OF RECOMMENDED PRODUCERS

in the bottle for a year or more. However, most of the Schaefer dry Rieslings are elegant and harmonious from the moment they are released.

For many decades the estate has singled out three of its best wines to be sold under 'brand' names; a Riesling Kabinett called 'Sonnentropfen' (drops of sunshine), a Riesling Spätlese called 'Schöne Anna' (beautiful Anna), and a Rieslaner Auslese called 'Schaefer's Haardtblume' (Schaefer's Haardt flower). This idea is only now catching on widely in Germany.

Weingut Dr Bürklin-Wolf

Bettina Bürklin (owner),
Georg Raquet (director).
Weingut Dr Bürklin-Wolf,
Weinstrasse 65,
D 6706 Wachenheim.
Tel: 06322 8955.

110 hectares/272 acres.
71% Riesling, 12% Müller-Thurgau, 4% Ehrenfelser,
2% Scheurebe, 2% Weissburgunder (Pinot Blanc),
2% Gewürztraminer, 2% Spätburgunder (Pinot Noir),
2% Silvaner, 3% other varieties.

The Bürklin-Wolf estate is one of the largest privately owned wine estates in the whole of Germany. It is almost as large as the very biggest of the Grand Cru Classé Châteaux of the Médoc in Bordeaux, yet instead of producing one or two wines as those estates do it currently offers a range of fifty! Given this, the quality level is quite remarkable. Excellent organisation, particularly in harvesting and pressing the grapes, is the secret of Bürklin-Wolf's high quality. However, the sheer number of different wines must be a problem in the cellar, and the slight sameyness of the estate's wines from some vintages seems to result from too much systematisation there.

The best wines from the estate are currently the dry Riesling and Weissburgunder wines, which can be really fine, with a Rheingau-like elegance. As a result of quite lengthy ageing in old wooden casks, these wines are usually mellow and drink well from the moment they are released. Best of all are the 'Selection

Albert Bürklin' dry Riesling wines and Sekt, a recently created range produced from Bürklin-Wolf's monopole vineyards. The traditional-style Spätlese and Auslese wines can also be very good indeed, and the very top Prädikat wines are often stunning. Bettina Bürklin recently completed her studies at the Geisenheim school, and is now joining the dynamic Georg Raquet in directing the estate.

Weingut Werlé

Hardy Werlé (director),
Otto Werlé (owner).
Weingut Werlé,
Altes Schlossel,
D 6701 Forst.
Tel: 06326 8930.

11.5 hectares/28.5 acres.
93% Riesling, 7% other varieties.

There can hardly be a wine estate in the Palatinate with a more perfect combination of beautiful wines and a beautiful estate house than this. The Werlés' estate is based in a large manor house, or small castle, in the middle of the oldest part of the wine village of Forst. All the Werlé Riesling wines ferment through by themselves to dryness (to between two and twenty grams of unfermented sugar per litre) in old wooden casks. The grape must or wine is given as little treatment as possible, and the result is wines of the highest elegance and great finesse.

The estate is largely run by Hardy Werlé, a charming and extremely friendly man only just into his thirties. He is determined to continue his family's long-standing commitment to the Riesling variety, and their tradition of making wines in an extremely unmanipulative manner. He will also continue the organic cultivation of the vineyards, which his father always practised. The estate's best wines are capable of *very* long ageing, and can still be fresh after more than forty years in the bottle.

Without doubt, the Werlé estate is one of the great unknown names of Germany. If they were in Burgundy the wine world would be knocking on their door!

Weingut Mossbacherof

Werner Klein (owner and director).
Weingut Mossbacherhof,
Weinstrasse 23,
D 6701 Forst.
Tel: 06326 264.

10 hectares/24.5 acres.
90% Riesling, 10% Gewürztraminer, Spätburgunder (Pinot
Noir), Scheurebe, Silvaner and other varieties.

The Mossbacherhof looks a rather sullen Victorian lump of a house from the outside, but to enter is to leave the familiar world behind and go back several centuries. The entrance hall and first tasting room are covered with baroque wooden panelling, and contain a small part of the collection of Klein family portraits. Across the hall on the other side is a mid-nineteenth-century sitting room containing dozens more paintings, then an exuberant rococo sitting room, followed by a Napoleonic lounge. The stairway is hung with Renaissance paintings and upstairs is an extraordinary rococo dining room normally only used for tastings for large groups. Knowing full well that all these things are originals, the visitor stumbles back down the stairs in an openmouthed daze to taste some wines.

Werner Klein makes wonderfully full-flavoured Rieslings, wines full of fruit and extract from the soil. Nearly all the wines are made in drier styles, always fermenting with their own yeasts. When they are fined only egg white is used, and many wines stay in wooden casks until shortly before the harvesting following the vintage. In short, for the last three decades and more Werner Klein has been making very traditional Palatinate Rieslings. His best Riesling and Silvaner wines are of exceptionally high quality.

Weingut Acham-Magin

Anton Acham (owner),
Anna-Barbara Acham (director).
Weingut Acham-Magin,
Weinstrasse 67,
D 6701 Forst.
Tel: 06326 315.

4 hectares/10 acres.
75% Riesling, 25% Weissburgunder (Pinot Blanc),
Spätburgunder (Pinot Noir), Kerner and Gewürztraminer.

Weingut Acham-Magin is one of very few estates in the Palatinate never to have made anything but dry wines. Anna-Barbara Acham, the young winemaker and director, has been hailed in Germany as one of the leaders of a new generation of young winemakers who completely reject the trend towards sweet wines of recent decades, but as Anna-Barbara says, 'First of all, though my ideas about winemaking are somewhat different from my father's, there was never a non-dry style here for me to reject! During the 1960s we had mainly older customers who had never drunk anything but dry wines. Then came the 1970s. We won a lot of younger customers interested in food and wine, which once again meant a demand for dry wines, and finally in the 1980s the almost nationwide fashion for dry wines came along.'

Anna-Barbara is lucky to have a wonderful cellar behind the charming courtyard in the centre of the estate buildings, which also house a popular wine bar. The oldest part of it dates from 1711, and here the estate's wines are fermented and matured, those from the classical grape varieties in old wooden casks. There is no deacidification, so the wines sometimes lie here for many months to round their assertive acidity. Consequently, the wines are never aggressive, though many need a couple of years ageing to show their best. There is no fining at all, either of musts or wines, and minimal filtration. Every Acham-Magin wine has a distinctive character which comes from the soil, the Ungeheuer wines being the heaviest and earthiest, and the Pechstein wines with an almost flinty tone, to take just two examples.

Weingut Georg Siben

Wolfgang Georg Siben (owner and director).
Weingut Georg Siben Erben,
Weinstrasse 21,
D 6705 Deidesheim.
Tel: 06326 214.

12 hectares/29.5 acres.
95% Riesling, 3% Ruländer (Pinot Gris), 2% Kerner.

The Palatinate is full of wine estates producing fine dry Riesling wines. Perhaps the most masculine Rieslings in the region are produced by Weingut Georg Siben. Wolfgang Siben is a very serious middle-aged man who is virtually a dry Riesling visionary (see p. 9). He dresses in extremely traditional fashion, with knee-breeches and a nineteenth-century-style narrow-collared jacket, and his office also looks as though it came straight out of the last century.

Herr Siben's approach to winemaking is a strange combination of faith in the virtues of the region's traditional style, and belief in science. His list contains about ten pages of information about the conditions during the last vintage, details of exactly how the wines were made, and chemical analyses of all the wines listed. A quick glance at these statistics reveals that the Siben wines are almost all bone-dry, have very high acidity levels, and a gigantic amount of extract. This extract, which comprises all the complex organic compounds and minerals in the wine, acts as a buffer to the acidity of the wines, and also contributes to the concentration of flavour. Wolfgang Siben's wines are never thin, rather they are tremendously powerful, firm, and at the same time many-faceted and complex; they are all *serious* stuff.

Wolfgang Siben feels that the problem for wines like his is that people's expectations of what a good dry white wine should taste like have been created by French wines. 'As a result people expect dry white wines to be full bodied – that is high in alcohol – round and soft. Our dry wines get their power from acidity and extract, rather than alcohol and oakiness. I am all in favour of the increasing demand for natural products, and if you make wines in the Palatinate as nature gives them to us, then they will be dry with a pronounced acidity. The same applies in Chablis, Champagne and the Loire. We have to get people to understand that our wines must also be like this.'

Weingut Reichsrat von Buhl

Michael Hiller (director).
Weingut Reichsrat von Buhl,
Weinstrasse 16–24,
D 6705 Deidesheim.
Tel: 06326 1851.

100 hectares/247 acres.
90% Riesling, 8% Müller-Thurgau, 2.5% Gewürztraminer.

Reichsrat von Buhl is, perhaps not surprisingly, the only German wine estate to be run by a native New Yorker who has graduated in philosophy and computer science, as well as in viticulture and winemaking! As one might expect from this, the estate promotes itself very dynamically, and the winemaking is technically well-nigh perfect.

This is a big change from the seventies when the estate lolloped along, and some superb, if old-fashioned, wines were produced next to some rather unbalanced ones. Today every von Buhl wine is crystal-clear, the great majority of them now being made in stainless steel tanks to retain every last bit of freshness. A large proportion of the current production is dry, which means bone-dry at von Buhl, or medium-dry, and many 'sweet' wines have little unfermented sweetness. The grapes are now harvested more for a nice acidity level which will result in elegant wines, than for a high level of ripeness. When grape musts are harvested which have only just enough sugar (i.e. potential alcohol) to be made as Kabinett wines, they are always chaptelised with sugar, and sold as QbAs. The von Buhl wines today are generally clean, dry, and racy. The production of Spätlese wines is small, and Auslese wines are the rarity they should be even in the Palatinate.

Michael Hiller is a tremendously active promoter of his wines, as well as of fine German wines as a whole. He spends a great deal of time travelling around Germany and abroad to present the von Buhl wines, often together with fine cuisine. However, he has not ignored the potential which the beautiful von Buhl estate buildings offer, where he regularly stages art exhibitions and concerts. As Michael says, 'It's a great way to bring people into the estate, but really the most important reason for doing this is to get people to realise that fine wine is part of culture, and should be valued as such. Nobody thinks that Liebfraumilch is a part of culture, and its price most certainly reflects that. I think it's important to show that we belong to a different world from that.'

For several years von Buhl have marketed a large proportion of their QbA wines as 'Reichsrat von Buhl Riesling QbA' in

Trocken, Halbtrocken, and sweeter versions. They are in the process of extending this to QmP wines.

Wegeler-Deinhard

Heinz Bauer (director).
Wegeler-Deinhard
(Gutsverwaltung Deinhard),
Weinstrasse 10,
D 6705 Deidesheim.
Tel: 06326 221.

18 hectares/44 acres.
74% Riesling, 17% Müller-Thurgau, 4% Scheurebe,
3% Gewürztraminer, 2% other varieties.

The Deinhard estate in Deidesheim produces classically full-flavoured and perfumed Palatinate Riesling wines. The style has changed a little in the last few years, with the wines being bottled a little earlier, which has made them slightly racier and a little less expansive than they once were. This has simply brought them in line with modern taste, and there has not been any emasculation of regional character.

Herr Bauer has a highly infectious natural good humour, which makes a visit to the estate a joy. In a region where nearly everyone seems 'well built', owing to the Palatinate tradition of enjoying food and wine in good quantities, it is rare to find someone of such slight build as Herr Bauer. He seems possessed of energies quite disproportionate to his size, though, and the estate's wines are clearly made with a real dedication to quality. With the Forster Ungeheuer vineyard now back in production after being reorganised and replanted (*Fluerbereinigung*), the estate once again has the chance to produce really fine Rieslings.

Scheurebe and Gewürztraminer have long been specialities, and fine, full-bodied dry wines (Spätlese Trocken and Auslese Trocken), and high-quality dessert wines are also regularly produced from these varieties at the estate.

Weingut Josef Biffar

Gerhard Biffar (owner and director),
Karl Früh (cellarmaster).
Weingut Josef Biffar,
Niederkircher Strasse 13,
D 6705 Deidesheim.
Tel: 06326 5028.

12 hectares/29.5 acres.
80% Riesling, 20% Weissburgunder (Pinot Blanc),
Gewürztraminer, Scheurebe and Müller-Thurgau.

Weingut Josef Biffar has one of the most beautiful vaulted cellars in the whole Palatinate. A cask tasting here with Herr Früh is quite an experience, it being hard to decide which has more character, the wines or the man! The Biffar wines are not the most elegant in the region, but the best are very satisfying, with a full Riesling fruitiness. The general quality standard is high because each year up to 40 per cent of the harvest is sold away as grape must. The style is very traditional, with almost every wine both fermenting and maturing in wooden casks, the majority of wines not being bottled until the weeks before the following harvest. In the press house stand two basket presses, one large hydraulic one, and another small hand press. These are no ornaments; the larger is used for the Spätlese and Auslese wines, and the smaller for the very top Prädikat wines.

If there is a criticism which can be justifiably made of the estate, it is that because of the long cask ageing the wines from ripe vintages tend to develop rather quickly. However, in difficult or poor vintages the Biffar wines can have a harmony and a ripeness that few in the area can match. The Gewürztraminer wines are amongst the best of the Palatinate, with the classic lychees and rose petals character of the variety, but never top heavy.

Von Bassermann-Jordan'sches Weingut

Dr Ludwig von Bassermann-Jordan (owner).
Geheimer rat Dr von
  Bassermann-Jordan'sches Weingut,
Kirchstrasse 10,
D 6705 Deidesheim.
Tel: 06326 6006.

50 hectares/123.5 acres.
97% Riesling, 3% other varieties.

The Bassermann-Jordan estate is totally committed to Riesling wines made in the most traditional way, fermented and matured in wooden casks as a matter of principle. With its excellent vineyards, and its cool, humid vaulted cellar of great size, it certainly has the right basis for making superb wines in this style. However, in spite of continuing to produce some wines which fully live up to its high reputation, the potential which is there is not achieved as often as it might be.

Of 'The Three Bs' of the Palatinate, that is Bürklin, Buhl and Bassermann, the latter currently produces the highest proportion of drier-style wines, with barely a third of its wines being in the sweeter style. Demand for these wines in Germany is such that the list virtually only offers wines from the last two vintages.

Weingut Müller-Catoir

Heinrich Catoir (owner and director),
Hans-Günther Schwarz (cellarmaster).
Weingut Müller-Catoir,
Mandelring 25,
D 6730 Haardt an der Weinstrasse.
Tel: 06321 2815.

17 hectares/42 acres.
34% Riesling, 15% Scheurebe, 5% Gewürztraminer,
4% Ruländer (Pinot Gris), 10% Müller-Thurgau,
3% Silvaner, 6% Kerner, 5% Rieslaner, 5% Weissburgunder
(Pinot Blanc), 5% Muskateller, 5% Spätburgunder, 3% other
varieties.

Weingut Müller-Catoir is one of the great unknown names of Germany. Although they produce very fine Riesling wines,

it is their specialities – Scheurebe, Gewürztraminer, Rieslaner and Muskateller – which make this one of the world's
great white wine estates. At Müller-Catoir the wines from each
of these grape varieties retain entirely their own character,
combined with an incredible elegance. However, while the pursuit of greater elegance in the Palatinate has often resulted
in rather neutral wines, at Müller-Catoir the opposite is
the case; their wines are almost bursting with flavour and
extract.

Heinrich Catoir is a firm believer in reductive winemaking,
winemaking which allows the wine minimal contact with the air,
and all the estate's wines are made in tanks. A tall man of about
forty, Heinrich Catoir is very sparing with his words, only
displaying any fervour when stating the first principle of his
winemaking: 'With every handling, every racking or filtration,
you take something out of the wine. In some cases you can
virtually ruin a wine in a few hours. For instance, Scheurebe
wines have a distinctive bouquet [This can be reminiscent of
grapefruit, blackcurrants, or even cat's pee] and with a harsh
filtration you can destroy this. Nothing you do in the cellar can
improve on what was in the grapes. In the cellar you have to
stand back as much as possible.' This philosophy is followed
through scrupulously. The Müller-Catoir wines are not deacidified, they are only racked once after fermentation (to separate
them from the dead yeast) and have the minimum level of
sulphur dioxide which will protect them from oxidation after
bottling.

Perhaps the estate's finest wines are their dry Muskateller and
Rieslaner wines. Muskateller is a very old variety now little
grown anywhere in Germany. As its name suggests it has a
grapy, perfumed Muscat character, but this is far more refined
than in the majority of French Muscat wines. It is a very difficult
vine to grow, the grapes often falling to the ground in poor
weather. It is also extremely easy to lose its classic varietal
character in the cellar, often without having any idea why or
how. Müller-Catoir generally make their Muskatellers as light
Kabinett wines, feeling that this brings out the varietal character
most strongly.

In contrast, their dry Rieslaner wines are massive, with up to
15 degrees of naturally achieved alcohol! These wines have

almost too much luscious apricoty richness, and give a sensation similar to that of looking at a landscape too expansive for the eye to take in. At this level Rieslaner wines are certainly too powerful in flavour for any food to compete with them. Rieslaner is a modern crossing, of Silvaner and Riesling, but is nothing like either. Very few growers outside Franconia (pp. 209–14) have it in their vineyards. The best sweet Auslese and higher Prädikat wines from Müller-Catoir are also quite magnificent.

Weingut Ökonomierat Rebholz

Christine Rebholz (owner),
Hansjörg Rebholz (director).
Weingut Ökonomierat Rebholz,
An der Weinstrasse 54,
D 6741 Siebeldingen.
Tel: 06345 3439.

9 hectares/22 acres.
35% Riesling, 13% Müller-Thurgau, 10% Gewürztraminer,
24% Spätburgunder (Pinot Noir), 10% Grauburgunder (Pinot
Gris), 5% Weissburgunder (Pinot Blanc), 5% Muskateller.

The Rebholz family's approach to winemaking has long been idiosyncratic almost to the point of eccentricity. For many years they have never used any sugar to build up the alcohol content of any of their wines (chaptelisation), nor any unfermented grape juice (Süssreserve) to sweeten any of their wines. As a result of this policy, and the coolish climate in the vineyards of Siebeldingen and Birkweiler high above the town of Landau, a large part of the Rebholz production is dry 'Landwein'. Landwein is the German equivalent of Vin de Pays in France, and it has been a designation which has caught on very slowly, except at Weingut Rebholz. There every wine under Kabinett quality is a Landwein. These wines are a bit of a shock to those raised on the idea that Palatinate wine is full and plump, for they are light and crisp; they normally have 8.5 to 9.5 degrees of alcohol, making them similar to dry Moselle wines in structure.

Hansjörg, who has been running the estate since his father's death in 1977, has winemaking abilities far beyond what his obvious youth would lead one to expect. The best wines from the estate, particularly the late-harvested Muskateller, Gewürztraminer, Riesling and Spätburgunder Weissherbst (rosé) wines have a startling brilliance, and a filigraine character which sets them quite apart from the majority of Palatinate wines. It should be pointed out that they can also have an equally startling acidity content, and in spite of the estate's rule about not adding any sweetness to the wines, they are not forced to bone-dryness. Every wine at the estate is allowed to find its own harmony. If a wine stopped fermenting with 30 or 40 grams per litre of unfermented sugar it would be left that way, and some of the late-harvested wines have this much sweetness.

Franconia

Franconia's problem is that its very continental climate can give it wonderful vintages when nothing very remarkable is produced elsewhere in Germany, but it can also suffer from spring frosts which decimate the crop. As a result, in spite of its size of 10,000 hectares/24,700 acres only a handful of the larger producers can export. This is not a real problem for the producers because since Napoleonic times Franconia has been incorporated into Bavaria, and the Bavarians patriotically drain the region's cellars quite effectively in spite of relatively high prices compared to other regions.

Franconia extends roughly from Aschaffenberg and Schweinfurt along the valley of the Main river, and to the east to the western slopes of the Steigerwald. On generally quite heavy soils the classic Franconia grape variety, the Silvaner, gives wines of considerable body and masculinity. The region's unbroken tradition for dry wines has sadly not been matched by an unbroken commitment to the classic grape varieties, and there is all too much of the inferior modern Bacchus, Optima and Perle vine crossings planted in the region. On the other hand Müller-Thurgau gives some of its best wines here.

The city of Würzburg sits at the cèntre of the region and epitomises its long tradition of rule by Catholic prince-electors (the principality of Castell was one of a few islands of Protestantism). Whilst this has long since been ended, older traditions of music, dance, recitation and literature thrive in a way not

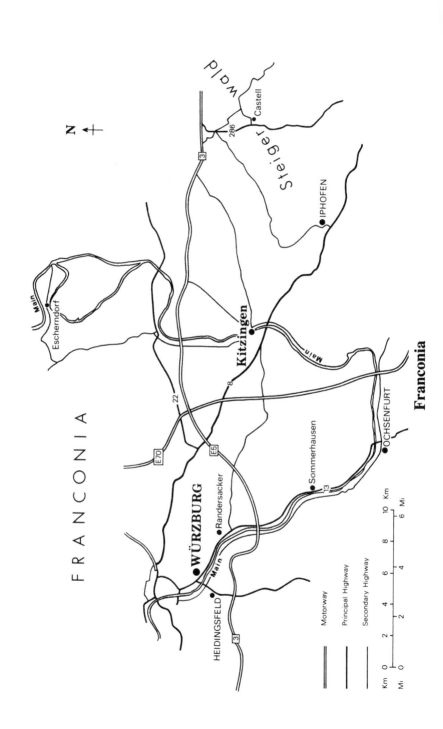

FRANCONIA

Franconia

matched by other regions of Germany. Franconian cuisine matches the earthiness of its wines, and has no truck with anything that even drifts in the direction of Nouvelle Cuisine! Franconia is well worth a visit to experience all these things, and to see the remaining trappings of its erstwhile autocracy, principally the massive 'Marienburg' fortress and dazzling rococo 'Residenz' in Würzburg.

Juliuspital Weingut

Horst Kolesch (director).
Juliuspital Weingut,
Klinikstrasse 5,
D 8700 Würzburg.
Tel: 0931 3084147/3084148.

160 hectares/395.5 acres.
26% Silvaner, 25% Müller-Thurgau, 12% Riesling,
8% Scheurebe, 7% Bacchus, 22% Traminer, Kerner,
Rieslaner and other varieties.

Since the establishment of the Juliuspital charitable foundation for the care of Würzburg's aged citizens in 1576, the wine estate it was endowed with to provide its income has had the reputation of being one of the most reliable estates in Franconia. However, from the end of the war until Horst Kolesch's arrival, it was often said that the very best Würzburg wines were not to be had at the Juliuspital. Since then the winemaking has been noticeably sharpened up, the wines being generally drier and crisper than before.

As a result even the Juliuspital's wines from execrable vine crossings such as Bacchus, which is sadly rather widely planted in Franconia, are clean and elegant. However, it is still the Silvaner, Traminer and Riesling wines which stand out. Riesling is not a typical grape variety for Franconia, but on the lighter limestone soils around Würzburg it does very well. Even then, it can hardly be compared to Riesling wines from anywhere else in Germany, having a distinctive assertiveness and richness. Put beside a light Riesling Kabinett from the Moselle, a Würzburg Riesling seems almost overwhelming in its fullness of flavour. It could also have nearly twice as much alcohol as the Moselle wine (i.e. 14 degrees)! Clearly, such wines are not for the faint-hearted.

The estate still makes nearly all its wines in wooden casks in its beautiful vaulted cellars under the Juliuspital hospital. The main gallery is over 250 metres long, Stück casks lining both sides into the distance. Today, however, the wines do not mature so long in cask, and are quite rapidly transferred into stainless steel tanks to await bottling. Very little unfermented grape juice (Süss-reserve) is used to sweeten the wines, the majority of which are made bone-dry.

Bürgerspital Weingut

Heinz Zeller (director),
Rudolf Friess (director).
Stiftung Bürgerspital zum Heiligen Geist
  Weingut,
Theaterstrasse 19,
D 8700 Würzburg.
Tel: 0931 50363.

140 hectares/346 acres.
25% Riesling, 20% Müller-Thurgau, 20% Silvaner,
35% Kerner, Scheurebe, Traminer, Ruländer (Pinot Gris),
Spätburgunder (Pinot Noir), Weissburgunder (Pinot Blanc)
and Schwarzriesling (Pinot Meunier).

The remarkable consistency in the quality of its wines which the Bürgerspital estate has maintained during recent years is based on its excellent vineyards. In marked contrast to their region as a whole, they never planted more than a few small experimental plots of the new crossings, and therefore stand in the lucky position of having almost exclusively traditional varieties, and the largest area of Riesling in the whole of Franconia. In many respects their winemaking is traditional and conservative; there is no deacidification except in very difficult years, and the wines from the grape varieties with acidity are always matured in wooden casks. More than half their wines are bone-dry; the remainder are made with a very modest touch of sweetness which does no more than round them off a little.

However, the Bürgerspital wines do not have quite the full

earthiness of the uncompromisingly traditional wines of the region. Those seeking elegance find this a great virtue, and would say that part of the real traditional style also involved a slight oxidation of the wine, which is best avoided. Those committed to wines with a crystal-clear regional identity will find the Bürgerspital wines impressive in their polished elegance, but lacking a little bit of earthiness, a little bit of soul.

Staatliche Hofkeller

Dr Heinz Martin Eichelsbacher (director).
Staatliche Hofkeller Bayerische Landesanstalt
  für Weinbau und Gartenbau,
Residenzplatz 3,
D 8700 Würzburg.
Tel: 0931 50701.

120 hectares/296.5 acres.
25% Riesling, 20% Müller-Thurgau, 10% Silvaner,
10% Spätburgunder (Pinot Noir), 35% Rieslaner, Scheurebe
and other varieties.

Of all the Würzburg estates, the Staatliche Hofkeller sticks most unswervingly to the traditional Franconian style. Their wines have a rich fruitiness, and a lot of mineral extract from the soil, giving them the full earthy character which is the mark of classical Franconian wines. For some this amounts to a lack of refinement, and certainly as a result of their relatively long cask maturation (up to a year) they do not often have the raciness of the Bürgerspital wines.

  If the question of which of the great Würzburg estates is the best is open to lengthy debate, the question of who has the finest cellar architecture is not. The Staatliche Hofkeller's wines are made in the cellar of the Würzburg Residenz, which is one of the most impressive pieces of rococo architecture in Germany (and the state of Bavaria, of which Franconia is a part, has an embarrassment of riches from that period). While Tiepolo was not invited downstairs to paint magnificent murals and ceilings here, the large galleries filled with wooden casks really do take one's breath away.

Weingut Hans Wirsching

Hans Wirsching (director),
Dr Heinrich Wirsching (director).
Weingut Hans Wirsching,
Ludwigstrasse 16,
D 8715 Iphofen.
Tel: 09323 3336.

45 hectares/111 acres.
30% Silvaner, 30% Müller-Thurgau, 10% Riesling,
10% Scheurebe, 20% Kerner, Traminer, Bacchus and
Portugieser.

The Wirsching brothers are masters of the modern style of Franconian wine. For them freshness is everything, and they use every technical means to retain it. The great majority of their wines are bone-dry, and fermented in tanks. Their best wines, the Silvaners from the excellent Julius-Echter-Berg vineyard, are always very fine, with an elegance that is quite remarkable for this grape variety and the area. Normally, on the heavy gypsum-marl soils of the Steigerwald, Silvaner produces hearty, substantial, distinctly rustic wines. To find such finesse in an area which really feels as though it has barely made it into the present century, where there are still plenty of wild boar to be seen and where wolves would not be out of place, seems slightly incongruous! The Wirschings' wines from other grape varieties are all good, but, in comparison to the Silvaners, a little less startling.

Baden

Baden covers an enormous area. Whilst it is possible to nip around the Rheingau from one grower to another at the opposite end of the region in one day, the same certainly is not possible here. It is over 400 km/250 miles from one end of Baden to the other, yet the vineyard area is only 14,930 hectares/36,880 acres. As a result there are huge variations in style and of grape varieties, and it is necessary to take the region to pieces to even begin to get a general picture of what sort of wines it produces.

The most northerly of its sub-regions is Badisches Franckenland, which is at the southern edge of Franconia, and whose wines are completely Franconian (generally dry, full-bodied and earthy) in style. This area is not part of the wine region of Franconia simply because it happens to fall within the German state of Baden-Württemberg rather than Bavaria, to which Franconia belongs.

Badische Bergstrasse–Kraichgau extends both northwards and southwards from Heidelberg along the west-facing slopes at the edge of the Odenwald forest. Here the principal grape varieties are Müller-Thurgau, along with Weissburgunder and Ruländer. These produce medium-bodied, quite elegant wines, sometimes of some distinction and finesse. Little of these wines leaves Germany, however.

Rather more important, and long since a proven producer of Riesling and Spätburgunder wines of both power and complexity, is the Ortenau. The Ortenau's vineyards, which lie between Baden-Baden and just south of Offenburg, are generally sloping to precipitous, and mostly on weathered volcanic soils of some richness. The best are situated in a couple of valleys which cut into the Black Forest mountains in an easterly direction. This provides sites facing due south, where Spätlese or even Auslese wines can be made from the late-ripening classic vine varieties almost every year.

The vineyards on the lower slopes of the Black Forest mountains going south from Offenburg to Freiburg form the Breisgau area, whose wines are less distinguished than those of the Ortenau but can also be good. Here, Müller-Thurgau makes up a significant part of the vineyard plantings, followed by the Pinot family of varieties.

Set apart from the Breisgau, and rising dramatically above the surrounding Rhine plain, are the Kaiserstuhl and Tuniberg. The former of these is the stump of a long-extinct volcano, the latter a large mass of chalk, and both have been covered by a thick layer of loess (a very fine sandy deposit). Here the Pinot family produce some of their most powerful and forceful wines. The tradition is for dry wines, with plenty of alcohol as a result of the excellent climate and vineyard sites here.

From Freiburg southwards to Basel on the Swiss border is the Markgräflerland. The soils here are once again much lighter and generally quite chalky, giving lighter wines than the Kaiserstuhl or Ortenau. The Gutedel grape has been grown here for centuries, though Weissburgunder, the other members of the Pinot family, and Gewürztraminer make the best wines. The countryside here is of gently rolling hills, with thousands of acres of fruit trees, particularly cherries, which clothe the landscape in blossom during the spring.

Finally there are the vineyards on the northern shore of Lake Constance. These are almost the lightest of the entire region: elegant Spätburgunder Weissherbst (rosé) and Müller-Thurgau.

If Baden has had a problem during recent years it is precisely that the region's wines are so diverse. Although the regional co-operative sells wines under the name of the region (Baden QbA) there is no one style for the whole region. To understand Baden's wines at all, one must understand the region area by area.

Winzergenossenschaft Sasbachwalden

Bruno Spinner (director).
Winzergenossenschaft Sasbachwalden,
Tal 2,
D 7595 Sasbachwalden.
Tel: 07841 4033.

220 hectares/534.5 acres.
50% Spätburgunder (Pinot Noir), 20% Klingelberger
(Riesling), 20% Müller-Thurgau, 10% Gewürztraminer and
Grauburgunder (Pinot Gris).

One of the most dynamic co-operatives in Baden is that at Sasbachwalden in Ortenau. The same thought and care which goes into their winemaking has also gone into the design of their new buildings. While the majority of German co-operatives have the appearance of anonymous plants which might produce microprocessors or toilet paper, here the building has been designed to blend in harmoniously with the numerous half-timbered houses in the village.

The speciality here is Spätburgunder which has been matured in new-oak barriques, and this is probably the best new-oak-matured Pinot Noir in Germany. Because of the strong oak character of these wines they would not be able to acquire AP numbers, so they have to be sold at Tafelwein. However, the

entire production of the best 1985 vintage barrique-aged Spätburgunder was sold to a single client (the excellent German wine
merchant Richard Heuser) for a very healthy price. Non-
barrique Spätburgunder is also produced, and this is aged in old
Stück casks. It too is of very good quality.

All the white wines are made in stainless steel tanks, are crisp,
very clean and typical. A large proportion of these are made in
drier styles.

Weingut Heinrich Männle

Heinrich Männle (owner and director).
Weingut Heinrich Männle,
Sendelbach 86,
D 7601 Durbach.
Tel: 0781 41101.

5 hectares/12.5 acres.
35% Spätburgunder (Pinot Noir), 14% Ruländer (Pinot
Gris), 16% Müller-Thurgau, 13% Scheurebe,
8% Klingelberger (Riesling), 8% Clevner (Traminer),
3% Weissburgunder (Pinot Blanc), 2% Gewürztraminer,
1% Würzer.

Herr Männle is known locally as 'Rotwein Männle' to distinguish
him from the other wine producers of the same family in
Durbach. Durbach is perhaps the most famous wine village in
the whole of Baden, and it is also the only one to be famous for its
Riesling wines. However, the Ortenau area of Baden as a whole
is just as famous for Spätburgunder red wines, and Heinrich
Männle is the current master of these.

His red wines have a long open fermentation in the skins as in
Burgundy, and are aged for a long time in cask. Indeed, he is
currently reverting to the *extremely* long cask ageing which his
grandfather gave the Spätburgunder red wines, that is twenty-
two months! The results of this are very impressive, the wines
becoming even deeper and more powerful in flavour (see p. 91
for the explanation of this), than the already fine red wines made
at the estate in the last few years. No red wines are made with less
than almost 12 degrees of alcohol, and a lot of selective harvesting is done to make small batches of red wine with 13 and more

degrees of naturally achieved alcohol. These have to be tasted to be believed.

It takes great determination and ambition to make wines like these, even with the highly favourable microclimate of Durbach, and Heinrich Männle applies the same qualities to his white winemaking. During a time when the fashion in Germany is for bone-dry wines, Heinrich Männle continues to make many ravishing sweet Auslese wines from a wide range of white grape varieties.

Weingut Salwey

Wolf-Dietrich Salwey (owner and director).
Weingut Salwey,
Hauptstrasse 2,
D 7818 Vogtsburg–Oberrotweil.
Tel: 07662 384.

10 hectares/24.5 acres.
47.5% Spätburgunder (Pinot Noir), 15% Ruländer (Pinot
Gris), 13% Müller-Thurgau, 7% Silvaner, 6% Riesling,
6% Gewürztraminer, 2.5% Freisamer, 1.5% Weissburgunder
(Pinot Blanc), 1.5% Muskateller.

Wolf-Dietrich Salwey's wines are an astonishing contrast to the full-bodied, plump, sweet style of wine which has been typical of the Kaiserstuhl area during recent decades. Herr Salwey's white wines are dry, exceptionally fresh and clean for his region, often with a 'Spritz' of carbon dioxide. The reason for the full-bodied nature of Kaiserstuhl is the remarkable microclimate of this long-weathered stump of an extinct volcano. Sitting in the middle of the Rhine plain, with the Vosges mountains to the west and the Black Forest to the east, the Kaiserstuhl as a whole is well protected from cold winds. The valley in which Oberrot-weil, Oberbergen, and Schelingen are situated is even more sheltered, giving their vineyards the most favourable climate for wine growing in the whole of Germany.

Most of the vineyards of the Kaiserstuhl have been terraced for centuries, owing to the steepness of the slopes, and reorgan-isation of many of these is creating very wide terraces which give the landscape a strangely surreal character. The soils in the best of these vineyards is tephrite, a volcanic rock rich in minerals. In many places this is overlaid with loess. Herr Salwey uses only organic fertilisation in his vineyards, the best of which produce his richly fruity Spätburgunder red wines. Some of these are now matured in small new-oak casks with very good results.

Herr Salwey also produces some of the finest dry Ruländer wines in the whole of Baden; wines with the perfect combination of richness and finesse. His fruit Schnapps (Eau de Vie) are quite remarkable; the best I have tasted anywhere in Europe!

Weingut Freiherr von Gleichenstein

Freiherr Hans-Joachim von Gleichenstein
  owner and director).
Weingut Freiherr von Gleichenstein,
Bahnhofstrasse 12,
D 7818 Vogtsburg–Oberrotweil.
Tel: 07662 288.

22 hectares/54.5 acres.
40% Spätburgunder (Pinot Noir), 35% Müller-Thurgau,
10% Grauburgunder (Pinot Gris), 2% Silvaner,
2% Muskateller, 2% Traminer, 2% Nobling,
3% Weissburgunder (Pinot Blanc), 2% Findling, 2% Riesling.

Freiherr von Gleichenstein, like his next-door neighbour Wolf-

Dietrich Salwey, makes the majority of his wines bone-dry, and ferments the great majority of his white wines in stainless steel tanks. They even have the same grape varieties and some vineyards next to those of each other. However, there is a sharp difference of style between them, Freiherr von Gleichenstein's wines almost invariably being more robust and assertive. The best have great power and substance. In particular the estate produces some of the best dry Müller-Thurgau wines I have ever tasted, and the top Spätburgunder Weissherbst wines will stun anyone who thinks that rosés can never be more than light, easy drinking wines. In contrast to the white wines, all the Spätburgunder red and rosé wines are matured in wooden casks. They have a very long fermentation on the skins, up to fourteen days, and are without doubt the most masculine red wines currently being made in Germany.

Hans-Joachim von Gleichenstein's estate is one of the few in the Kaiserstuhl with beautiful buildings, though these are somewhat (literally) overshadowed by the wonderful park-like garden; the perfect place to sit and taste their wines. He and his wife really love fine cuisine, and their wines are made for it. Many Michelin-starred restaurants are among their customers.

Zentrallkellerei Badischer Winzergenossenschaften

Armin Göring (director).
Zentralkellerei Badischer Winzergenossenschaften,
D 7814 Breisach.
Tel: 07667 82202.

45% Müller-Thurgau, 20% Spätburgunder (Pinot Noir),
10% Grauburgunder (Pinot Gris), 5% Gutedel (Chasselas),
5% Riesling, 15% other varieties.

ZBW is the gigantic Baden regional co-operative, taking all the grape production of fifty village co-operatives, and part of the production of another forty-five, pressing, vinifying, and marketing them. Its gigantic winemaking facility outside Breisach, the largest in the whole of Europe, makes over a third of all Baden wine. Most of this is sold under the regional name, either alone or in conjunction with a grape variety, e.g. Baden Gutedel. These wines have been forcefully marketed in Britain lately, but the line taken by the advertising, and the packaging of the wines, has rightly upset a lot of German producers. The advertisements talked about how Baden is unique among the German wine-producing regions in falling into EEC wine-growing category 'B' (along with Champagne, the Loire and Alsace), and how its wines are therefore necessarily better. The words 'Estate Bottled' printed in large letters on the labels of its new range have infuriated others, who say it is absurd for such mass products to be called estate-bottled.

In fact, ZBW also produces a range of fine-quality wines in small quantities which might seem to deserve this title. These are mostly from the best vineyards in the Kaiserstuhl, and are made in a small winery in the centre of Breisach. These wines, nearly all dry, can be of very good quality, with strong varietal character. It is a shame that no more than a few of them have so far been exported.

Weingut Hermann Dörflinger

Hermann Dörflinger (owner and director).
Weingut Hermann Dörflinger,
Mühlenstrasse 7,
D 7840 Müllheim.
Tel: 07631 2207.

5.5 hectares/13.5 acres.
50% Gutedel (Chasselas), 15% Müller-Thurgau, 5% Silvaner,
30% Spätburgunder (Pinot Noir), Weissburgunder (Pinot
Blanc) and Grauburgunder (Pinot Gris).

Gutedel is easily the most important grape variety of the Markgräflerland area of Baden, accounting for about 40 per cent of the region's vineyard area. It produces a very different wine here from the Chasselas of the Savoie in France, or those of Switzerland where the vine and wine are called Fendant, altogether lighter and much fresher with a very slight muskiness. Probably the best Gutedel wines of the Markgräflerland come from Hermann Dörflinger who often harvests early to get as much fresh fruitiness as possible, who never deacidifies any of his wines – 'with our good climate that's really crazy!' – and ferments all his wines through to bone-dryness.

This uncompromising dry-wine philosophy is nothing new, for Herr Dörflinger's father and grandfather did exactly the same. He has introduced some important new ideas, though, like new-oak ageing for his best Grauburgunder wines, and the red wines are fermented longer on the skins to achieve a remarkable depth of colour in good vintages. Though his red wines are definitely serious stuff, they are often quite low in alcohol, and their delicacy of flavour can come as quite a shock after the fine colour. Easier for non-Markgräfler palates to get excited about are the superb Weissburgunder and Gewürztraminer wines, which combine elegance with rich concentrated varietal flavours, and other flavours I have never come across in wines from these varieties before.

Herr Dörflinger is a great enthusiast, and absolutely committed to quality. Small estates like this are thin on the ground in Baden, and this is one of the best.

Winzergenossenschaft Auggen

Emil Krumm (director).
Winzergenossenschaft Auggen,
An der B3,
D 7841 Auggen.
Tel: 07631 4045.

240 hectares/593 acres.
60% Gutedel (Chasselas), 10% Müller-Thurgau and Silvaner,
30% Spätburgunder (Pinot Noir), Weissburgunder (Pinot
Blanc), and Grauburgunder (Pinot Gris).

The Auggen co-operative is really a model village co-operative, epitomising all the virtues of the strong co-operative movement in Baden. The new winery, in which the wines have been made since the 1980 harvest, is ultra-modern. The serried ranks of stainless steel tanks are typical of the region, where even a slight oxidative influence can leave white wines flabby. The oak casks which used to live in the co-operative's old building in the village have not been thrown away, though; they now occupy a corner of the air-conditioned cellars where the red and rosé (Weissherbst) wines are made. The pressing, fermentation and filtration technology are all exceptionally modern. The new fermentation tanks recently installed for the red wines should considerably improve them; the one weak area of Auggen's range.

The finest wines of this area are undoubtedly the Weissburgunder and Spätburgunder Weissherbst, which the rather chalky soils suit perfectly. At Spätlese level these wines have real complexity and finesse, and are not too alcoholic (12 degrees). The Gewürztraminer wines can also be very fine, distinctly more elegant and less domineering than the majority of those from Alsace. Gutedel is, however, the basis of the Auggen co-operative's production, and like the other wines is fermented to dryness. It makes a very satisfying straightforward wine.

Staatsweingut Meersburg

Hermann Häussermann (director).
Staatsweingut Meersburg,
Seminarstrasse 6,
D 7758 Meersburg/Bodensee.
Tel: 07532 6085.

60 hectares/148 acres.
45% Spätburgunder (Pinot Noir), 38% Müller-Thurgau,
5% Weissburgunder (Pinot Blanc), 4.5% Ruländer (Pinot
Gris), 3.5% Traminer, 1% Riesling, 3% other varieties.

The Staatsweingut Meersburg is situated in the magnificent baroque Reithof palace which stands at the top of the steep northern bank of Lake Constance (Bodensee). On a clear day its director, Herr Häussermann, can see from his desk a large part of the estate's precipitously steep vineyards along the lakeshore, right across the lake and beyond to the Alps. Because of this extraordinary view many visitors to the Staatsweingut Meersburg tell him he has the most beautiful office in the whole of Germany!

Because these are the most southerly vineyards in Germany one might expect the Bodensee wines to be very full and ripe, even tending to be over-ripe and plump. However, the normal water level of Lake Constance is 395 metres/1000 feet above sea level, and the estate's monopole Olgaberg vineyard rises to 530 metres/1350 feet, making it the highest in Germany. This, combined with the moderating influence of Lake Constance's glacial water and the light glacial moraine soils, results in wines of surprising elegance and delicacy, with the kind of refreshing ripe acidity more normally associated with the northern regions of Germany. While the tradition here is for dry wines, the mists which frequently form over the lake in the late summer and early autumn mean that a good number of *Botrytis*-affected dessert wines are also produced (1983 was the last great vintage for these).

Spätburgunder has been the dominant vine variety here since Elbling and Gutedel (Chasselas) were judged inferior and thrown out over two hundred years ago. Because of the ease with which *Botrytis* develops here (breaking down the colouring matter in the skins), the majority of these grapes are used to produce rosé (Weissherbst) wines. Since Herr Häussermann's arrival a couple of years ago an increasing number of these, and the white wines, have been made in the traditional dry style.

Württemberg

Württemberg is a widely scattered region of 9,845 hectares/ 23,425 acres centred around the large towns of Heilbronn and Stuttgart, and extending along the sides of the valley of the river Neckar, and its tributaries the Kocher, Jagst, and Tauber. Its wines are quite different in character from those of all the other German wine-producing regions, partly because of the different grape varieties such as the red Trollinger and Lemberger which are not grown in any of the other regions. The heavy marl-clay soils in the greater part of the region (otherwise limestone) also significantly influence the wines. In combination with the continental climate this gives them a full, sometimes plump character.

Traditionally, Württemberg white and red wines have undergone a natural second, or malolactic, fermentation – it is the only region where this has been a normal occurrence and is an accepted part of winemaking for many producers. Riesling, the most important white wine variety in Württemberg, with malolactic fermentation character is quite a different beast from Riesling with high acidity and low alcohol on the Moselle. If the latter is something one has become used to, then the Rieslings from this region might be a big shock. However, today there is generally more careful control of fermentation, and increasingly the wines of this region only undergo a second fermentation if this is what the winemaker decides upon.

As in Baden, the co-operatives are very strong in this region, and also often quality-minded. In spite of their well-organised production, because the average Württemberger's wine consumption matches his prodigious chauvinism, little wine from this region escapes from the state of Baden-Württemberg, let alone from Germany.

Schlossgut Hohenbeilstein

Eberhard Dippon (director).
Schlossgut Hohenbeilstein,
D 7141 Beilstein.
Tel: 07062 4303.

9 hectares/22 acres.
30% Riesling, 30% Trollinger, 40% Lemberger,
Schwarzriesling (Pinot Meunier) and other varieties.

In recent years under the direction of Herr Dippon the small Schlossgut Hohenbeilstein estate has produced some of the best red wines in Württemberg, and the whole of Germany. There is no use of new wood here, just extremely conscientious traditional German red wine making, with a strong emphasis on varietal character and intense fruit flavours. The great majority of the wines are dry, but even those which are not have very modest amounts of sweetness, such that the red wine's fruit is never masked by sweetness. The best red wines are probably the Lembergers, which need several years of ageing to show their best.

226

BADEN AND
WÜRTTEMBERG

N

↑FRANKFURT

67
E4
●Mannheim
Neckar
HEIDELBERG
E12 Sinsheim
N37
Angelbachtal
KRAICHGAU Michelfeld
Neckarsulm ●Affaltrach
Bruchsal Schwaigern HEILBRONN
Neipperg● Flein●
Karlsruhe Beilstein
Neckar 27 Klein-
35 Bottwar
3 E70
PFORZHEIM● Vaihingen ●LUDWIGSBURG
E11
BADEN-BADEN●
Stuttgart●
RHEIN

Motorway

Principal Highway

Secondary Highway

Km 0   10   20   30   40   50 Km
Mi 0   10   20   30 Mi

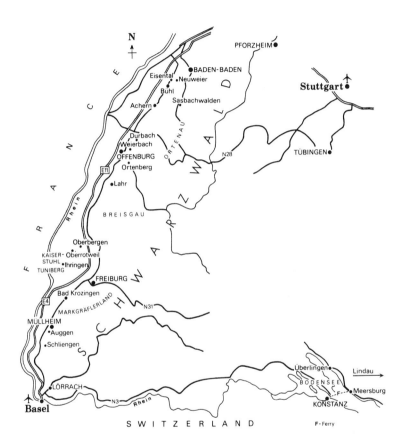

Baden and Württemberg

Weinguter Graf von Neipperg

Josef-Hubert Graf von Neipperg
(owner and director).
Weingüter und Schlosskellerei Graf von
  Neipperg,
Schloss,
D 7103 Schwaigern.
Tel: 07138 5081.

29 hectares/71.5 acres.
23% Lemberger, 22% Riesling, 17% Schwarzriesling (Pinot
Meunier), 10% Spätburgunder (Pinot Noir), 10% Trollinger,
8% other varieties.

The Neipperg estate is one of the oldest wine estates in Germany, and one of the most traditional in its winemaking. In the seventeenth century they imported the Lemberger grape variety, then known as Blaufrankisch, from Austria. It has since spread throughout Württemberg, and beyond (some interesting Lemberger wines are being produced in Czechoslovakia), and along with Spätburgunder produces most of the serious German red wines. All the estate's red wines have a classical open fermentation on the skins, and are then matured in old Stück casks, as they have been here for centuries. Unusually for Württemberg, all the white wines are also matured in old casks rather than in tanks. The majority of the wines, both red and white, are dry, and except for Auslese and higher Prädikats the remainder are medium-dry. The estate's finest wines are, as its history might suggest, the Lemberger red wines, which from good vintages like 1976, 1979, 1983, or 1985 have real power. These can easily stand comparison with the equally fine red wines from Graf Neipperg's other red wine estate, Château Canon-La-Gafellière in St Emilion.

Schlosskellerei Affaltrach

Dr Reinhold Baumann (owner and director).
Schlosskellerei Affaltrach–Dr Reinhold
Baumann KG,
Am Ordensschloss 15,
D 7104 Obersulm–Affaltrach.
Tel: 07130 557.

7.5 hectares/18.5 acres.
24% Riesling, 14.5% Kerner, 21% Trollinger,
12% Müller-Thurgau, 9.5% Clevner, 8.5% Spätburgunder
(Pinot Noir), 3.5% Lemberger, 2.5% Traminer,
1.5% Dornfelder, 1.5% Muskateller, 1.5% other varieties.

Schlosskellerei Affaltrach's vineyards only provide a small part of its needs, and 250 small growers are the main source for its grapes. The majority of its wines are light dry Trollinger red wines, and rather fuller medium-dry Rieslings. However, what has made the estate famous are its remarkable dessert wines. These have been made from all its major grape varieties since 1969, but Trollinger icewines are a great speciality. Pink Eiswein may sound absurd, but the result is delicious, if expensive. A great deal of Sekt (sparkling wine), both red and white, is also produced.

These specialities are all very interesting. The only wines from Schlosskellerei Affaltrach which can be disappointing to palates used to full-bodied red wines are the Trollinger red wines. These are typically light in colour and body for the variety. The Lemberger and Clevner red wines are altogether more serious.

Glossary

Acidity. For most wine-drinkers 'acid' is a negative word, meaning sharp and aggressive. However, acidity is an essential
element in the structure of all wines, without which they are
flat, heavy, and formless. There is an important difference
between fruity, or tartaric, acidity, and unripe, or malic
acidity. Both kinds are found in German wines, and *some* of
each is necessary for good balance, though in good-quality
wines the ripe tartaric acidity is in the majority. When this is
the case, the wine can have much more acidity than is normal
for the wines of other countries, but will be lively, refreshing,
and capable of long maturation in the bottle, rather than being
simply 'acid'. If a German wine has a lot of unripe malic
acidity, and very little ripe tartaric acidity, then it will have the
tartness of unripe apples and be sharp. Though such wines can
also sometimes age for a long time, they rarely ever reach a
good harmony.

Alcohol. German wines are famous for being low in alcohol, but,
in spite of this, alcohol is a crucial element in their make-up.
While dry white wines from the Loire tend to have 12 or more
degrees of alcohol, dry Rhine wines normally have between 10
and a little more than 11 degrees of alcohol, and dry Moselle
wines less still. The same wines made in a sweeter style will
have at least one degree of alcohol less still. A fine Moselle
Auslese can have as little as 7 degrees of alcohol. It is a
common mistake to suppose that only alcohol makes wines
more powerful; white wines can have power which comes
from alcohol, oak flavours (tannins), acidity, and mineral
extracts. German wines gain their power principally from the
latter two sources. However, in southern Germany very high
alcohol white wines can be made. An Auslese Trocken from

the Palatinate, Baden or Württemberg may have as much as 15 degrees of alcohol.

Alleinbesitz. See *monopole.*

Anbaugebiet. There are eleven 'Anbaugebiet', or wine-growing regions, in Germany. An increasing amount of German wine is being sold under these regional names, often in conjunction with the name of a grape variety, e.g. Rheinhessen Silvaner, Rheinpfalz Weissburgunder. Until recently QmP wines could not be sold under the Anbaugebiet names, but, following a recent change in the law, both QbA and QmP wines can now be sold under regional designations of this kind.

AP number. All German quality wines have to receive an AP number, or Amtliche Prufungs Nummer, before they can be sold as QbA or QmP. The fact that a German wine bears one of these numbers says no more than the words Qualitätswein or Qualitätswein mit Prädikat, since these terms cannot appear on the label unless the wine has passed the AP testing. This testing assesses only whether the wine is of acceptable quality and typical for its grape variety and region. Sadly, very poor quality but typical wines sometimes seem to receive an AP number, whilst atypical wines of very high quality do not.

Auslese (QmP). Directly translated, Auslese means selectively harvested, a selection of the very ripest bunches or berries. In spite of many wine drinkers' expectations, Auslese wines rarely have more than a touch of *Botrytis* character, and often have none. Only in exceptional vintages like 1967 and 1976 are considerable quantities of botrytised Auslese wines produced. Auslese wines should be really ripe and concentrated in flavour. In Germany opinions are divided as to whether it is a good idea to ferment these wines to dryness, since from the beginning (the last years of the eighteenth century) Auslese was traditionally used as a designation for high-quality wines with some sweetness. Auslese Trocken wines are generally full-bodied, but should not be alcoholic in the way that powerful Chardonnay wines can be.

Barrels, casks. Wooden barrels are still widely used in Germany as vessels for fermenting and maturing wines. Generally they are old, and do not give any wood taste to the wine. The reason for maturing wines in them for a number of months is the gentle contact with air which a wine in barrel has through the wood of the cask. This softens and mellows wines, at the same time developing their aromas.

There are two different sets of traditional German barrel sizes still in use today. In the Moselle, Saar, and Ruwer the 'Füder' (1000 litres) is the basic barrel size, with 'Halbfüder' (500 litres) barrels also being widely used. In the Rhine regions the 'Stück' (1200 litres) is the basic barrel size, with 'Halbstück' (600 litres), and 'Doppelstück' (2400 litres) casks also being in widespread use.

Quite distinct from these barrels, and very new on the German wine scene, are 'barrique' barrels. These are 225 or 228 litre barrels of *new* wood generally imported from France. They are used to give both red and white wines an oaky taste, and they also assist the development of red wines in other ways. When winemakers talk about oak-ageing they are usually referring to this type of cask maturation.

Barrique. See under *barrels.*

Beerenauslese (QmP). A Beerenauslese, or BA for short, should be an Auslese made from a selection of individual berries. Such wines are extremely costly to make. For example, Weingut Fritz Haag's (see p. 32) 1985 Riesling Beerenauslese required 140 man-days of picking for 180 litres of wine! BAs from the traditional grape varieties should be extremely rich and concentrated, and will almost invariably be quite sweet and show at least some *Botrytis* character. In recent decades BAs have tended to be made very sweet with a low alcohol level (6 or 7 degrees), but recently there has been a trend back to the less sweet and more alcoholic traditional style. Beerenauslese can only be made from the traditional grape varieties in very good vintages (from top vineyard sites only), or in excellent vintages.

Bereich. A Bereich is a sub-area of a wine-producing region (Anbaugebiet), and is invariably named after the most famous wine town or village within its extensive boundaries. e.g. Bereich Bernkastel (Moselle), Bereich Nierstein (Rheinhessen). The problem with this is that generally speaking only QbA wines of very ordinary quality are sold under Bereich names; wines from lesser areas which are given the good image of a famous wine village's name. This devalues these famous names. It will be a good day when the Bereich names are withdrawn, and such wines are sold under the names of the regions instead.

Böckser. This German word is used to refer to a range of faults which affect wines' bouquet. In particular it is used to refer to hydrogen sulphide and other sulphides, which give wine a smell reminiscent of bad eggs. Poor winemaking is the usual cause, but some vintages are more prone to this problem than others.

Botrytis. Botrytis cinerea is a fungus which lives on vines. It over-winters in the bark covering the vines' stems, spreading out from there in June. If it reaches the grapes before they are ripe, grey rot results, and the winemaker will have to work hard to get a clean-tasting wine. If *Botrytis* reaches the grapes when they are ripe, its effect is positive. This is called 'noble rot', or 'Edelfäule' in German. Though nobly rotten grapes look rotten and shrivelled in the negative sense, this shrivelling results in the concentration of the grape juice. Wines made from heavily botrytised grapes are rich and usually sweet or very sweet. Noble rot is the method by which the great dessert wines of Sauternes are made, as well as the Beerenauslese and Trockenbeerenauslese dessert wines of Germany.

Bottle age. Fine German wines, and particularly Riesling wines, can mature for at least as long as any other fine wines, red or white. The bottles must be laid horizontally in a dark cool place (ideal temperature about 8°C), and not disturbed. There is no point in bottle-ageing simple-quality German wines, since they do not have the acidity structure which enables fine German wines to develop in bottle. Bottle age gives white wines a mellow, honeyed character, and an almost musty tone that the Germans call 'Firne'. This might sound like bad news, but a touch of Firne only adds to the complexity of the wine.

Carbon dioxide. Carbon dioxide produced as a by-product of alcoholic fermentation remains dissolved in the wine if it is not disturbed too much. This gives many wines from the northern regions of Germany a slight sparkle, or 'Spritz', which adds to their vivacious charm. Carbon dioxide produced by a second alcoholic fermentation in the bottle (or in tank) creates the sparkle or 'mousse' in sparkling wines. These bubbles will be small and long-lasting, whereas they will be big and short-lived if the sparkle in a wine is due to carbon dioxide injected into the wine just before bottling.

Casks. See *barrels.*

Cellar work. Cellar work is everything that the winemaker does after the grapes have been pressed. See *barrels*; *centrifuge*; *chaptelisation*; *deacidification*; *filtration*; *fining*; *racking*; *reductive winemaking* and *Süssreserve.*

Centrifuge. Though used less and less in Germany, centrifuges are still an important item of wine cellar equipment there, and around the world. They are used to remove coarse and fine particles suspended in grape musts and wines by centrifugal force (the same principal as the salad shaker). Their disadvantage is that they tend to knock some of the stuffing out of the wine while removing the particles which make it hazy; wines which have been centrifuged tend to taste thin. In an ideal world centrifuges would only be used to help clear musts and wines if the grapes had been in poor condition at harvest. A large-scale wine producer is virtually forced to use them more systematically, to deal with the large volumes of must and wine which he has to clarify.

Chaptelisation. Chaptelisation, or 'Verbesserung', is the addition of sugar to grape must/juice or fermenting wine so that the finished wine has a higher alcohol content than it would naturally have. It is normal practice in much of France, top Bordeaux wines being chaptelised eight or nine years out of ten, for example. It is also used in Germany, and is necessary for at least 50 per cent of the Riesling wines from the more northerly regions. It is less necessary in the south of Germany where the grapes ripen more easily.

Charta. Charta wines are dry Rheingau Rieslings which have passed a series of rigorous quality tests. Though there are more than thirty producers of these wines, they can be recognised instantly from their common capsule, bottle, and back labels, all bearing the Charta estates association's double romanesque arch emblem. The analytical criteria which Charta wines have to satisfy mean that they have excellent ageing potential, and will accompany a wide range of foods very well.

Deacidification/Entsäuerung. Artificial reduction of the acidity content of German wine. This can be necessary in poor vintages, but is a big mistake with the wines of ripe vintages, however much acidity they have. Sadly, this is something not well enough understood in Germany, and far too many wines are deacidified, with the result that they are flat, lacking fruitiness and vigour.

Doppelstück. See under *barrels.*

Durchgegoren. This word means that the wine has fermented through until all the sugar has been converted into alcohol by the yeast, or the yeast has given up working. The word is proposed by some German producers as an alternative to 'Trocken' the present German term for dry wines, with the claim that it is more precise, since it would preclude producers deliberately making Trocken wines with a few grams of unfermented sugar. However, in a warm, above-ground cellar wines will ferment through until less than one gram per litre of sugar remains, while in some cold subterranean cellars wines will naturally stop fermenting when a considerable amount of sweetness remains. 'Durchgegoren' would therefore be no more precise than the present term. In many parts of France the producer decides by taste what is a dry, medium-dry, or sweet wine (e.g. Vouvray). Surely this should be allowed in Germany too?

Earthy. A term applied to wines that have a distinctive fruity character reminiscent of the smell or taste of earth. Many of the subtle variations in flavour and aroma between wines of different vineyards are the result of different earthy tones in the wines. The wines of some regions are associated with particular tones that come from the soil, for example the slatiness of Moselle wines, which is quite similar to the 'flintyness' of some Pouilly Fumé wines from the Loire, though more subtle.

Edelfäule. See *Botrytis.*

Einzellage. Einzellage are individual vineyards. An Einzellage may be smaller than 1 hectare/2.47 acres in extent (e.g. the Warpolzheimer Gärkammer in the Ahr valley, see Weingut J. J. Adeneuer, p. 146). It may also be over 100 hectares/247 acres in extent, which is clearly much less precise. These very large Einzellage are generally the result of the amalgamation of what were several individual vineyard sites under the most famous of their names during the years since the introduction of the 1971 wine law. For example, from the 1987 vintage the wines of the Ockfener Herrenberg vineyard in the Saar valley can be sold under the name of its much more famous neighbour, the Ockfener Bockstein. Several successful lawsuits have been fought against these changes, most notably that by Weingut Joh. Jos. Prüm (p. 126) and Deinhard (p. 131) against the expansion of the world-famous Wehlener Sonnenuhr vineyard. Surely, it only makes sense to put an individual vineyard name on a label if the quality of the wine is very high and the vineyard name is of some renown, instead of on every wine, as had become the German tradition? See also *monopole*.

Eiswein (QmP). Eiswein, or icewine, is a special category of German dessert wine which must be of at least Beerenauslese quality. It can be made only from frozen grapes picked in the early hours of the morning, preferably during the weeks immediately after the main harvest. Eiswein is normally made in vintages where BA or TBA is not possible owing to a lack of *Botrytis* (e.g. 1973 or 1983, which were both great Eiswein vintages). These wines are quite different from dessert wines made through *Botrytis*, having a great concentration of clean fruit flavours, without the honeyed character of *Botrytis*. They also tend to have *very high* acidity, and need decades of ageing in the bottle to show their full glory. As young wines they make a fine aperitif, and have enough power to stand up to strongly flavoured desserts (e.g. mango or pineapple dishes).

En primeur. For many years the top châteaux of Bordeaux have offered a proportion of the latest vintage for sale in the spring after it has been harvested, well over a year before it is bottled. The customer does not receive the wine until after it has been bottled. This is called 'en primeur' selling, and it is also practised on a small scale by a number of German estates who offer their top wines of the preceding vintage for sale at auction in the spring or early summer following the vintage.

Extract. Extract consists of all the substances that make up a wine apart from water and alcohol. If any unfermented sugar in the wine is subtracted from this, the 'sugar free extract' which remains consists of all the minerals, acids, and complex

organic compounds which are so crucial in forming the taste
and aroma of the wine. Some of these substances are extracted
from the soil, and some are manufactured inside the vine,
during the ripening process.

Fermentation. Grape juice, or must, is turned into wine when
fermented by yeasts called *Saccharomyces cerevisiae*. In this
process glucose is converted through a series of about forty
chemical reactions into ethyl alcohol and carbon dioxide. This
carbon dioxide gives many German wines a slight natural
sparkle, or 'Spritz'. Alcoholic fermentation also has a number
of by-products which have an important influence on the
character of the wine. Of these, glycerine (an oily, sweet-
tasting compound) and acetaldehyde (the substance which
gives sherry its distinctive smell and taste) are the most
important. See also *malolactic fermentation*.

Filtration. Along with fining, filtration is one of the two methods
of clarifying wines. The principle is just like that of sieving
ingredients when cooking, though on a microscopic scale.
Filters fine enough to remove any micro-organism from wines
now exist. In general too much filtration is done in Germany,
and too many wines are made rather neutral in taste as a
result. However, the very top German producers do less
filtration than almost any other white wine producers in the
world.

Fining. The fining of white wines to clarify them is not absolutely
essential, and some German growers try to avoid it (see
Weingut Lingenfelder, p. 89). The principle of fining is that a
fine powder or liquid suspension of the right substance will
attract or adhere to microscopic particles of various solids in
the wine, and, as it falls through the wine, will remove them
from it. However, fining agents also tend to take some flavour
out of the wine. Bentonite, for example, is very aggressive to
the fruitiness of wines.

Firne. See under *bottle age*.

Fruity. There is no more misused word when people talk about
German wines than 'fruity'. All too often people say, 'I don't
like German wines, they're too fruity', when what they mean
is that the wines they have tasted are too sweet for them. In
fact all wines, red, white, rosé, sweet or dry, should be fruity.
Without fruitiness a wine is thin and unattractive. One of the

wonderful things about German wines is the sheer variety of fruit flavours they can have: white and yellow peaches, apricots, apples, redcurrants, blackcurrants, gooseberries, ripe lemons, grapefruits, figs, dates, mango, guava, and pineapple, just to name those which can be found in a variety of Rielsing wines.

Füder. See under *barrels.*

Goldkapsel. There is no legal control in Germany over the use of gold capsules. Some estates, such as Weingut Dr Wagner in the Saar (p. 239), put gold capsules on all their wines, just as a normal part of their packaging. However, with the wines of the VDP estates in the Moselle, Saar, and Ruwer a gold capsule is used to distinguish a Spätlese or Auslese wine of particularly high quality. Confusingly, two lengths of gold capsule are used for differentiation. However, few wines bearing such special capsules from these estates are less than excellent; in this context a gold capsule means quality.

Grosslage. A collective site, that is, a name which can be used for wines from a number of individual vineyards. Some Grosslage names, like Niersteiner Rehbach (Rheinhessen) or Bernkasteler Badstube (Moselle), work quite well since they can only be used for wines from vineyards that belong to the village which forms the first part of the Grosslage name. However, other Grosslage names such as Niersteiner Gutes Domtal (Rheinhessen) and Bernkasteler Kurfürstlay (Moselle), are applicable to wines from a lot of inferior vineyards far from the villages which form the first part of their names. These Grosslage have exactly the same problem as the Bereich names. They are a confidence trick which can be pulled on the consumer, owing to the complexity of Germany's system of classifying its wines. This should be stopped!

Halbfüder. See under *barrels.*

Halbstück. See under *barrels.*

Halbtrocken. Medium-dry German wines almost invariably bear the word 'Halbtrocken' on the label. Halbtrocken wines from the northern regions of Germany which have a refreshing acidity are often dry in taste. This is the taste balance of Charta Rheingau Riesling wines, for instance. A German wine which is Halbtrocken contains not more than 18 grams per litre of unfermented sugar. Unfortunately, as with the designation Trocken, Halbtrocken means something quite different when applied to sparkling wines. A German sparkling wine which is Halbtrocken will have between 33 and 50 grams per litre of unfermented sugar, which tastes sweet.

Hock. The word for Rhine wines invented by the Victorians, and derived from the name of the wine town of Hochheim in the Rheingau (with which Queen Victoria's name is particularly associated). 'Hock' is still a designation which can be used for Rhine Tafelwein, or QbA wines from any of the Rhine regions.

Kabinett (QmP). The lowest grade of the QmP scale, and always a light wine whether dry or sweet. Indeed, Kabinett wines from the northern half of Germany are the lightest quality wines in the world. Many German wine producers regret that owing to the popularity of Kabinett wines they cannot do away with this grade. They feel that nearly all these wines would be better if they had some sugar added to them and were fermented to a slightly higher alcohol level.

Landwein. Landwein is the German equivalent of Vin de Pays, and has higher minimum standards than for Tafelwein (of which it is technically a sub-category). A maximum level of sweetness is set for Landwein at 18 grams per litre, so they are always dry or medium-dry in style. Like Vin de Pays or Vino da Tavola, Landwein has to be sold under regional names, though these are not identical to the regional names for QbA or QmP wines; e.g. 'Altrheingauer Landwein' comes from the identical area from which Rheingau QbA or QmP wines originate.

Lieblich. The German word for the sweet style of German wines that we are all familiar with. 'Vollmundig' is also used sometimes to refer to this style.

Malolactic fermentation. A kind of fermentation quite different and distinct from normal alcoholic fermentation. That German wines rarely undergo this second fermentation, while French wines normally do, is one of the major causes of the clear difference between them. Malolactic fermentation converts the unripe malic acid in a wine into the softer lactic acid. This makes white wines smoother, and gives them an oily, richness. It is an essential element in making red wine, and more and more German red wine producers are now using it.

Microclimate. Microclimate refers to the subtle differences in atmospheric conditions between one side of a hill and the next, the land right next to a river and that further from it. The reality of these differences can be seen by looking at how lichen and moss tend to grow only on the north-facing side of trees. Clearly, the south-facing sides of hills and trees are warmer and drier than the north-facing sides. Most German wine-producing regions are undulating or hilly, hence the importance of microclimatic differences between neighbouring vineyards. This, and the role special soil types play, are the most important reasons why the wines of certain vineyard sites have acquired a special reputation.

Monopole. An Einzellage, or individual vineyard, entirely in the possession of a single grower. For example, the Kesselstatt estate in Trier owns vineyards in many places on the Moselle, Saar, and Ruwer, including the whole Josephshöfer vineyard in the village of Graach on the Moselle. There are also a few estates like Maximin Grünhaus in the Ruwer, and Schloss Vollrads in the Rheingau, where the estate name is identical to the name of the monopole vineyard it owns. Both types of 'monopole' are referred to in German as an 'Alleinbesitz'.

Must/grape must. Fully pressed grape juice.

Noble rot. See *Botrytis.*

Oak-aged. See under *barrels.*

Oechsle. The ripeness of grapes in Germany is measured on the Oechsle scale, which is an expression of the density of the grape juice, or must. The Oechsle level of grape juice is reached by taking its specific gravity and then dropping the 10 at the beginning of this value. For example, grape juice with a specific gravity of 1080 has 80 degrees Oechsle.

Ortsname. As vested interests would make it difficult to change the law to abolish Bereich and Grosslage names, many German wine producers have recently started to sell wines under village names, e.g. Weingut Breuer's 'Rüdesheimer Riesling QbA Trocken' (a dry Rheingau wine). Such wines must come 100 per cent from the vineyards of the village named, so that a Piesporter QbA must be 100 per cent from Piesport vineyards, whereas a Piesporter Michelsberg QbA (a wine sold under a

Grosslage name) may contain not one drop of wine from Piesport's vineyards. The return to village wines is therefore to be loudly applauded.

Oxidation. German winemakers, more than those of almost any other country, fear the oxidation of their wines through too much contact with the air. Oxidation causes wines to lose their fruitiness, to become flat in taste, and to acquire a brown tinge. See also *reductive winemaking* and under *barrels.*

Prädikat. See *Qualitätswein mit Prädikat.*

Press. Various types of presses are used in Germany to extract the juice from the freshly harvested grapes. The oldest type is the so-called basket press, a vertical cylinder composed of wooden slats joined by metal rings. Today the fashion is for pneumatic presses which use only very gentle pressure, though horizontal screw presses are also used by many producers. The same grapes pressed in different types of press will give musts that taste and look slightly different. The choice of which type of press to use is part of winemaking.

Qualitätswein/QbA. Qualitätswein, or QbA, is a 'quality' wine from a delimited region or from a smaller geographical designation (i.e. it may be anything from a regional to an individual vineyard wine). Together with Qualitätswein mit Prädikat, or QmP, it is the equivalent of Appellation Contrôlée in France, DOC in Italy, or DO in Spain. The addition of sugar to the grape juice or fermenting wine to increase its alcohol level (chaptelisation) is permitted, but not obligatory, for QbA wines. QbA is a problematic category because it includes everything from cheap Liebfraumilch made from vineyards in the southern Palatinate where yields of up to 24,000 litres per hectare/10,000 litres per acre have been possible, up to fine individual vineyard Riesling wines made at yields one quarter of that, or even less. There is a gigantic difference in the depth of flavour, sophistication, and price between these two extremes. However, both are legally Qualitätswein, and carry an AP number to say that they are of an acceptable standard and typical for their region. The restrictions on yield which are currently being introduced in Germany will do something to narrow this chasm, but not enough.

Qualitätswein mit Prädikat/QmP. As with QbA wines, QmP wines have to be analytically and taste tested for an AP

number, which guarantees that they are of acceptable quality
for their grade in the QmP system and that they are typical for
their region. The major difference between QbA and QmP
wines is that the latter cannot have sugar added to them before
or during fermentation to build up the alcohol level. These
wines can be dry even if they bear a designation traditionally
associated with sweet wines. Spätlese and Auslese Trocken
(dry) or Halbtrocken (medium-dry) are not only possible, but
can be quite superb if made from a traditional grape variety.
The differentiation between the QmP grades is made solely on
the sugar content of the grapes at harvest. See also *Kabinett*;
Spätlese; *Auslese*; *Beerenauslese*; *Trockenbeerenauslese* and
Eiswein.

Racking. After a wine has finished fermenting it must be
separated from the dead yeast at the bottom of the tank or
cask. This is done simply by pumping the wine into a new cask
or tank, often filtering it at the same time.

Racy. An adjective often used in this book as a term of high
praise. It refers to wines with a rich, but definitely not aggressive, acidity which animates the fruitiness of the wine, giving
it intensity of flavour. This is what Riesling wines are all
about!

Reductive winemaking. Wines made in new or old wooden
barrels have continuous slight contact with the air through the
barrel. For this reason cask maturation is referred to as
oxidative winemaking, which means something quite different from oxidation (which only results when the wine has
much more contact with the air than it can gain through a
barrel). This has been 'out' for some decades, in favour of its
opposite: reductive winemaking. This means the making of
wines in fibreglass, concrete, or stainless steel tanks. Here the
wine has almost no contact with the air, it develops much more
slowly, and quite different chemical reactions take place.

Regional designations. For QbA and QmP wines there are
several levels of regional designation. These, in ascending
order of specificity, are: Anbaugebiet, Bereich, Grosslage,
Ortsname and Einzellage (*qq.v.*).

Sekt. German sparkling wine is known as 'Sekt'. It ranges from
poor-quality products made from cheap imported Italian and
French wines to high-quality individual vineyard German

wines. Sekt is usually sold under the designation 'Qualitäts-schaumwein' or simply 'Sekt'. If the words 'Deutscher Sekt' or 'Product of Germany' also appear on the label, or if it carries the designation 'Sekt bA', then the base wine was entirely of German origin. *German* sparkling wines can be of quite ordinary quality, or as fine as all but the greatest Champagnes. Their style is very different from Champagne, though, and they generally do not have the yeastiness, richness, high alcohol, or slightly oxidised character of Champagne. Instead, the emphasis is on clean fruitiness and flowery bouquet. The best examples come either from wine estates that consistently market sparkling wines alongside their still wines (e.g. von Buhl in the Palatinate, or Maximin Grünhaus in the Ruwer), or from small companies specialising in sparkling wine production (e.g. Reuter & Sturm in the Rheingau, or Mabillon in the Saar).

Spätlese (QmP). Directly translated, Spätlese means late-harvested, and the law insists that these wines are what they say; Spätlese quality cannot be harvested until at least seven days after the official beginning of the harvest in a region. They are always made from fully ripe grapes, and should always have a good amount of body and a real depth of ripe fruitiness. They should never be heavy wines, and even if fermented through to bone-dryness should not be too powerful to drink with food. Indeed, quite the opposite; a Spätlese Trocken or Halbtrocken is probably the ideal German wine to drink with high-class modern cuisine. Spätlese wines have been systematically made since the last quarter of the eighteenth century, the principle of late-harvesting having been discovered at Schloss Johannisberg in the Rheingau in 1775.

Spitzenwein. 'Peak Wine'. This word generally refers to the top Prädikat dessert wines, Beerenauslese, Trockenbeerenaus-lese, or Eiswein.

Spritz. See *carbon dioxide.*

Stück. See under *barrels.*

Sulphur. Sulphur, in the form of sulphur dioxide gas dissolved in water (sulphurous acid), has been used in winemaking as a disinfectant and anti-oxidant for over five centuries. It is impossible to make white wines of modest alcohol content that will stay fresh without it, and any wine with a significant amount of sweetness needs a good measure of it before bottling. By the time the wine is drunk this should have become 'bound' in the wine, and be no problem. However, a young sweet Auslese or Sauternes will often have noticeable sulphur dioxide, which causes a stinging sensation in the nose and at the back of the throat. A few people are actually allergic to sulphur dioxide in wine, but the majority are not harmed by it.

Süssreserve. Unfermented, clarified grape juice, which is added to German wines (it is also widely used in New Zealand and some other countries) to sweeten them before bottling. It is more widely used than the other method of making sweet wines, the interruption of the fermentation by separating the wine from the yeast, since it allows more precise control over the result.

Sweet. The most difficult thing about writing on wine is to decide what to describe as tasting sweet or dry, since people's ideas on this point vary so much. Also, some wines with no analytically detectable sugar can taste sweet because they have a lot of alcohol and glycerol (a natural by-product of fermentation), and little acidity. This is often the case with Chardonnay wines from warm climates. A German wine with considerable unfermented sugar and very racy acidity will probably taste drier than a Chardonnay of this type.

Tafelwein. Tafelwein is the German equivalent of Vin de Table, or Table Wine. It is the lowest quality category, and these wines may be a blend of wines from any combination of the EEC countries (EEC Tafelwein), or from Germany (Deutsche Tafelwein). In either case the quality will be very ordinary. The one exception to this is wines which have to be sold as Tafelwein because they have been deemed too untypical to qualify for QbA or QmP status (see Schlossgut Diel p. 54, and Weingut Lingenfelder, p. 89).

Tanks. See *reductive winemaking.*

Tannin. This is a normal component in all red and white wines. In red wines it plays a very important role as part of the structure of the wine that enables it to develop if it is laid down, but it is also present in all white wines. Many German winemakers do all they can to reduce the tannin content of their white wines, but a small amount can help give the wine depth and power. In large quantities, tannin has a mouth-drying and puckering effect, like stewed tea.

Tartrates. These are the small, completely harmless crystals or 'Weinstein' which fall to the bottom of many fine German wines. Wines made from grapes affected by *Botrytis* often have a *finer* white deposit too. This is called 'Schleimsäure-kalk' in German, and is equally harmless.

Trocken. Dry German wines sometimes bear the word 'dry' on the label, for example Deinhard's and Scholl & Hillebrand's excellent 'Riesling Dry' wines, but more often the word 'Trocken' is used to denote dryness. A German wine which is Trocken contains not more than 9 grams per litre of unfermented sugar (not more than 4 if it is from Franconia). Unfortunately Trocken means something else on a bottle of German sparkling wine, or 'Sekt'. A German sparkling wine which describes itself as Trocken will have between 17 and 35 grams per litre of unfermented sugar. The upper end of this range tastes really quite sweet.

Trockenbeerenauslese (QmP). Trockenbeerenauslese, or TBA for short, is traditionally a wine made from a selection of shrivelled berries at an advanced stage of *Botrytis* infection. A well-made Riesling, Traminer, Spätburgunder, Scheurebe, or Rieslaner Trockenbeerenauslese is as rich, intense, and lusciously sweet as any wine can be. In quality it should be on a par with a top Sauternes of a fine vintage. Such wines are great rarities, since the necessary degree of *Botrytis* infection only develops very rarely. When they can be made, the yields for such wines are microscopic, a mere 2–5 hectolitres per hectare/80–200 litres per acre (less than half that at Château d'Yquem, the top Sauternes producer). Although wines of this style have been made at the great aristocratic estates of the Rheingau since the late nineteenth century, TBA was not made in the Moselle until 1921, and in Württemberg, Franconia and Baden until still later.

VDP. The VDP, or 'Verband Deutscher Prädikats- und Qualitätsweingüter', is the national quality wine estates' association. It was founded in 1910, and in spite of several name changes has maintained a consistent policy of promoting quality German wines. In recent years it has become more active in extending its activities outside Germany's borders. It has also tightened its quality monitoring system, so that the VDP eagle emblem on a bottle of German wine can be relied upon as a sign of high quality.

Verbesserung. See *chaptelisation.*

Vintage. It might seem obvious that a vintage-dated bottle indicates that the wine it contains comes exclusively from the grapes grown in one season. However, German wine law allows up to 15 per cent of the wine in a vintage-dated bottle to come from other vintages. Few of the estates recommended in this book have ever gone in for any such blending between vintages.

Volatility. Volatile acidity, or acetic acid, is present in all wines in very small quantities as a by-product of fermentation. In botrytised wines it is invariably present in higher concentrations. This is vinegar, so, obviously, a large quantity has a very negative effect on wines. Luckily this final stage of oxidation of wines does not often occur, but the first stage of oxidation is rather more common. This is a substance called acetaldehyde, which is what gives sherry its distinctive smell. One of the reasons why sulphur dioxide is added to wines is to remove this substance, which might otherwise give the wine a sherry-like tone and impair its fruitiness.

Vollmundig. See *lieblich.*

Weissherbst. The German for rosé. Weissherbst wines must be 100 per cent from the grape variety stated on the label, and can be made as a QbA, or at any of the QmP grades.

Yeast. See *fermentation.*

Index

189, 199, 203–4, 207–8, 215,
218, 228, **232**, 237, 239, 243,
245
Auslese, Dry/Trocken, 185, 189,
204, 207–8, 231–2, 237
Australia (wine regions), 89
Austria (wine regions), 113, 228
Auxerrois, Pinot (grape variety),
166
Avelsbacher Altenberg (Saar), 117
Ayler Kupp (Saar), 48, 117

Bacchus (grape variety), 10, 102,
209, 211
Bacharach (Middle Rhine), 146–7
Bacharacher Hahn, 147
Bad Dürkheim (Palatinate), 197–8
Bad Kreuznach (Nahe), 53, 152,
156
Baden, ix, 10, 21, 26, 29, 106–9,
214–24, 232, 246
Balance (sweetness/acidity), 36,
49, 78, 153–4, 174
Balbach, Weingut Anton, 178, 187
Barr, Andrew, 91–2
Barrique (barrels), 38, 55–6, 58–9,
86–8, 90–1, 101, 108, 112, 183,
185, 194–5, **233**
Barth, Weingut Hans, 70
Basedow Wines (Australia), 89
Bassermann-Jordan, Dr Ludwig
von, 206
Bassermann-Jordan'sches
Weingut, Dr von, 206
Bauer, Heinz, 204
Bavaria, 102, 209
Beaune (Burgundy), 1
Becker, Hans-Josef, 75–9
Becker, Dr Helmut, 61
Becker, Maria, 75, 77–8
Becker, Weingut J. B., 75–8
Beerenauslese (QmP grade), 8, 11,
39, 55–6, 73, 75, 93, 96,
100–1, 104, 124, 138, 163–4,
181, 183, 195, **233**, 237, 244
Beethoven, 115
Bentonite, 102, **238**
Bernkastel (Moselle), 7, 42, 117,

120, 123, 129, 134
Bernkastel, Bereich, 32
Bernkasteler Badstube, 44
Bernkasteler Doctor, 7, 130–1, 148
Bernkasteler Kurfürstlay, 24, 239
Berry Bros & Rudd (wine
merchants), 1
Biffar, Gerhard, 205
Biffar, Weingut Josef, 205
Bingen (Rheinhessen), 148, 150,
178, 180–1
Bingen Scharlachberg, 181
Bischöfliches Konvict, 135
Bischöfliches Priesterseminar, 135
Bischöfliche Weinguter, 135
Black Forest, 215, 218
Blending, 16, 18, 26
'Blue Nun', Liebfraumilch, 2,
15–16, 89
Bodenheim (Rheinhessen), 184
Bohn, Friedel, 178, 189
Bonn, 145–6
Boos, Gernot, 159–60
Boppard (Middle Rhine), 146
Bordeaux (wine regions), 1, 5, 31,
33, 40, 63, 65, 68, 74, 89, 102,
105, 110–11, 132, 171, 198,
237
Bordeaux, winemaking, 19, 54, 87
'Boris', restaurant, 158
Botrytis (noble rot/Edelfäule), 73,
79, 95–6, 104, 122, 224, 232–3,
237
Bottling, 36, 76
Brandstetter, Heinz, 181
Braun, Peter, 185–6
Braun, Weingut Heinrich, 185–6
Brauneberg (Moselle), 4, 32–7, 44
Brauneberger Juffer, 33, 36
Brauneberger Juffer-Sonnenuhr,
33, 35–6
Breiling, Ludwig, 143, 145
Breisach (Baden), 215
Breuer, Bernhard, ix, 59, 61, 64–6,
101
Breuer, Weingut Georg, 61, 64–6,
101, 241
Brokers, 16

Red wines, German, 76–7, 79,
85–7, 105, 108–14, 146–8,
166, 183, 194, 216–20, 222–3
Regional character of wines, 19–29
Regional designations, **243**
Regional – varietal wines, 3, 14, 17,
25–9
Reh, Annegret, 134
Reh Group, Günther, 135
Reichensteiner (grape variety), 59,
168
Reil (Moselle), 117, 120
Reinhartshausen, Weingut Schloss,
170
Ress, Stefan, 167–8
Ress, Weingut Balthasar, 69,
167–8
'Reuter & Sturm Classic', 175
Reuter & Sturm Sektkellerei,
175–6
Rheingau, 1, 3, 14, 19, 21, 59–79,
101, 107, 147–8, 150, 156–78,
197–8, 214, 246
Rheingauer Weinkellerei, 69
Rheinhessen, 14–15, 17, 19, 22–3,
79–88, 178–91, 196
Rheinhessenwein, PR
organization, 23
Rheinpfalz, *see* Palatinate
Rhine/Rhein, river, 22, 145, 159,
183
Rhine Terrace/Rhein Terasse,
178–9, 183–90
Rhône (wine region), 105
Richter, Dr Dirk, 132
Richter, Horst, 132
Richter, Weingut Max Ferd.,
132–3
Richter, Wolfgang, 135
'Dr Richter's Riesling', 132
Riedel, Weingut, 165
Riedel, Wolfgang, 165
Rieslaner (grape variety), 102,
104–5, 206–8, 211–13, 246
Riesling (grape variety), 4, 8, 12,
14–15, 23–4, 28, 33–40, 42,
44–101, 105–9, 114, 117–78,
180–2, 184–91, 193–206,

208–9, 211–20, 235, 242;
character of, 34–5, 83–4, 99
Riesling Dry, blended wines, 3, 17,
24–5, 53, 246
Riesling wines, maturation in cask,
38–9, 83–4, 100, 128, 169–70,
205–6, **232–3**; maturation in
bottle, 34–5, 49–50, 64, 73–5,
79, 99–100, 142, 156, 160, 163,
173, 199, **234**
Rietburg, Winzergenossenschaft,
26–8
Romans, 38, 137
Romantic movement, 145
Rosé wines, 147, 209, 220, 224, 246
Royal family, English, 158
'RS'/Rheinhessen Silvaner, 23, 29,
180
Rüdesheim (Rheingau), 1, 3, 64–6,
158, 161–2, 173
Rüdesheimer 'Berg', 19, 63, 65–6
Rüdesheimer Berg Schlossberg, 65
Rüdesheimer Bischofsberg, 161
Rüdesheimer 'Oberfeld', 66
'Rüdesheimer Schloss', restaurant,
158
Ruländer (grape variety), 54–6, 74,
86, 88–9, 106–8, 109, 114, 150,
169, 178, 181–5, 187–9,
193–5, 201, 206, 208, 212,
215–23; character of, 107
Runck, Carlo, ix
Ruwer, 24, 37–41, 117, 143–5

Saar, 6, 19, 22, 24, 46–50, 116–17,
134, 136–43
Saarburg (Saar), 6, 47, 141–2
Saarburger Antoniusbrunnen, 48
Saarburger Kupp, 48–9
Saarburger Rausch, 48–50, 117
Saarstein, Weingut Schloss, 142–3
Saint Emilion (France), 110–11,
228
Salm, Ludwig-Otto, 152
Salm-Dalberg'sches Weingut,
Prinz zu, 3, 152–3
Salm-Salm, Michael, Prince, ix,
152–3